Whitewashing Britain

WHITEWASHING BRITAIN

Race and Citizenship in the Postwar Era

KATHLEEN PAUL

Cornell University Press

Ithaca and London

First published 1997 by Cornell University Press
First printing, Cornell Paperbacks, 1997

Printed in the United States of America

Library of Congress Cataloging-in-Publication Data

Paul, Kathleen, 1964–
    Whitewashing Britain : race and citizenship in the postwar era / Kathleen Paul.
        p.   cm.
Includes bibliographical references and index.
    ISBN-13: 978-0-8014-8440-7 (pbk. : alk. paper)
    ISBN-10: 0-8014-8440-5 (pbk.: alk. paper)
    1. Great Britain—Emigration and immigration—Government policy
2. Citizenship—Great Britain.   3. Racism—Great Britain.   4. Great
Britain—Politics and government—1945–1964.   I. Title.
    JV7633.P38   1997
    325.41'09'045—dc21

                                                            97-5410

Cornell University Press strives to use environmentally responsible suppliers and materials to the fullest extent possible in the publishing of its books. Such materials include vegetable-based, low-VOC inks and acid-free papers that are recycled, totally chlorine-free, or partly composed of nonwood fibers. For further information, visit our website at www.cornellpress.cornell.edu.

Paperback printing   10   9   8   7   6   5   4

For my Dad

Contents

Illustrations

Preface

"Race" and migration have been among the most hotly contested issues in British society since 1945.[1] Traditional research has focused on migrants from the "New Commonwealth" countries of India, Pakistan, and the West Indies. According to the standard account, popular racism against these people created Britain's "race relations problem" and compelled Harold Macmillan's Conservative government to alter the expansive formal nationality policy that allowed free entry into the United Kingdom to all British subjects, and to introduce legislation in 1962 designed to stem the flow of "coloured immigration" into Britain. The official picture thus shows a liberal elite forced by an illiberal public to change the formal nationality policy. In recent years this traditional view has begun to be challenged.

This book takes its place among the challengers. It does so by examining the nationality, demographic, and migration policies conceived and implemented by successive British governments in the postwar era, specifically in the years 1945 to 1965, a period for which extensive public records are now available. This book broadens both the substance of the historical debate and its conceptual boundaries. It sets postwar nationality, race, demography, and migration in a political context by showing how these issues were integral parts of the larger imperial and foreign policies of successive British governments. Using a comparative approach to British migration studies, the book examines the four principal migrant groups of the postwar period: emigrating United Kingdom residents, immigrating European aliens, migrating citizens of Ireland, and migrating subjects and citizens from the colonies and Commonwealth.

UK policy makers adopted a different strategy toward each of these four migrant groups. Residents of the United Kingdom were financially encouraged to emigrate from Britain to the self-governing parts of the empire. Continental aliens were recruited from refugee camps to work in Britain's basic industries. Irish citizens were encouraged to migrate to Britain and given all the privileges of citizenship despite their alien status. And colonial citizens migrating in search of work found that they were not wanted by their country of citizenship. At first glance, the different strategies adopted toward the four groups suggest confusion in postwar nationality and migration policy. After all, successive British governments spent a great deal of money attracting over 600,000 European aliens to work in Britain while spending an equally large amount to facilitate the emigration of 1.5 million UK residents to the dominions, all the time resisting the independent migration to Britain of thousands of colonial citizens of color.

In fact, the politics of citizenship was not the result of confusion but rather reflected competing communities of "Britishness" which challenged the policy-making elite's presentation of a single and singular British imperial national identity. Proclaiming equality as the universal nationality policy enabled policy makers to propagate the image of the British Empire as a liberal, civilizing institution. In reality, this facade of equality was fractured along several lines. *Whitewashing Britain* is most acutely concerned with the inequalities caused by the significance accorded skin color, for it was this significance that had the most direct and immediate effect on concepts of British nationality.

The understanding of the world's population which made skin color the definitive signifier of group and national identity resulted in different communities of Britishness which reflected separate spheres of nationality. "Racialization" created a fundamental contradiction between an inclusive legal nationality policy—the formal definition of who had the right to enter the country—and an exclusive constructed national identity—the informal notion of who really did or could belong. Thus, despite an imperial nationality and the facade of equality, the policy-making elite perceived emigrating UK residents, immigrating continental and Irish aliens, and migrating subjects of color as belonging to different communities of Britishness. As a result, each group experienced Britishness in a different way, their access to material wealth, education, and privilege conditioned by where they were perceived to "fit" within the hierarchy of Britishness.

The book also addresses the relationship between policy makers and the politics of nationality and migration. The evidence reveals that successive postwar governments undertook an active role in the creation and manipulation of British nationality and migration policy in order to further larger political objectives. Chapter 1 examines the 1948 British Nationality Act, which, with its generous grant of the rights of citizenship to all members of the British Empire, was designed to maintain Britain's unique position as a metropolitan motherland and to demonstrate to the world that the United Kingdom was still the center of a great commonwealth of nations, even as certain parts of that commonwealth began to assert their independence. Chapter 2 looks at the government-sponsored emigration of UK residents to other parts of the empire/commonwealth. Both Labour and Conservative administrations conceived of this migration as a means of boosting the "Britishness" of each dominion and thereby strengthening Britain's position as an imperial power. Chapter 3 explores the initiatives undertaken by the Clement Attlee government to recruit foreign workers for jobs in Britain. Expecting them to fill gaps in the labor force in the short term, policy makers clearly also expected these aliens to become British subjects in both form and substance in the long term. Chapter 4 analyzes the migrant experience of Irish aliens and finds that their entry to Britain was facilitated by a perception common to both Labour and Conservative administrations that labor was a commodity to be disposed of according to the interests of the nation-state. Both continental and Irish aliens were admitted because their entry was perceived as likely to be advantageous to the UK economy and because they passed an unwritten test of racial acceptability.

By contrast, as Chapter 5 details, the entry of British subjects of color was qualified and circumscribed by policy makers' racialized understanding of population. Chapter 6 continues the exploration of race, analyzing the policy-making elite's growing frustration with increasing colonial migration and the steps taken to reduce it, in effect limiting the practical rights of subjects of color. These measures consisted of a variety of administrative devices to control migration and an educative campaign designed to inculcate among the resident UK public the dangers of uncontrolled inward colonial migration. There were no formal directives or official offerings of hate literature. Rather, the campaign revolved around the reconstruction of British subjects as immigrants, the transformation of immigrants into "coloureds," and the problematization of "coloured immigration." Formal control of colonial migration to Britain came in 1962 with the passing of the Commonwealth Immigrants Act. This act did not resolve all the confusions and contradictions within the politics of citizenship, however. Chapter 7 updates the story of British nationality and finds that the discourse of separate spheres of nationality and the existence of different communities of Britishness remain as real today as in 1945. Clearly, concepts of British nationality which had race at their core were not initiated by popular forces in the early 1960s. Rather, such concepts had their origin at least as early as 1945 and were the creation of a policy-making elite that manipulated notions of identity and definitions of citizenship and massaged public opinion in order to preserve a constructed national identity, a useful labor supply, and a demographically and politically strong empire/commonwealth. The ramifications of this series of policy decisions are still being worked out today. The need for labor which prompted recruitment from among the refugees of Europe and in the employment exchanges of Ireland is perhaps the most positive aspect of the demographic incoherence of the postwar period. Individuals in need of refuge and employment found some degree of economic prosperity within a labor-hungry Britain. That their acceptance came at the expense of others' rejection can hardly be laid at their door. Less happily, an enduring and outdated fascination with empire contributed to Britain's postwar economic decline and played a role in Britain's halfhearted commitment to European unity. And most unhappily of all, modern Britain is still plagued by past perspectives that categorized some Britons as more British than others. Facing the fact that successive governments did not want them and tried to reclassify them as something other than British, British subjects of color still have to fight to identify themselves as British. They do so within a domestic community many of whose members, thanks to successive legislative acts, have come to understand race as a natural divider and nationality as an accidental commonality.

Analyzing UK emigrants, European refugees, Irish citizens, and colonial subjects in a comparative and political framework raises significant questions about the fluidity of national identity and the politics and economics of migration. In this context, my work contributes to the current international debate on what constitutes membership in a society.[2] Much of the contemporary literature on citizenship has been inspired by the plight of guestworker populations in Europe and illegal aliens in the United States. The central question is whether the rights of citizenship should be extended to all residents regardless of whether they are citizens of the country in which they live, or whether access to citizenship should be opened up in order to provide access to rights. Those arguing the former case believe that membership in a state is to be assessed no longer by one's citizenship but by the level of one's participation in the society.[3] Thus, by their longtime social and economic involvement in their countries of residence, immigrants have become members regardless of formal nationality. As members, they are entitled to all the privileges of citizenship including the right to become a citizen in law if they so desire. Others plead the case for dual citizenship, reasoning that European nations should recognize that their guests have come to stay and this is the most practical way of dealing with them.[4] Whatever the particular proposal, however, the majority of theorists maintain that it is dangerous for democratic nation-states to include in their population large numbers of individuals who have no vote and are unrepresented in the political process.

In all these debates Britain remains a little apart because, as one theorist sees it, while other countries debated the admission of immigrants to citizenship, Britain alone was discussing the admission of citizens as immigrants.[5] Yet Britain provides a significant case study both because the democracy of the British state is no less endangered and because the British debate is situated within the lines of citizenship. For although division is traditionally made between citizens and aliens, the British postwar case would appear to suggest that formal citizenship matters less than the constructed national identity. In this postwar British case, the formal policy should have rejected the aliens and retained and accepted the citizens, but the informal identity did precisely the opposite: immigrating white aliens were recruited as members and citizens for their perceived potential to become British, and white UK residents were directed to the Commonwealth in order to maintain Britishness abroad as members and citizens of the wider British community. Meanwhile, migrating citizens of color were rejected as members of British society because they had never been and could never become "really" British. This demographic pattern suggests that resolution of the "immigrant and refugee problem" across Europe, including Britain, relies less on legislative change and the institution of formally expansive nationality policies and more on a concerted effort to redefine the national identity as more inclusive. This book will perhaps contribute to the groundwork for this expansive renewal by illustrating the constructed nature of national identities and by demonstrating that it is the nature of migration to remake a society and the fate of societies to be remade.

This book is all the better for bearing the imprint of the great many friends, colleagues, and family members with whom I have shared the past six years. My first thanks go to those who supervised the project in its early stages. In particular I thank Jim Cronin. His intellectual support, friendly encouragement, and continuing interest in my work have been of enormous influence in my development as a scholar. I am indebted to Peter Weiler for his inspiring example of intellectual integrity, his thorough and constructive criticisms, and his continuing counsel. My thoughts upon Irish communities the world over owe much to Kevin O'Neill, who generously shared his views and time. I thank Andy Buni for first suggesting that I should pursue advanced graduate study. And finally, I owe Carol Petillo a great deal. Her demanding academic standards and unfailing supportive enthusiasm did much to shape both this book and my notion of scholastic excellence.

In the spirit of true collegiality, several individuals took the time to comment on my research. Laura Tabili provided constant affirmation of the validity of my work as well as offering suggestions that forced me to expand my understanding of race and identity—no small matters in a book of this nature. Bob Carter also generously shared his scholarship with me, and Zig Layton-Henry and Jim Walvin each offered constructive criticism. My thanks at Cornell University Press to the readers, the editorial staff, and to Roger Haydon, whose continuing enthusiasm for the topic was matched only by the professionalism he brought to its final production.

A number of people facilitated the completion of this book at the University of South Florida. Bob Ingalls not only read the entire piece in double-quick time, returning it with a host of thoughtful and critical comments, but he has also been a constant source of friendship and wise counsel. In addition to being a good friend, Laurel Graham read (and reread) significant sections of the manuscript, offered much insightful commentary, and thereby helped improve the whole. Ward Stavig offered both firm friendship and critical suggestions on work in progress. Giovanna Benadusi provided intellectual comradeship and practical advice. Jeff Lipkes proofread the entire book at minimal notice. I am grateful to John Belohlavek and Lou Perez Jr. for their constructive readings of my work in its early stages, to Gail Smith for her assistance with the photographs and much else besides, and to Sylvia Wood for her practical support. My particular thanks to those other departmental and university colleagues whose presence contributed to an environment supportive of research. My gratitude goes too to fellow migrants to Tampa who helped build a community: Jeffra Flaitz, Jenny Friedman, Joele Ingalls, Fraser Ottanelli, Jan Robert, Ella Schmidt, and Kelly and Brenda Tipps.

My initial research was funded by a Boston College Dissertation Fellowship, and a USF Research and Creative Development Grant provided the necessary funds to finish. I thank both institutions. I am grateful to the staff of the following libraries and archives: the Public Record Office, Kew; the Institute of Commonwealth Studies, University of London; the University of Warwick Modern Records Centre; the Polish Institute and Sikorski Museum; the Polish Library; the Museum of London; the Harold Cohen Library, University of Liverpool; and the British Library at Colindale.

Some of this material was previously published in the following articles: part of the Introduction and Chapters 1 and 2 in "British Subjects and British Stock: Labour's Post-War Imperialism," *Journal of British Studies* 34 (April 1995); portions of Chapter 4 in "A Case of Mistaken Identity: The Irish in Post-War Britain," *International Labor and Working-Class History* 49 (April 1996). I thank the editors for permission to reuse this material here.

Both in York and in Boston I have been fortunate in those with whom I have shared the study of history and those in whom I have found good friends; by making life more pleasant, they made this research easier to produce. Special thanks to Evelyn Neuber for her all-encompassing friendship and to Martin Wolfendon and Martin Wray for their London hospitality. I am indebted to Marie and Mike Jones for investing financially in my graduate career when I could not afford to do so, to Michael Paul for brotherly and scholarly advice, to Terence Paul for his editorial suggestions, to Stephen Paul for his moral and practical sustenance, and to John Paul for his infectious enthusiasm for my life abroad. John and Michele, Stephen and Maria, Marie and Mike, Mike and Anne, and Terence and Rita have together provided me with a familial community of the strongest kind. I thank Marie in particular. Her absolute confidence in me and my abilities has contributed much to anything I have achieved. My greatest debt is to my father, John Paul, and to my late mother, Mary Paul, not only for working all their lives to sustain this community but for their profound influence on my life. Together, they taught me to question, demonstrated the value of hard work well done, and encouraged me to strive for my highest goals. I owe them more than can be neatly summarized. My final expression of thanks goes to Brian Keaney. I have benefited enormously from his intellect and enthusiasm and the generosity of spirit which encouraged him to share these with me. He and this book entered my life at the same moment. He has borne the consequences of that dual meeting with great patience and good humor and it is in large part thanks to him that it now seeks a wider audience.

KATHLEEN PAUL

Tampa, Florida

The Road from 1945

*E*lected in July 1945, Clement Attlee's Labour government was as determined to preserve the British Empire and Commonwealth in peace as Winston Churchill had been to preserve it in war.[1] This aspiration derived not just from a desire to retain imperial glory but also from the perception that the empire/commonwealth offered concrete political and economic advantages to Britain. In political terms, the empire substantiated Britain's claims to a seat at the top table of international powers. Sir Orme Sargent, Permanent Under Secretary at the Foreign Office, for example, believed that only by remembering that "we are still the centre of an Empire" could Britain challenge the apparent perception of the United States and the Soviet Union that "Great Britain is now a secondary power and can be treated as such." It seemed clear to Sargent that "if we cease to regard ourselves as a World Power we shall gradually cease to be one" and that it was Britain's responsibility to combat this "misconception."[2] In addition to the long-term value of securing Britain's equality with the United States and USSR, the empire/commonwealth also offered some immediate economic benefits to Britain. Imperial preferences and the sterling area offered a financial buffer against Britain's true plight of accumulated wartime debt and major infrastructural damage and neglect.[3] Australia and New Zealand provided dollar-free sources of meat, wheat, timber, and dairy produce and, with Canada, took in over 40 percent of British exports. Given these perceived political and economic benefits, one may understand why Labour believed preservation of the empire/commonwealth to be an essential component of British economic and political reconstruction.

For a variety of reasons, however, the task in 1945 was less maintenance than reconstitution. First, it seemed that just at the moment when Britain needed them most, some of the strongest and oldest members of the Commonwealth were moving away. The 1931 Statute of Westminster formally recognized the equality of Australia, Canada, New Zealand, South Africa, and Eire with Britain and, as a consequence, provided that rulings of the imperial Parliament in London no longer had automatic jurisdiction in the dominions.[4] Less than ten years later, Canada signed the Ogdensburg Agreement, which constituted the first alliance between a member of the Commonwealth and a foreign power. The treaty signified Canada's perception that its strategic needs and future interests lay more directly with the United States than with Britain. Likewise, the Japanese attack on Pearl Harbor and the later fall of Singapore led policy makers in both Australia and New Zealand to look for support from the United States in addition to, or even in place of, Britain.[5] In short, as one scholar has pointed out, by 1945, "in different ways, each dominion had shrugged off a good deal of its pre-war subservience to Britain, discovered vital interests which its imperial connections could not provide for and developed new international ambitions and relationships hardly envisaged before 1939."[6]

Second, six years of war had threatened colonial relations. In pursuit of greater efficiency but at the cost of increased hostility toward the imperial system, the tactic of management from a distance had been replaced by much closer contact between the British state and colonial producers. The onset of peace had provided little respite as, in response to desperate economic circumstances in Britain, the Labour government demanded both increased colonial exports and greater contributions to the sterling area. The Colonial Development Corporation, established in 1947 to "re-establish and indeed improve upon the pre-war position in which exports of primary produce from the colonies to America were among our principal earners of dollars" was but one manifestation of the seriousness with which Labour viewed colonial resources.[7] In the long term the corporation was intended to promote colonial development, but in the short term the Cabinet assumed that all dollars earned would be spent in the sterling area and so work to Britain's advantage. Some colonies had resources of a different kind. In the years immediately after the war, for example, the idea of a "Euro-Africa" that would harness British, European, and colonial resources and so contribute to British independence from both superpowers became the subject of a lengthy series of negotiations with the French government.[8]

Third, the postwar retreat from India, Burma, Ceylon, Palestine, Greece, and Turkey diminished both the size of the empire and its potential influence. On the one hand, these withdrawals appear to suggest Labour's acceptance of the approaching end of empire. On the other hand, the need to acknowledge certain political and economic realities perhaps served to highlight the need to build and maintain the empire in any other way possible. In May 1947, for example, in the context of these changes, Attlee wrote of the need to find a new "formula which will enable the greatest number of independent units to adhere to the Commonwealth." A year later Labour feared that India and Pakistan's withdrawal from the Commonwealth following their adoption of republican constitutions would damage the Commonwealth's "prestige and influence in the world." Believing that Western Europe needed the support of non-European countries if it was to remain independent of both the Soviet and US blocs, Labour tried hard to find a formula that would allow the republican countries to remain associated with the Commonwealth. This flexibility suggests that Labour perceived the decline of formal empire not as a retreat but as part of a greater challenge to retain influence by refashioning external linking apparatus.[9]

Thus, on assuming office the Attlee government faced a situation in which the perceived benefits of the empire/commonwealth could be retained only by triumphing over several practical difficulties. For economic and political reasons, neither oppression nor castigation were available as policy options; the Attlee government therefore needed innovative strategies if it was to maintain the imperial system. The game was the same, but the rules had changed: the empire/commonwealth had to be preserved as a basis for international prestige and economic fortune, but gunboat diplomacy and outright domination were to be replaced by colonial economic development and equality among dominion nation-states. Labour sought tools that might refashion the links holding the empire together and thereby recognize the changing nature of the empire/commonwealth while preserving the special relationship of each territory with the United Kingdom. Even as Labour embarked upon its imperial project, however, demographic, economic, and labor crises within Britain made the task more difficult.

The apparently declining birthrate had generated much discussion since the early twentieth century, sparked by the failure of between 40 percent and 60 percent of recruits for the Boer War to pass the physical exam, and fueled by a variety of publications and societies. The carnage of World War I exacerbated the fears, and had the money been available, a fertility census would likely have accompanied the regular census in 1931. Over the course of the next decade, popular newspapers bewailed "the peril of the empty cradle," and described the "tumbling birth-rate" as the "fundamental long-term problem" for the future.[10] The government meanwhile enacted the Population (Statistics) Act in 1938 to facilitate demographic planning. Commanding the attention of various public figures, the birthrate and apparent subsequent population decline remained an issue during the war. Speakers nearly always perceived a direct link between Britain's leadership role and the "dwindling birthrate." Sir William Beveridge, outlining plans for Britain's future welfare state, advocated an increase in the birthrate as a means of ensuring the survival of the "British race."[11] MPs questioned whether Britain could "for all time proudly and somewhat arrogantly sing about Britainnia ruling the waves, if . . . our numerical strength to maintain that ruling is gradually shrinking."[12] Home Secretary Herbert Morrison believed the birthrate constituted one of two great question marks overshadowing Britain's future.[13] And Winston Churchill as Prime Minister warned that Britain's "future as a nation . . . future as the centre of a great Empire alike" depended on an improvement in the birthrate.[14] Intertwined with these fears about the quantity of the United Kingdom's population were fears about its deteriorating quality. The *Times* was only one organ that suggested that the aging of the population and "the inverted birth rate," with "poorer and less successful sections of the community" producing more children than "the more prosperous and more successful sections," were of greater import than the population's total size.[15]

For the first half of the twentieth century, then, population decline was linked to ability to perform the job of empire, with the implicit assumption that only a rising population of the right kind would be adequate to the job. Against this background, Churchill, declaring that the "destiny of our country . . . depends upon an ever-flowing fountain of healthy children," appointed a Royal Commission on Population in 1944. The commission's brief was to examine population trends in Britain, to determine likely consequences of those trends, and to suggest ways in which the trends could or should be influenced by government. The findings of the commission proved extremely relevant to the postwar politics of citizenship, for the commissioners extended their report to cover the birthrate not just in the United Kingdom but throughout the empire, and the relationship between the birthrate and imperial migration.

If the demographic crisis had its origins in the nineteenth century, the postwar economic crisis had its immediate roots in World War II. Victory had been achieved at the expense of the national debt and the balance of payments. The desperate state of the economy and the shortage of labor became apparent within a few months of the war's end. In October 1945 the Trades Union Congress (TUC) reported that "we are meeting the problem of manpower scarcity at every turn, and the whole of the vital services of this country are very near breaking point."[16] Although 335,000 POWs were already employed in Britain, the TUC estimated that 585,000 would be needed if urgent reconstruction and agricultural production were not to be "seriously affected."[17] In January 1946, in its first economic survey, the government forecast a labor shortage estimated variously at between 600,000 and 1.3 million and a balance-of-payments deficit of £750 million.[18] By 1947 officials gloomily asserted "that we do not have enough resources to do all that we want to do. We have barely enough to do all that we *must* do"—that is, to find the means to buy imports previously paid for by overseas investments and to repair industrial infrastructure that had been neglected for six years. To put these basics right would be a "huge job of work."[19] In addition, the new Labour government had committed itself to a progressive social program. The Cabinet concluded that the nation's greatest problems showed themselves most plainly in the shortage of manpower to meet requirements.[20] More troubling, the industries seriously affected by the labor shortages were the high dollar earners critical to the reconstruction and export effort—coal mining, textiles, agriculture, steel, and construction.[21] Staffed during the war by directed labor, these industries were sufficiently "unattractive" with regard to pay and conditions that it was thought unlikely that many prewar employees would return in the absence of controls. Early reports from the Royal Commission on Population offered little hope of respite. The commission predicted a fall of 200,000 in the working-age population by 1959.[22] According to the commission, this drop was worrisome not merely for the economic consequences of an imbalance between producers and consumers but because an absence of youth could lead to the loss of "the qualities that make for progress."[23] The overall prospects seemed sufficiently gloomy for the commissioners to conclude that "the need to increase the working population is not temporary; it is a permanent feature of our national life." The fuel and convertibility crises of winter 1946 and summer 1947 perhaps best exemplify Britain's plight. A combined labor and coal shortage in the midst of the worst winter of the century brought the entire country to a halt for several days. Both industrial and domestic consumers endured electricity rationing under freezing conditions. Popular newspapers graphically depicted the "state of emergency," urging readers to conserve power as a "duty to your country" and calling on the government to face "the problem of labour shortage with courage and determination."[24] The situation continued to worsen, and by the summer of 1947 the "manpower" crisis had been the subject of many Cabinet discussions. It was equaled in severity only by the government's deepening financial crisis. The US loan negotiated in late 1945 had provided a temporary respite, but the subsequent convertibility of sterling in July 1947 had a disastrous effect on the UK economy, starkly revealing its fragility. In addition to this run on the pound, exports fell steadily in 1947, so that by July the trade deficit was $500 million a month.[25]

While Britain's balance-of-payments deficits were real enough, they and the labor shortages stemmed less from a cut-and-dried lack of resources than from a conflict that would permeate both Labour and later Conservative administrations and the politics of citizenship: the desire to earn international recognition as a great power versus the need to reconstruct the domestic economy. In Cabinet debates Chancellor of the Exchequer Hugh Dalton argued strenuously for the reduction of the armed forces as a means of "freeing up" labor for the civilian sector. Dalton's initiatives were blocked, however, by those of his colleagues who regarded a well-stocked military as essential to imperial and great-power status.[26]

Other Cabinet conflicts derived from a divided commitment to planning as an economic tool. Following Dalton's lead, Emanuel Shinwell, Minister of Fuel and Power, advocated a statutory wage policy as a means of increasing general productivity and drawing labor into industries traditionally made unattractive by low pay or poor conditions. Likewise, other ministers called for greater economic planning, for without such control "we could not expect to secure all the advantages which might be derived from a fully-planned economy." Minister of Labour George Isaacs and Home Secretary Herbert Morrison, rejected the proposals, fearing that they "would turn every wage negotiation into a political issue, and in addition undermine the whole basis of wage determination by consent."[27] Likewise, the Attlee administration chose not to increase the labor supply by imposing female civilian national service or by delaying the raising of the school-leaving age.[28] Thus, the postwar labor "crisis" was not only about an absolute shortage of numbers but also about a shortage of workers willing to work under existing conditions, together with disagreements over the use to which the available labor should be put.

Despite this complexity, the government did implement certain strategies as evidence of its "courage and determination" to increase the size and productivity of the labor force. In March 1946 the Ministry of Labour launched a domestic productivity drive, calling on all workers to "fill the ships," so that the government might "fill the shops." "Lend a Hand on the Land" schemes as well a fifteen-day exemption from school for Scottish children provided temporary labor for essential short-term harvest work. The government undertook an extensive publicity campaign in order to draw workers to "essential" but unattractive industries, employing newspaper advertisements, posters, leaflets, exhibitions, film and radio pieces—all proclaiming the benefits and virtues of, for example, "a well-paid man's job" in the mines. More concretely, increased wages, the installation of baths and other amenities, a five-day week, and exemption from national service were all part of the effort to increase the mining labor force.[29]

A similar publicity campaign was intended to draw women back into the labor market by convincing them of the severity of the crisis facing Britain and the importance of their contribution. To facilitate female employment and recognizing women's continued obligations in the home, the Ministry of Labour encouraged employers to offer schoolday shifts, part-time work, and child care.[30] The textile industry went even further in its efforts to recruit married women back to work by arranging for traveling shops to visit the mill or even, as in Lancashire, taking care of the "Monday wash" with on-site laundries. The new Chancellor of the Exchequer, Sir Stafford Cripps, met with the editors of women's magazines to explain the economic difficulties facing the nation. He also asked that fashion and beauty editors solve some of the day-to-day problems of women, such as the protection of permanent-wave hairstyles from the steamy atmosphere of the mill.[31] As had been the case in wartime, this appeal to women to enter the work force was only partially liberatory. The language employed and the terms offered confirm that the government regarded women as members of a reserve labor force who could be called upon in extraordinary circumstances to step outside their "normal" sphere of home and family and take up paid employment.[32]

Further relief for the civilian labor force came in the form of the October 1947 decision to reduce the armed services by almost 300,000 by March 1949.[33] The same month, having thus far resisted calls for total planning, the government took a small step in this direction by instituting a Control of Engagement Order. Under the terms of this directive, all men between eighteen and fifty and all women between eighteen and forty, unless gainfully occupied, and with certain exceptions, had to obtain employment through a labor exchange. This practice enabled exchange officers to "guide [people] into jobs where they can best contribute to the improvement of the country's economic position."[34] Three months after the order's implementation, the Cabinet noted some significant successes. Coal mining, which had seen a fall of 4,000 in the work force from October to December 1946, witnessed an increase of 4,200 during the same period a year later. Similarly, agriculture lost 3,000 workers in the last three months of 1946 but gained 1,000 in the same period in 1947.[35] Even more startling than the benefits of direction was the absolute increase of 600,000 in the total UK working population from mid-1939 to December 1947. This was largely due to the entry of women into industrial, particularly textile, employment. In October 1947 alone, 8,950 additional women were recruited to the textile industry, following an average monthly increase of just 2,450.[36] In spite of these successes, however, critical industries continued to report acute labor shortages, and the government thus persisted in its efforts to locate additional sources of labor.

This, then, was the situation in 1945: imperial realignment, demographic crisis, financial difficulty, and labor shortage. For a multiplicity of reasons, the Attlee Cabinet and permanent officials in the Ministry of Labour and the Colonial, Home, and Dominions Offices gradually came to see migration and nationality as potential solutions to at least some of their problems. Confirming a universal British nationality for all British subjects and sending "British stock" emigrants abroad offered subtle, yet effective means to shore up the imperial system without offending dominion or colonial sensibilities, or indeed the formally antiimperialist position of the United States. At the same time, recruiting aliens for work in Britain might reduce labor shortages that otherwise threatened to cripple the economy and hamper emigration schemes. Though not without their internal contradictions—emigrating British subjects robbed the UK economy of potential labor, incoming aliens imposed considerable financial burdens at a time of fiscal crisis, and Irish citizens fought to be categorized as neither subject nor alien—these steps appeared to place nationality and migration under policy makers' control. The advent of independent colonial migration began a new chapter in migration policy, however, as British subjects of color exercised the migration rights confirmed in the British Nationality Act. Over the course of the next half century, both Labour and Conservative administrations would discover the difficulties involved in trying to control migration and manipulate nationality.

Subjects and Citizens

The politics of citizenship in postwar Britain first began to take visible and effective form in September 1945 when the Canadian government announced its intention to introduce new legislation on Canadian nationality. The Attlee government's initial reaction was mixed: the proposed form of the bill offered a practical means of resolving some of the inconsistencies in the universal nationality policy by which the whole British Empire was allegedly governed; yet at the same time, by changing the root of allegiance, the bill threatened to impair imperial strength and unity. Over the course of a year's worth of discussions, however, Labour ministers and their officials transformed the Canadian bill from a potentially divisive blow into a mechanism for further securing imperial harmony and unity. By the end of the negotiations, the ambitions of the policy makers had enlarged again, and the resultant 1948 British Nationality Act became a means of securing Britain's role at the center of an empire/commonwealth and securing the continuing dependence of parts of that empire.

The transformation from crisis to opportunity was not achieved without some costs. Indeed, so determined were Labour ministers to accomplish their goals that they underplayed the significance of their actions at the time. This political modesty has made it easy for subsequent historians to underrate the importance of the 1948 act. An alternative reading of the public record suggests that it was the opening ploy in the game of citizenship politics in postwar Britain, which involved a variety of players but essentially revolved around two simple rules: Britain must maintain international influence while balancing several different, competing communities of Britishness within a single empire. The British Nationality Act at the time seemed a triumph for Labour.

It bolstered Britain's international stature by maintaining imperial harmony without imposing too much strain on either limited US goodwill toward empires or on the United Kingdom's own limited financial resources. Its success suggested that the politics of citizenship was an easy game to win. In reality, policy makers had just begun an adventure involving citizenship, subjecthood, national identity, and migration from which their successors have not yet extricated themselves, the United Kingdom, or indeed Britain's imperial possessions.

I

Since at least the seventeenth century, the power to interpret and manipulate British and imperial nationality has rested with the Parliament at Westminster, not with British subjects or citizens themselves. In that century, a court ruling known as Calvin's Case effectively determined how British subjecthood was acquired and what obligations subjects had, but made no provision for subjects' rights. In effect, as Ann Dummett and Andrew Nicol assert, the "feudal law of lord and subject," which carried rights and obligations on both sides, was broken. From this moment on, rights of citizenship and the practices customarily associated with nationality, such as free entry into the country and the franchise, would become attributes or privileges subject to the whim of Parliament and, thanks to the absence of a written constitution, unprotected in law.[1]

In deciding which privileges to grant and to whom, Parliament, or more realistically, the government of the day, has historically been influenced by a variety of economic, political, religious, racial, and social factors. In terms of empire, up until 1962 successive governments consistently chose to emphasize equality by treating all British subjects the same, regardless of where in the empire they habitually resided. Symbolizing this universal equality was the common status of British subject—a term that carried much prestige and, according to a 1930 Cabinet memorandum, had "for generations been well-known and recognized throughout the civilised world."[2] At the center of this common subjecthood and status was the doctrine of personal allegiance to the Crown as "the link which bound the whole empire together."[3] Whether born in Kingston, Ontario; Kingston, Jamaica; or Kingston-upon-Thames, one was a British subject of the imperial Crown and shared a universal British nationality. With this nationality came customary rights: all British subjects could freely enter the United Kingdom, vote for Parliament when resident there, and take up employment. As noted, however, these rights were neither automatic nor inalienable; they derived from Parliament's gift.

The common status of British subject had been confirmed in the 1914 British Nationality and Status of Aliens Act, which in turn stemmed from a 1911 imperial conference called in an attempt to standardize confusing naturalization procedures throughout the empire. Prior to 1914, for example, an alien naturalized as a British subject in Australia remained an alien under New Zealand law, and while UK law recognized children born of British parents outside the empire as British subjects, Canadian law did not. Irregularities such as these, while not fundamentally damaging to the empire/commonwealth, nevertheless represented tiresome ripples in the fabric of unity. Thus, in an effort to ensure that "a British subject anywhere is a British subject everywhere," the 1914 act established uniform procedures for naturalization of aliens and confirmed the *ius soli* principle of nationality, whereby all individuals born within "His Majesty's dominions and allegiance" automatically acquired British nationality at birth.[4] The act affirmed the existence of a common status—British subjecthood—and established a common code—the means by which all members of the British Empire acquired their primary nationality and became British subjects. The code was based on the principle that all those born or naturalized within the empire possessed only one nationality. Embedding the principle of theoretical equality in the formal nationality policy enabled UK policy makers to tout the British Empire/Commonwealth as a universal, united institution centered upon the United Kingdom.

Under the umbrella of British subjecthood dominions were granted space within which to construct local nationalities. These local citizenships carried weight only in the territory of creation, however, and were designed to satisfy the dominions' increasingly strident declarations of autonomy and restrictive immigration preferences. They were not intended to inspire loyalty or express national, or even imagined, communities. For Parliament, residents of the empire were British subjects first and local citizens second. Throughout the interwar years, dominion nationalism periodically challenged the concept of a single imperial nationality by pushing ever harder for formal recognition of local citizenships. By 1930 Home Office officials feared that "the 'extreme' dominions may succeed in securing for their own nationality such a degree of international recognition that British nationality. . . will be ousted altogether" with the overall effect being to "destroy an important legal bond between the different members of the Commonwealth." The problem, as perceived by the Home Office when preparing for the 1930 imperial conference, was to find some means of reconciling the competing imperial and dominion nationalities "so as to preserve a common status *as a nationality* which all the nationals of each member of the Commonwealth will possess."[5] In the event, the 1930 conference reaffirmed the primacy of British subjecthood and the common code.[6] Despite the universalism suggested by this conclusion, it remained open to dominion governments to create their own class of nationals and to discriminate among other British subjects in such matters as immigration, access to the franchise, and appointment to offices. Despite these real infringements on equality, however, the formal imperial nationality policy continued to emphasize the universal rights of British subjects. In particular the right to enter the United Kingdom remained secure for all British subjects. The Home Office considered this imperial generosity in the face of dominion self-interest a necessary price to pay for the role of parent.[7]

And yet, despite the apparent belief in a universal nationality and the proclamation of equal rights for all, the governing elite's own conflicting interpretations generated a great many practical infringements of theoretical equality. Hypocrisy is not solely to blame; conflicts inherent in a multinational empire played a part, as did the essential contradiction of professions of equality from a hierarchical body.

Among the many forms of imperial inequality, three of the most important were differences based on gender, class, and skin color. Women, for example, could not transmit their status as British subjects to their children; nationality could descend only through the male line. Equally compromising, by the 1914 act, British women automatically lost their nationality upon marriage to an alien, and alien women marrying British men automatically became British. This policy was based on the twin assumptions that, as men were heads of the family, so must they define its nationality and that women were incapable of loyalty to both their marriage beds and their passports. During the 1914 parliamentary debate only one Member of Parliament protested this measure. The vast majority concurred that to allow separate nationalities for husbands and wives "would depart from the practice of the civilized world."[8] These practical qualifications suggest that women belonged to the empire only through their husbands and that they were in effect subsidiary subjects. Women's practical equality was further circumscribed by their presumed roles as reproducers of the labor force rather than as wage laborers in their own right. This presumption contributed to female economic dependency by limiting independent wage work and allowing access to benefits or social rights as wives and mothers rather than as independent citizens. Women's reliance on men's income was part of a vicious circle of female exclusion since it was extended to imply total dependency and thus suggested an absence of the independence and self-reliance deemed essential for responsible citizenship.[9] Instead, women were encouraged to learn the craft of motherhood in order to produce good "citizen sons" for the empire, a prescription of duties which further separated them from possession of their own citizenship.[10]

The theoretical equality of the imperial nationality was similarly compromised by social class. Until 1948 the franchise was based on property ownership, and throughout the first half of the twentieth century and for many generations before, mortality rates were higher for the working class than for any other economic group and educational levels were lower. Members of the governing elite consistently regarded members of the working classes as inferior to middle- and upper-class citizens. The high medical exam failure rate among potential recruits for the Boer War, for example, together with the higher birthrate of the working classes alarmed many MPs, journalists, and reformers, who publicly feared for the decline of the "British race."[11] These concerns at a time when working-class subjects were in fact reproducing at a rate sufficient to ensure the continuation of the "British race," suggest that the governing elite perceived some members of the British Empire as more desirable, more equal, than others. Some observers have suggested that the institution of social rights in the twentieth century—pensions, unemployment insurance, health care, education—mitigated the effects of class inequalities by providing a common base of citizenship in which all citizens participated. Yet while these institutions did contribute to a rise in the standard of living for all social groups, social citizenship, by providing the appearance of equal opportunity, legitimated the outcome of continuing economic inequality.[12] Thus, even after the institution of a full-scale welfare state in the postwar era, the image of a single imperial nationality with universal rights for all clashed with the reality of economic inequality.

The equality of subjects of color of all classes was compromised throughout the empire/commonwealth by a racialized understanding of the world's population. That is, social relations within the empire were structured according to perceived immutable genetic characteristics producing "naturally occurring, discrete breeding population[s]."[13] In the case of the British Empire, racialization produced a hierarchy whereby British and European populations or races were regarded as superior to African and Asian. Maintained through a rigid system of discrimination and prejudice and incorporating perceived cultural, social, religious, and political distinctions in addition to physical ones, the imperial hierarchy served both to justify and to facilitate control. The effect was an empire of white governors and black governed, in which British subjects of color were repeatedly prevented from practicing their customary rights of subjecthood. Free migration within the empire/commonwealth, for example, was generally restricted by immigrant poll taxes, literacy and English-language tests, and administrative checks on migrating subjects of color.[14]

Thus despite the existence of an imperial nationality, working-class subjects, subjects of color, female subjects, and other "outsiders" all found their access to material wealth, education, and privilege severely limited by economic, gender, and "racial" status.[15] These practical divisions within a theoretically universal subjecthood suggest competing definitions and communities of Britishness which reflect separate spheres of nationality: an inclusive formal nationality policy and an exclusive informal national identity. The formal policy instituted as one means of maintaining and justifying imperial control over time developed sufficient symbolic and nonrational resonance to become naturalized as an imagined community of imperial "Britishness." The informal national identity imagined a different community of "Britishness" which included only white residents of the United Kingdom and privileged middle- and upper-class men within that.[16]

II

In late 1945, with the Canadian government's announcement that it planned to introduce a bill defining Canadian citizenship, the vision of a single, universal, and equal nationality throughout the empire again came under attack and in a manner more serious than ever before. This time, unlike 1930, Canada refused to withdraw or even delay its legislation to preserve the imperial nationality.[17] World War II had not only weakened the imperial link; it had strengthened the Canadian vision of the essential component parts of independence. Canada's proposed bill threatened imperial credibility both by clarifying and codifying what was actually ambiguous and contested and by doing so in a way particularly threatening to Britain's position as the imperial center. The Canadian bill reversed the emphasis on imperial nationality by making Canadian citizenship the primary nationality and making British subjecthood a secondary status, almost a fringe benefit. The practical effect of this radical inversion of principles, wrote Cabinet Secretary Sir Norman Brook, would be to "drive a coach through the 'common code' principle of British Nationality."[18] Citizenship, not subjecthood, would constitute the shared basis of the Canadian national community. Residents of Canada would still be British subjects, but only by virtue of their Canadian citizenship rather than as members of the British Empire per se. Home Secretary Chuter Ede recommended that Westminster cooperate with Canada's "radical alteration," likely to be adopted by other dominions in the near future, by producing a UK bill along similar lines.[19]

Assessing the significance of the 1948 act, some legal historians have tended to concentrate on the changes it wrought to the administrative "tree," overlooking the "forest" of imperial preservation.[20] The technical changes were indeed important and contributed to Ede's acceptance of the bill. In his first statement to Prime Minister Attlee, Ede noted that the new scheme offered a practical alternative to the persistent irregularities of the common code, which appeared "to be breaking down."[21] In reality these inconsistencies could probably never be resolved because they derived from the internal contradictions inherent in universalizing categories such as empires, subjects, and citizens. Nonetheless, both the Home and Foreign Offices saw a new nationality bill as an opportunity to straighten things out and to reaffirm an appearance of uniformity. Thus the Home Office proposed a common treatment of married women's nationality (an idea supported by the only female Cabinet member, Ellen Wilkinson), and the Foreign Office and Board of Trade favored a new bill because it would facilitate the making of treaties and trade agreements by formally establishing in whose name such treaties were being concluded.[22] Furthermore, an interdepartmental committee of officials recommended adoption of the new framework of nationality in the hope that it would do away with the delays inherent in a system that relied for its operation on consultation among all Commonwealth members.[23] Thus, at the most practical level, Britain participated in Canada's new citizenship scheme as part of its ongoing coordination of imperial nationality policy.

Although Ede remained conscious of the practical advantages of participation, however, he advocated cooperation primarily because of his concern about the "forest" of imperial preservation. In his opinion, past difficulties concerning the imperial nationality had been caused by Britain's determination to retain the common code. Switching to an alternative method therefore seemed to offer the best way to achieve consensus with other Commonwealth members.[24] Thus, "with a view to maintaining the common status of British subject unimpaired throughout the Commonwealth," Ede proposed "a meeting of experts" from all the Commonwealth countries to consider "the far-reaching issues raised by the Canadian action."[25] Meanwhile, Ede worked to establish the United Kingdom's position, which by the summer of 1946 focused less on practicalities and increasingly on the need to avoid division among Commonwealth members and to retain the common status of British subject throughout the empire. In a major statement to the Cabinet in July 1946 Ede and Dominions Secretary Christopher Addison (Viscount Addison of Stallingborough) declared that it was "virtually imperative" that Britain participate in the new scheme. Failure to do so would split the Commonwealth "into two camps" with regard to nationality, and the division "would be found to become more marked with the passage of time." Furthermore, abstention might offend dominion governments, prompting them to "give way to demands from within for completely separate nationhood and to drop the common status . . . thus severing the main link in the allegiance to the Crown which the common status implies." Avoiding "this undesirable situation" was a "paramount necessity."[26] UK participation would provide safeguards to protect the universal nationality from "becoming an easy victim of an upsurge of nationalistic feeling in any particular dominion."[27] In response to Ede and Addison's argument, the Cabinet established a ministerial committee chaired by Ede and comprising Addison, Lord Chancellor Jowitt, Colonial Secretary George Hall, Secretary of State for India and Burma Lord Pethwick-Lawrence, and Attorney General Sir Hartley Shawcross. Reporting back to the Cabinet a month later, the committee emphasized both its belief in the "great importance" of maintaining "the common status of British subject" and its fear that not to place it upon an alternative basis could lead to the eventual dissolution of the Commonwealth.[28] Faced with this prospect, the Cabinet uniformly endorsed the committee's recommendation that the United Kingdom participate in the new scheme by passing a nationality bill in line with Canada's.[29]

Had the resultant 1948 British Nationality Act only prevented dissension and secured harmony among Commonwealth members, historians of imperial policy might well have judged it a success. As it was, the Attlee government turned an un-looked-for Canadian initiative into a proactive tool of imperial policy. Under the terms of the act, London recognized the right of dominion governments to create national citizenships, which would then provide access to the common, imperial status of British subject. The Attlee government even followed this principle itself by creating its own area of citizenship—the United Kingdom and Colonies. Yet at the same time the Labour government chose to ignore all these newly created citizenships by emphasizing that in UK law all British subjects remained equal. The Parliament at Westminster would continue to consider the imperial nationality of British subjecthood the only nationality that mattered. Unlike the Canadian government, the UK government made no distinction between its own citizens and the larger class of British subjects. This major privilege resulted once again in equality of status and rights throughout the empire: all were equally entitled to live and work in Britain. This generosity was not accidental. When he was first recommending that the Canadian system be adopted, Ede had emphasized as an advantage that "it would still be possible for the United Kingdom to continue to grant free right of entry into this country to all British subjects from whatever part of the Empire they come, a privilege which has, I think, contributed to the loyalty and solidarity of the Empire."[30] Echoing these sentiments, Sir Hartley Shawcross noted Britain's "special responsibility" as the "historical Motherland" and explained that "the Bill's whole purpose is to maintain the common status, and with it the metropolitan tradition that this country is the homeland of the Commonwealth."[31] By keeping migratory routes revolving around Britain, and by remaining the only Commonwealth country not to privilege citizen nationals above other British subjects, the bill reinforced the island's distinct position: England remained the center to which members throughout the empire would be drawn and the Westminster Parliament remained first among equals.

The bill appeared to be a perfect compromise. It appeased dominion nationalism by recognizing the right of territories to legislate their own citizenship laws and the dominions' "equality of status with this country."[32] Even as it recognized dominion equality, however, the bill also asserted the United Kingdom's right to legislate *its* own citizenship laws, which it exercised in choosing to offer all national privileges to all imperial subjects. The dominions could hardly complain; they retained the prerogative to offer the same generosity. London knew that they were unlikely to do so, however, since many dominions already had restrictive immigration policies in effect. Thus, the 1948 act incorporated Canada's growing autonomy by refashioning something of the external appearance of the imperial relationship while sustaining much of the substance of existing relations. As a result, what Lord Chancellor Jowitt perceived to be a "vital" link between Commonwealth members was preserved, "the conception of an all-pervading common status, or nationality . . . the mark of something which differentiates the family from mere friends."[33] Preservation of this common nationality constituted one means of retaining bonds between the family members despite visible signs of independence. The 1948 act thus changed the manner of acquiring British nationality in order that the nationality itself, and the United Kingdom's position as central provider, might be preserved.

If Canadian, Australian, and New Zealand nationalism could be pacified through national citizenships, the nationalism of more recent dominions, such as India and Pakistan, required additional attention. In early 1948, the governments of both countries objected to the act's use of the term "British subject" to describe the common nationality, perceiving it as suggestive of subordination and inequality. In order to placate these fears, Labour agreed that countries unhappy with the traditional language employ the alternative title of "Commonwealth citizen." Ede and the new Commonwealth Relations Secretary Philip Noel-Baker hoped to deprive of ammunition nationalists eager for an excuse to leave the Commonwealth. Ironically, this accommodation, originally designed at the instigation of India and Pakistan, would be used against their citizens in the very different imperial and Commonwealth climate of a decade later.[34]

III

The 1948 act succeeded in satisfying the varying expressions of nationalism throughout the Commonwealth while preserving the common status of British subjecthood. In spite of this mighty achievement of imperial policy, however, the Attlee government was compelled to follow the intent of the Canadian legislation by identifying an area of national citizenship, membership in which would provide access to British subjecthood. Unlike Ottawa, however, London did not confine itself to a territorial or geographical definition of citizenship. The 1948 British Nationality Act created a new political entity—the United Kingdom and Colonies (UKC)—whose residents shared a common citizenship. This new area of citizenship clearly collided with the intention of the Canadian legislators that each component part of the empire/

commonwealth should enjoy its own national citizenship. In this respect it represented another attempt to ensure the maintenance of a strong and united empire/commonwealth to serve as the basis for Britain's international political aspirations.

Responsibility for determining the manner of Britain's participation in the new nationality scheme was given to an interdepartmental working party, chaired by the Home Office and including representatives from the Dominions Office, Foreign Office, India Office, and Colonial Office. Discussion quickly centered on the colonies and four possible ways of accommodating them. From the outset, the Home and Foreign Offices favored the institution of a citizenship of the United Kingdom accompanied by separate citizenships for each individual colony. This "completely logical" scheme could "be easily understood and appreciated."[35] These two departments rejected three other possibilities. Abstaining from the creation of national citizenships, though popular with the Colonial Office, was regarded by the rest of the committee as impractical in light of the need to recognize dominion equality. Creating two citizenships, one for all the colonies as a group and one covering the United Kingdom alone, was rejected as "politically impossible" for fear that the distinction "would be resented as a sign of inferiority" by colonial residents. A single combined United Kingdom and Colonial citizenship was likewise rejected "on the grounds that the United Kingdom plus the Colonies is such an artificial entity that it would not be politically practicable to propose it."

Initially, the Colonial Office had hoped that its arguments would persuade the government to abstain from the whole scheme. When it seemed unlikely that this view would prevail, officials maintained that political complications in the colonies could be best avoided by a plan adhering as closely as possible to "existing and traditional forms"—effectively the combined UKC option so disliked by the Home and Foreign Offices. The Colonial Office took this position in the belief that the significance of nationality went beyond the practicalities of geography, nomenclature, privileges, and duties. Rather, as "a symbol of common loyalty and equal status," nationality, and the common status of British subject, constituted one of the main arteries between motherland and colony which "no opportunity should be lost to strengthen."[36] Thus, if the colonials were to continue to regard themselves as British, they must share a single nationality with the United Kingdom. Other representatives of the working party disagreed. Speaking for the Home Office, Sir Oscar Dowson said that to confer "UK citizenship upon the inhabitants of a remote island thousands of miles away seemed to be a violation of geography and common sense." Responding for the Colonial Office Sir Kenneth Roberts-Wray countered that "the conferment of a separate citizenship upon every colony" as sought by the Home Office plan "would lead to absurd results."[37] Other committee members reminded the Colonial Office that the bill changed only the manner by which the common nationality was acquired, not the status of British subject itself. The Colonial Office responded that perception was as important as reality and that the dual centers of loyalty created by the bill would be confusing for colonial peoples. Above all, new citizenships "would interrupt the direct link" between the United Kingdom and the colonies and "would obscure what is common, and throw into relief what is individual and separate." The Colonial Office perceived this differentiation between center and periphery to have dangerous long-term implications, providing "politicians . . . moved by extreme views, whether in the direction of nationalism or communism" with "ready-made material for political agitation."[38] Thus, for the Colonial Office, preservation of the common nationality was linked to preservation of the empire/commonwealth in its current form and under continued British influence.

Unable to reach a unanimous decision, officials prepared a memorandum for the Cabinet which acknowledged five possible solutions to the "very thorny problem" but suggested that only three merited "serious consideration": the creation of separate citizenships for the UK and each colony; abstention from the whole scheme; the creation of a citizenship for the UK but not for any colonial territory, the inhabitants of which would participate as British subjects *simpliciter,* with no intervening citizenship status. The memo omitted the combined UKC option, rejected as "too artificial an entity for citizenship purposes." In its presentation of the possibilities available, the paper articulated the by now obvious "clash of interests" between Colonial and Dominions Offices: nonparticipation threatened dominion relations, while logical participation threatened colonial relations. Attempting to appease the demands of both departments, the working party recommended in favor of the compromise third alternative—the creation of a citizenship for the United Kingdom and the retention of a simple British subject status for colonial residents. To mollify colonial resentment of superior UK status, the working party suggested that colonial subjects be made UK citizens either upon entering the territory of the United Kingdom or after two years residence.[39]

The recipient of the memorandum, Sir Alexander Maxwell, Permanent Under Secretary at the Home Office, disagreed with the working party's findings. Maxwell thought the compromise alternative "involved a most unfortunate differentiation between the Colonies and the rest of the Commonwealth . . . and seemed almost bound to give an impression in the Colonies that theirs was to be an inferior status." Therefore, notwithstanding difficulties of nomenclature and geography, Maxwell directed the committee to reconsider the Colonial Office arguments for a combined UKC citizenship. During discussion, committee members rapidly adapted themselves to Maxwell's reasoning. The Dominions Office acknowledged that such a citizenship would meet its needs, and Dowson now acknowledged that the combined option "had certain advantages," expressing "exactly the relation of the UK and Colonies as one single unit in the British Commonwealth" and clearly fitting "the conception of this all-embracing citizenship."[40] With Maxwell's intervention and subsequent concessions, the Colonial Office won the day. Attempts were made to find a less clumsy terminology than "citizen of the United Kingdom and Colonies" but such suggestions as "citizen of Greater Britain," "citizen of the British Realm," "citizen of the Empire," and "British Crown citizen" seemed slight improvement and so the original, for all its awkwardness, remained.[41] Thus, when the so-called Experts' Conference met in 1947 to discuss Commonwealth nationality, the debate was primarily technical, as others have noted. This kind of a meeting was possible, however, only because the UK representatives had already worked out a firm and clear position.[42]

IV

Although UK officials achieved their goals at the Experts' Conference, their firm and clear position came under attack closer to home during the parliamentary debate on the bill in 1948. Partly as a function of being in opposition but primarily out of attachment to an imperialist heritage, Conservative MPs criticized the bill for undermining the imperial nationality by ending the period when "birth within the King's Dominions and allegiance automatically confer[ed] the proud status of a British subject."[43] Viscount Hinchinbrooke (Victor Montagu) accused the government of republicanism and of trying to reduce popular attachment to the throne.[44] Even as they condemned the bill for apparently weakening imperial links, however, Conservative MPs and peers objected yet more strenuously to the creation of a combined UKC citizenship. Implicit within their arguments was a perceived distinction between the familial imperial community and the political imperial community of Britishness. Although "deeply anxious that everything should be done to maintain the intimacy between the various parts of the Commonwealth," David Maxwell-Fyfe, a future Home Secretary and Lord Chancellor, did not consider citizenship to be an appropriate term to describe "the immense variety of people" caught within the institution of the UKC. In his argument that citizenship should not be equated merely with parliamentary sovereignty but should rather be based on "some homogeneity and some true community of interest and status," Maxwell-Fyfe clearly distinguished between the larger legal entity of the British Empire and the smaller informal community of true Britons. Employing the metaphor of family which would reappear so often in postwar discussions of migration and nationality, Maxwell-Fyfe denounced the combined citizenship since "the ordinary citizen" did not have "a feeling of special unity with the inhabitants of a colony," though there may be "a first cousin in the dominions with whom he has played in his Grandfather's house."[45] The same image of a formal empire bound by law but not by kinship appeared in Lord Altrincham's (Sir Edward Grigg) description of the new citizenship as "not real, because the peoples of the Colonial Empire are not united with us, or with each other, by the ties of which true national citizenship is made." Given that the "colonial peoples" were tied in every legal sense to the United Kingdom, what was missing must have been a nonlegal or informal sense of community and mutual acceptance of equality. Articulating this perceived sense of difference between colonial and UK residents, Altrincham denounced the bill as "a departure into complete and utter unreality," which ignored the bonds of "like to like."[46] Other members focused on the apparent discrepancy between colonial and dominion residents. Hinchinbrooke, so concerned for the popularity of the Crown, feared yet more that colonial residents were being granted "a higher nationality" than dominion residents, who while they became citizens of their own countries immediately, could become UKC citizens only after two years' residence in the United Kingdom.[47] Likewise, Altrincham maintained that the status of an Australian or Canadian would be "inferior to that of millions of members of entirely primitive societies, whose contribution to the development of the Commonwealth is in no way on a par with his." These complaints bore the implicit assumption that dominion residents, though living outside the territorial borders of the nation-state, were yet the true children and builders of empire and therefore somehow closer to the United Kingdom. The statements of these members of the Conservative party revealed the conflict between the separate spheres of nationality represented by the informal national identity and the formal nationality policy. The Conservatives resolved this conflict very easily by elevating sentimental attachment to the familial community of imperial Britishness above metropolitan obligation to "British" colonial possessions. In their criticisms, the Tories hit upon the pragmatism of the 1948 act but failed to understand that the policy was intended to shore up the empire rather than oversee its decline.

Labour justified the bill as necessary to show "our fellows in the Dominions . . . that we are in fact recognising [their] equality of status with this country." According to Ede, such changes as the bill brought about were inevitable if the "great, loyal confederation of people" known as the British Commonwealth of Nations, was to be maintained as "a living, growing organism."[48] Attorney General Shawcross defended the creation of the UKC citizenship as a legal necessity inasmuch as the colonies were subject to the sovereignty of Westminster. With this defense, Labour relied on the imagined political community of imperial "Britishness" to defend a practical policy—maintenance of the empire/commonwealth. Within this imperial political community, however, lay the informal national identity that consigned colonial citizens to a dependent inferiority. Ede emphasized that the government rejected any notion of inequality between "people in this country" and "the coloured races of the Empire." He went on to say that the creation of the UKC citizenship was a means of giving "backward peoples . . . a feeling that on the homespun dignity of man we recognize them as fellow citizens." Labour's object, which this bill made clear, was "to raise them to such a position of education, of training, and of experience that they too shall be able to share the grant of full self-government which this House has so generously given during the last few years to other places." Likewise, the Lord Chancellor believed Britain "responsible for [the] peace, order, and good government of our colonial territories," but distinguished "between our own people and the people for whom we are trustees."[49] Thus, in Labour's postwar imperialism, everyone was a British subject but some subjects were more British than others.

Despite differences in presentation and a Labour emphasis on paternalistic development, imperialist ideology on both sides of the House shared common origins. Members of the political elite, both Labour and Tory, subscribed to a racialized understanding of the empire's population which deemed race, rather than skin color, to be an unmodifiable genetic characteristic. It reified race as a biological reality instead of recognizing it as a social construct. According to this racialized interpretation of demography, the world's population could be broken down into discrete collectivities of racial types, each following genetically determined social and cultural patterns of behavior.[50] Thus, for both Labour and Conservative politicians, white-skinned British subjects were different from dark-skinned ones not just in terms of physical features but in terms of culture, intelligence, and other constructed attributes.

In addition, this racialized understanding of the world's population constructed national identities for the policy-making elite. For the most part, phenotypical features were assumed to correspond to national borders. Thus the UK population was presumed to be "white" and the Jamaican population presumed to be "black." White Jamaicans would generally be perceived as descendants of UK residents or, more poetically, as the sons and daughters of the empire. In much the same way, white emigrants to Australia had captured the title of Australian, leaving "native" or "primitive" for the indigenous Aborigines. Thus the policy-making elite's constructed national identity incorporated skin color, presumed genetically determined cultural and behavioral patterns, and claimed national titles based on these constructions. For example, residents of the United Kingdom were assumed to be white, Christian, conservative, and the true custodians and owners of the title "British." These differences between racial and subsequently national groups were presumed to be ancient and fixed, the root of hierarchical differentiation within the imperial population.

Within this hierarchy UK culture was deemed superior to all others. The colonials were "primitive of mind," "backward," a "responsibility," and not "our own people." The interdepartmental working party's first dismissal of a common citizenship had been largely based on the belief that there was no "natural" link between the colonies and the United Kingdom. Even the Colonial Office couched its argument for a combined citizenship in terms of responsibility and politics, not a "Britishness" shared by the two populations. In this context, the postwar political elite clearly had an idea about the true identity of the real British people. Colonial residents of the newly formed United Kingdom and Colonies might have been formal citizens of the new territory and might be deserving of respect and human rights, but they were not really kith and kin; real family ties lay with "brothers and sisters" in the dominions, not "friends" in the colonies.[51]

Immediately after the war, however, British subjects of color were granted UKC status, confirming their membership in the imperial political community of Britishness. Committed to the principle of colonial welfare and development, hopeful of potential political and economic advantage, Labour was most of all eager to convey an image of a strong and united empire/commonwealth. In short, in 1948 the larger vision of a universal imperial nationality outweighed racialized difference. Indeed, in the context of what has been seen as "the second colonial occupation," when the economic ties between Britain and the colonies tightened, the institutionalization of colonial individuality and a loosening of the political bonds would have been madness.[52] In fact, at a time when other changes were being forced on London, retaining as much as possible of the empire offered the best chance of sustaining enough power and influence to keep Britain among the great powers. As the Colonial Office also prophesied, anticipated Indian independence and strains already felt in Malaya and elsewhere in Southeast Asia made it unlikely that the imposition of separate national citizenships would long pass unregarded and unused by colonial nationalists in search of a basis on which to build popular nationalism.

Both the internal deliberations and subsequent public discussions of the 1948 act reveal that the decision to create a single community of the United Kingdom and Colonies was a political maneuver designed to ward off potential calls for colonial independence. Similarly, acquiescence in the dominions' national citizenships was seen as a concession that would enable these countries to remain within the Commonwealth. In both cases, universal subjecthood and common citizenship were designed to maintain subordination within the imperial system, and thus, ironically, they compromised the very equality that they allegedly heralded. Further compromising this equality were the racialized ideology of the governing elite and the competing communities of "Britishness" which revealed themselves in the negotiations surrounding the 1948 act. Labour succeeded in papering over these separate spheres of nationality, but in the following years the onset of independent colonial migration, the recruitment of aliens for work in Britain, and the revival of imperial migration would make it much more difficult to conceal the cracks.

In addition to constructing an imperial nationality around restless dominions and colonies, the 1948 Nationality Act carved out a unique relationship with Irish aliens resident in Britain which is detailed in Chapter 4. The act also restored women's right to retain their British nationality on marriage to an alien. This change, in line with policy in other Commonwealth countries, responded to women's demands during the past several decades.[53] The act did not entirely remove gendered stereotypes from British nationality, however. Under the terms of the new law, in order to prevent "women of very undesirable character" from arriving in Dover and marrying the first man they saw, alien women marrying British men no longer automatically became British.[54] And the transmission of citizenship, and thus subjecthood, continued to be confined to the male line. Thus, the community of female Britishness continued to suggest dependence and inequality.

Throughout the parliamentary debate, the Attlee government attempted to demonstrate continuity and avoid offending the dominions by emphasizing that the bill changed nothing. The same people eligible for British subjecthood prior to passage continued to be eligible for it after passage. The full truth, however, was that the bill changed the manner of acquiring British nationality, devised a scheme to permit Irish aliens to benefit from British nationality, extended the rights of women with regard to nationality, provided an alternative title for British subjects unwilling to accept the term, and most significant in terms of Labour's larger foreign-policy objective of securing British influence, created a mechanism for strengthening the empire/commonwealth. Given all of these achievements, the 1948 British Nationality Act may well be seen as a superior instrument of Labour's imperial policy. By the time it became law on 1 January 1949, the second strand of Labour's imperial policy, the sponsored emigration of British subjects, was already fully operational.

CHAPTER 2

Emigrating British Stock

In the fifteen-year period 1946 through 1960, out of a total population of 47 million, annual UK emigration averaged 125,000.[1] While some of these migrants went to foreign parts, 80 percent went to Australia, Canada, New Zealand, South Africa, and Southern Rhodesia. In total, these "old" or less euphemistically termed "white" dominions received over 1.5 million UK residents in the fifteen years after World War II. This significant movement of people did not happen accidentally; it reflected official policy. Within six months of taking office, Clement Attlee's Labour government had implemented a vision of imperial migration by negotiating sponsored schemes with Southern Rhodesia, South Africa, and Australia. New Zealand joined the fray in 1947, and although Canada waited until 1951 to organize a formal scheme, UK residents wishing to emigrate to Canada before that date found their path facilitated by the Canadian authorities' informal, but no less real, enthusiasm for British immigrants. Upon its assumption of office in October 1951, Winston Churchill's Conservative government demonstrated its backing by continuing to facilitate dominion recruitment efforts and by renewing the legislation that funded imperial migration. Although only the Australian scheme received a specific UK subsidy, each of the principal receiving countries benefited from a great deal of indirect UK government funding and significant official public support.

Postwar Britain's imperial migration policy is noteworthy in four respects. First, it involved a significant volume of population. Second, it revealed the many competing imagined communities of Britishness at work in the postwar British Empire/Commonwealth. Throughout the negotiations surrounding the various sponsored migration schemes and in the debates about the general merits of imperial migration, parliamentarians and civil servants consistently referred to transporting or transplanting "British stock." This language, together with eligibility qualifications, illustrates that although all British stock were British subjects, the political elites of the United Kingdom and the "old" dominions did not consider all British subjects to be British stock. Rather, policy makers conceived of separate spheres of nationality: residents of the empire with a white skin and European cultural descent were British stock; residents of the empire with a skin of color and African or Asian heritage were British subjects only. Thus, within a political community that included all members of the empire/commonwealth, there existed an exclusive familial community defined by blood and culture. Although metaphorically whole, this familial community was in practical terms further divided according to whether subjects resided inside or outside the United Kingdom. These separate spheres of nationality and competing communities of Britishness can be conceptualized as overlapping circles of belonging. White-skinned Europeans living in the dominions would be considered members of the political community of Britishness, the imperial family of Britishness, and the community of British stock. Dark-skinned Africans, West Indians, or Asians living in colonies or dominions would be considered members of the political community of Britishness only. And at the center of these three circles was the domestic community of Britishness which consisted of white-skinned residents of the United Kingdom, who were always presumed to be of European descent.

Britain's postwar migration policy was also notable for the extraordinary degree of confidence it manifested among the policy-making elite in the strength, resilience, and desirability of all levels of Britishness, but particularly the Britishness of emigrating British stock. Successive Labour and Conservative administrations remained secure in their conviction that the emigrating British stock would retain allegiance to Britain and membership in both the imperial and familial communities of Britishness. The total absence of concern about potential conflicts of loyalty, particularly in light of the new national citizenships being instituted at the time, demonstrates the political elite's conviction that the right policies could contain dominion nationalism within the rubric of British subjecthood.

Finally, the imperial migration is significant because it illustrates the commitment of successive administrations to the empire/commonwealth as a viable entity worthy of receiving large quantities of one of postwar Britain's scarcest resources—labor. Policy makers' acquiescence in, even facilitation of, the loss of this labor highlights the significance postwar governments attached to the imperial ideal. Labour and Conservative governments sent British stock to the dominions both to strengthen the links between Commonwealth members by maintaining the Britishness of the whole and to increase the stature of the British Empire by boosting economic development through demographic growth. Together, these efforts to shore up the imperial system were designed to provide a basis for the maintenance of Britain's international position at a time when the United Kingdom alone could not compete economically and politically with the superpower status of the United States or the Soviet Union.

These imperial objectives were sufficiently strong in the immediate postwar period to overcome otherwise prohibiting factors such as an acute labor shortage, a desperate financial crisis, and widespread fears that the UK population was failing to reproduce itself. In 1950 Attlee's government, followed by a series of Conservative administrations, began to give more and more attention to these factors. Although the number of departing UK residents held steady through 1962, both parliamentarians and civil servants were increasingly haunted by the specter of economic and demographic loss and the potentially unfavorable consequences for UK domestic interests. The public record reveals a perpetual battle among officials consistently struggling to balance the perceived political advantages of British stock emigration against the recognized economic disadvantages of the loss of young subjects and citizens. Thus, within less than two decades, fundamental assumptions of the postwar years were opened to question.

I

Emigration from the United Kingdom to parts of the empire and Commonwealth was a well-worn tradition by 1945. The numbers had probably been at their highest in the second half of the nineteenth century when over a hundred thousand people annually departed Britain for foreign and imperial shores.[2] The vast majority of these emigrants left under their own steam, but many received financial and administrative assistance either from philanthropic societies or from the state and its agencies.[3] Within the broad field of state-sponsored emigration there were three major policy shifts over the course of 150 years. Between 1850 and 1918, the general objective behind state assistance was to facilitate the departure of individuals deemed burdensome to society, such as the convicts transported to Australia and paupers given free passage.[4] Whatever the character or circumstances of the emigrant, however, the motivation of eighteenth- and nineteenth-century UK governments remained the same: to relieve congested social and economic conditions in the United Kingdom. Beyond a general preference for migration within the empire, little thought was given to the future welfare of the emigrants or the colonies.[5]

Public reaction to state assistance was mixed. Philanthropic bodies and churches tended to see the schemes as offering the pauper a fresh start, whereas manufacturers and employers regarded emigration as a drain on labor resources and a likely cause of higher wages.[6] Equally ambiguous was the response of the receiving countries, which, though eager for settlers, feared that newcomers in need of assistance represented an inferior type.[7] Partly as a result of this ambivalence, state assistance was given to only a very small proportion of emigrants in the nineteenth century.

The ambivalence dissipated after the First World War with the Coalition government's establishment of the Oversea Settlement Committee designed to promote the emigration of veterans and their dependents to the dominions. In a period of little unemployment, David Lloyd George's government was less interested in getting rid of paupers than in promoting dominion population growth, strengthening the bonds of family, and securing "the outposts of Empire."[8] For their part, Australia, New Zealand, Canada, and South Africa exchanged a nineteenth-century reluctance to accept Britain's castoffs for a twentieth-century enthusiasm for the island's exports. During the three years of the scheme's operation, approximately eighty thousand UK veterans and dependents took advantage of its provisions.[9]

In addition to assisting in the departure of veterans, the OSC recommended that dominion governments adopt a proactive approach to the "immensely important problem of the best distribution of the population of the Empire." The result was the 1922 Empire Settlement Act, which empowered the Secretary of State to cooperate with any dominion government, public authority, or private organization to promote the emigration of "suitable persons" to His Majesty's Dominions overseas. Although a secondary purpose of the act was to provide an outlet for surplus population, the Oversea Settlement Committee and the Dominions Secretary consistently emphasized that the "first and foremost" purpose was "to build up the strength and wealth of the Empire as a whole by the better distribution of its population."[10] In the first decade after passage, the scheme relocated 404,000 UK residents at a direct cost to the Treasury of £6.7 million.[11] Proof that the act was indeed not a palliative for unemployment came in 1931 with the onset of economic depression and significant UK unemployment, when in-migration exceeded out-migration. Despite this apparent decline in popularity, the interwar Conservative administrations continued to support the principle and practice of imperial migration, appointing the Oversea Settlement Board in 1936 to advise on long-term migration policy and in 1937 renewing the Empire Settlement Act for another fifteen years.

In its first report in 1938 the Oversea Settlement Board established what would prove to be the parameters of a debate that would continue through the postwar era. At a time when other nations and peoples had allegedly begun to covet dominion territory, the board highlighted the need to maintain the "British character" of the dominions. At the same time, however, the board acknowledged that continued emigration on a large scale posed a potential demographic risk to the United Kingdom. Caught between these two competing demands, the board found the interests of empire more important and recommended in favor of continued migration.[12] In 1919 the absorption of surplus population had been perceived as a secondary benefit of imperial migration: by 1938 the loss of population through emigration had come to be seen as a necessary evil.

As the probable outcome of the Second World War became apparent and the Coalition wartime government began to consider the likely shape of the postwar world, state policy toward imperial migration entered its third phase. As we have seen, one of the consequences of World War II was the growing practical independence of the dominions from the United Kingdom. Building on interwar strategies, wartime policy makers recognized in migration a means of combating this independence. Populating the empire with "British stock" would ensure that even as the dominions asserted their political autonomy, their cultural and economic links would still tie them to Britain. Equally significant, both Labour and Conservative members of the governing coalition believed that a strong empire/commonwealth would be a key factor in determining Britain's postwar role in the international arena. Whereas the United Kingdom's population of 47 million was dwarfed by the superpower populations of the United States and the Soviet Union, an imperial population of 650 million could command attention.

These considerations were at play in Cabinet discussions as early as 1942, when Prime Minister Winston Churchill suggested that at the war's end willing soldiers should be allowed to demobilize wherever in the empire they happened to be. Clement Attlee, Dominions Secretary in the Coalition government, agreed, claiming that the war had "shown the need for larger populations in the Dominions if the British Empire is to exercise a strong influence in the post-war world."[13] Two years later, at a meeting with dominion prime ministers, Minister of Labour Ernest Bevin advocated not simply the free demobilization of British soldiers but their resettlement and subsequent maintenance in the dominions as part of a grand imperial defense strategy.[14] Even as they perceived imperial political advantage, however, ministers revisited the parameters established by the Oversea Settlement Board six years earlier. Though questioning whether the country could "afford to lose good young men and women in large numbers," Lord Cranborne, the future Lord Salisbury who, as Commonwealth Relations Secretary, would advocate so strongly against admitting British subjects of color to the United Kingdom, concluded now in favor of imperial migration on the grounds that "the interchange of blood between one part of the Commonwealth and another must tend to strengthen the whole and to multiply the links that hold it together."[15] The Paymaster General disagreed, fearing that "with all the social services we have promised to the old, we cannot afford to get rid of people of the age and type most likely to work and breed."[16] Although recognizing the validity of these fears and acknowledging that Britain could hardly afford to "send its best stock abroad" as the birthrate declined, the Cabinet concluded in favor of imperial migration, reasoning that the numbers were unlikely to be large and that migration "was a valuable means of strengthening the cohesion of the British Commonwealth." Special note was taken of the possibilities of encouraging the emigration of "surplus" women.[17] Public face was given to these private convictions in the summer of 1945 with the publication of a White Paper that proclaimed imperial migration to be "essential to the future happiness and prosperity and even . . . the survival of the British Empire."[18] Despite this unequivocal public support, only a few months later ministers of the newly elected Labour government found themselves balancing the presumed political and strategic benefits of imperial migration against the practical economic loss of labor, just as some of them had done between the wars. They found in favor of government-funded migration, reasoning that the subsidy would not be large enough to promote new migration but would facilitate departures already decided upon.[19] Over the next six years, in its practical implementation of policy, Labour far exceeded this somewhat guarded approval of imperial migration.

II

Although postwar emigrants departed for a wide variety of destinations, both inside and outside the empire/commonwealth, the government supported only migration within the empire. In practical terms, this support manifested itself in the renewal of the Empire Settlement Act in 1952, 1957, and 1962 and the institution of schemes designed to increase imperial migration. In geographical terms, support focused on emigration to the five dominions that either instituted sponsored migration schemes or at least facilitated or encouraged British stock migration. Southern Rhodesia, South Africa, Australia, New Zealand, and Canada each adopted a different approach to imperial migration reflecting each nation's particular perception of its demographic needs. Put together, however, the detailed account of each dominion's imperial migration history provides a composite picture of the aggressive recruiting conducted in postwar Britain as well as the subsequent wave of departures.

Though its checkered relationship with sponsored migration limited its portion of assisted emigrants, Southern Rhodesia in January 1946 was the first country to open a formal scheme. Despite the intentions of its creators, this scheme for the free passage of skilled and professional workers never came into operation because Salisbury deemed that the 250 self-financing emigrants leaving for Southern Rhodesia each month were sufficient and there was no need to supplement the numbers with individuals in need of assistance.[20] So great was the flow of migrants to Southern Rhodesia in fact, that two years later, in 1948, Salisbury imposed financial qualifications on even free migrants in order to give the economy an opportunity to catch up and to ensure the financial stability of those arriving.[21] By 1950, however, a percentage decline in UK immigration relative to other countries prompted Salisbury to relax general immigration controls for UK residents while tightening them for other nationalities and to recruit UK migrants directly for employment as police, military instructors, civil servants, and skilled artisans.[22] In 1951, still eager to increase the immigration of "British stock" workers in construction and engineering, the Southern Rhodesia government inaugurated a second scheme. By giving a refund of thirty pounds to selected immigrants, the 1951 Assisted Passages Scheme was intended to increase the annual UK immigration rate from 3,000 to 6,000.[23] Just a year later, however, an economic downturn in Southern Rhodesia led to a temporary restriction on all immigration and subsequent introduction of national quotas. Although the quota for the United Kingdom and Republic of Ireland was fixed initially at 1,500, UK officials estimated a true annual immigration rate of approximately 3,500 by 1960. According to Southern Rhodesia's own figures, a total of 82,178 UK residents immigrated between 1946 and 1960.[24]

In 1946, under the leadership of General Jan Smuts, South Africa instituted a scheme for state-sponsored (but not financially assisted) "British stock" immigration which netted almost 28,000 emigrants in 1948 alone. The election of an Afrikaner government that same year, however, prompted a change in policy. In order to obtain "a more scientific selection," intending emigrants could enter the union only on the direct authorization of the South African government. This restriction effectively limited UK migration to staff required by existing British firms, others with special skills, or those with guaranteed employment. The Afrikaner government wanted to preserve the numerical superiority of the Afrikaners over the British element (roughly 3 : 2) and focused upon the recruitment of Dutch, German, and to a lesser extent Italian immigrants, who were "likely to become good Afrikaners."[25] In addition, South Africa, like Southern Rhodesia, believed assisted immigrants to be unsuitable because they were unlikely to be able to maintain the standard-of-living differentials between black indigenous and white immigrant communities thought necessary to South African society. Despite these preferences, a steady flow of "British stock" immigrants brought 125,676 into the country from 1946 to 1957. Although leaving the Commonwealth, South Africa reinstituted immigration programs for skilled and professional Britons in 1960.[26]

During the wartime discussions of migration, only the Prime Minister of

Interest in emigration among service personnel and their families ran high even before the opening of free and assisted passage schemes. Note the pleasant images suggested by the promotional literature and the rank of the window-shoppers, December 1945. (The Hulton Deutsch Collection.)

Australia had initially shown sufficient interest to sign a formal agreement, commenting that "suitable migrants of British stock would be a valuable accretion to his country's strength." Subsequent negotiations between the Australian and UK governments, which began in late 1944, bore fruit on 6 March 1946 with the announcement of the Free and Assisted Passage Schemes, which provided selected UK residents with free transportation to Australia, temporary housing, and assistance in finding employment. Financed jointly by the UK and Australian governments, the schemes derived their authority from the Empire Settlement Act and differed only in requiring a contribution of ten pounds from adult civilians (teenagers paid five pounds and children went free) whereas veterans received free passage. All veterans, including women, were eligible for the scheme, regardless of occupational or marital status, but civilians were recruited primarily from skilled and semiskilled trades, with preference given to single persons under forty-five. Initially, because of a housing shortage in Australia, the scheme worked by matching a UK applicant with an Australian nominee who agreed to provide housing and frequently a job.[27]

In 1950, with the supply of nominees running low, and wanting to increase "British stock" migration to 100,000 per year, Canberra launched a program for UK residents prepared to live in hostels and work in an approved industry. After less than three years, the scheme collapsed, however, plagued by tales of poorly maintained hostels, insufficient and ill-cooked food, an outbreak of rioting, a spate of evictions, and general resistance to the notion of British people living in camps.[28]

Undaunted, the Australian government instituted new measures designed to stimulate the flow of migrants in the latter half of the decade. Local communities in Australia were encouraged to "bring out a Briton" by offering sponsorship and accommodation. The "Nest Egg" scheme relaxed nomination requirements for Britons with a small sum of capital at their disposal. To encourage family migration, the five-pound contribution for teenagers' passages was abolished, and to overcome the shortage of shipping, assisted passages by air were provided at no extra charge. Finally, the Australian government opened additional migration offices in major provincial cities such as Edinburgh, Manchester, Belfast, and Birmingham. These efforts produced an annual emigration rate of 43,000 by 1960 and a total emigration for the period 1946 through 1960 of 566,429. Of this total 380,426 received free or assisted passages at a direct cost to the UK Treasury of £3.8 million.[29]

During a wartime election campaign, the New Zealand National Party, playing on popular fears of "the expanding Japanese Empire," promised that if elected it would raise New Zealand's population to 5 million within ten or fifteen years after the end of the war. Once in office, however, in recognition that reaching this target would require an annual immigrant flow of 70,000, the National Party adopted a more cautious approach to immigration.[30] Not until May 1947 did New Zealand institute Free and Assisted Passages Schemes for "British stock" veterans and civilians. Wellington paid the entire cost of resettlement, including passage, in order to retain a free hand in emigrant selection and to spare London additional financial burdens. The schemes initially recruited skilled single men and women aged up to thirty-five working in construction, engineering, or agriculture, but within a few years the requirements broadened to include married couples up to forty-five years of age working in the same industries and with one or two children. The restrictions slowed the start of the emigration stream, but by 1952 the average annual rate of immigration from the United Kingdom had reached over ten thousand, about a third of whom received financial assistance. This flow remained steady until 1958, when a contraction in the New Zealand economy prompted a temporary withdrawal of assistance, but by 1960 New Zealand authorities were again offering financial aid to selected UK migrants. The cumulative result of these efforts was the emigration to New Zealand between 1946 and 1960 of 151,730 UK residents.[31]

Canada's initial involvement in imperial migration consisted mainly of war brides. A reluctance to accept migrants in need of financial assistance and a fear of upsetting the French Canadian population by favoritism toward British immigrants inhibited the institution of free or assisted schemes, and the imposition of currency controls in 1948 limited the flow of independent migrants.[32] Nevertheless, large numbers of emigrants found their path smoothed by the readiness of the Canadian authorities "to accept any British immigrants who are able to satisfy certain simple requirements."[33] In late 1951, eager to fuel an economic boom with the right kind of "stock" but still trying to avoid the taint of charity, the Canadian authorities instituted a loan program whereby British, Irish, and certain other European people were advanced passage and resettlement costs to be repaid without interest over time.[34] These steps paid off, and in the eight years from 1946 to 1954, over 300,000 "British stock" immigrants came to Canada. Though large, this figure constituted only 33 percent of total Canadian immigration during this period, and there were repeated calls for greater British immigration.[35]

In late 1955, in an effort to lure large UK families, the Canadian government both extended the loan scheme and effectively agreed to extend family allowances to immigrants immediately upon arrival.[36] The urgency of the demand for British migrants in the postwar period is perhaps best exemplified by the Canadian Agriculture Minister's offer to give Britain a thousand bushels of wheat for every British immigrant.[37] Perhaps in part because of these additional measures, perhaps, as some newspapers speculated, partly in response to the debacle of Suez, 1957 was a boom year for emigration to Canada, with over twenty thousand applications per week submitted to the London and Liverpool offices of Canada House. National and provincial newspapers ran stories persuasively describing "the lure of the New World" with photographs of UK residents "queuing for Canada."[38] So great was the flow that an "Air Bridge to Canada" was instituted to help relieve pressure on shipping.[39] All told, just under 109,000 British stock immigrants entered Canada in 1957, 39 percent of the total.[40] In the last years of the decade, partly in response to a downturn in the Canadian economy, partly as a consequence of the high number of immigrants in previous years, emigration to Canada decreased to between 20,000 and 25,000 per year.[41] Nevertheless, despite apparently inhibiting factors such as the absence of any formal agreement with United Kingdom authorities and a reluctance to take "charity" cases, total UK emigration to Canada between 1946 and 1960 was 582,787.[42]

In addition to independent and sponsored adult migration, the postwar era witnessed the last gasp of child migration, primarily to Australia. Suspended during the war, child migration schemes originated under the auspices of the 1922 Empire Settlement Act. Over twenty years later, the Australian government announced plans to bring in around seventeen thousand child migrants, of whom it hoped the greater portion would be British, and the New Zealand government offered a home to any British child orphaned by the war.[43] In the context of new philosophies about child raising which suggested that children fared better in family rather than institutional settings, however, and in the wake of the establishment of the welfare state, UK local authorities proved reluctant to export the three thousand British war orphans in their care. Much more likely to emigrate were children in the care of voluntary societies, particularly Roman Catholic.[44]

Religious and secular voluntary bodies regarded emigration as a way to improve prospects for orphans, children born of unmarried parents, children whose parents were unable to provide for their offspring, and children from "broken homes." An interdepartmental official committee on migration policy supported the departure of such children on the grounds that "the young migrant makes the best migrant," that this class of children was the most likely, if left in the United Kingdom, to become a burden on the state, and that a child emigrant constituted less of a financial loss to Britain than an adult.[45] Official support for the principle and practice of child migration manifested itself in the provision of free passages and clothing and maintenance grants which lasted through the child's sixteenth birthday (all supplied under the auspices of the Empire Settlement Act). To this, dominion governments contributed settlement grants and maintenance payments. The voluntary societies themselves made up any shortfall as well as paying for the costs of the administration of their schemes. Despite the financial contribution, UK authorities largely left management of the schemes and the placement and supervision of the children to the voluntary societies.

By the mid-1950s, however, the program ran into problems. Despite general support for the practice, some officials questioned whether the sponsored departure of children "of fine physique and good mental equipment" (the type most preferred by the host nations) was to Britain's advantage and recommended instead that emigration should be restricted to children "with an unfortunate background" in greater need of a fresh start.[46] The Home Office voiced similar doubts, particularly in light of Australia's propensity to house children in institutions, and suggested that adoption in the UK or resettlement with some family member offered a better life.[47] By contrast, noting the relatively small number of children emigrating and believing that a great many children under local authority care would make suitable emigrants, the Oversea Migration Board (a pro-emigration advisory board composed of MPs)

A party of boys and girls traveling to Australia under the auspices of the Fairbridge Society, December 1948. The adult escorts and the children would most likely have met for the first time just a few days prior to departure. (Courtesy of the Harold Cohen Library, University of Liverpool.)

persuaded the Commonwealth Relations Office to sponsor a fact-finding mission to Australia to report on the living conditions and experiences of postwar child migrants. It was hoped that favorable accounts would stimulate greater local authority participation in child migration schemes. The effort backfired when the mission told of barrackslike facilities, overcrowding, understaffing, poor training, and a general lack of "appreciation of a child's need for affection, for roots in a home with a family atmosphere, and for adequate contact with the world outside the institution." Referring to the report as "embarrassing," "hasty," and likely to put "the cat amongst the pigeons," some UK officials urged that it not be published.[48] It was, however, and support for child emigration further declined. Indeed, in 1956 the interdepartmental committee on migration policy suggested that had it been "untrammelled by precedent" it might not have recommended either child migration or the existing methods of operating it. As it was, the committee linked future financial assistance to the voluntary societies with the societies' commitment to move away from institutional care. Five years later, this same committee recommended that Australia assume Britain's declining financial obligations for schemes that were in any case drawing to a natural close. Overall, in the twelve-year period 1946 to 1960, approximately three thousand children emigrated under the auspices of the voluntary societies at a direct cost to the UK Treasury (excluding passages) of just under £300,000. The decline is manifested in the figures for 1960, when just sixty-eight children emigrated and only 20 percent of places available in Australian institutions for British children were occupied.[49]

In addition to child migration societies, two other voluntary organizations concerned themselves with the promotion of imperial migration. Founded in 1919, the Society for the Oversea Settlement of British Women effectively operated as the female arm of the Dominions Office, advising professional women, mainly teachers and nurses, on positions in South and Central Africa. UK officials believed that the services of the society were worth the annual grant-in-aid it received from the government since its efforts helped ensure that emigrating women were of a high quality and thus unlikely to strain consular services and likely to enhance Commonwealth goodwill. In the postwar period 8,352 women sailed under its auspices, though by 1960 it was beginning to lose favor with officials. Still very much in favor at this time was the second principal nongovernmental agency concerned with the emigration of adults, or rather youth. The Big Brother Movement facilitated the emigration of boys aged between fifteen and nineteen—"some of the best material for successful settlement"—by providing each with a Big Brother sponsor upon arrival. Originally founded in 1924, the movement restarted its activities after the war, and with grants from both Canberra and London, it was responsible for the emigration of 2,898 boys from 1945 through 1960.[50]

The combined efforts of the dominion governments, the voluntary societies, and successive UK governments resulted in a total "British stock" migration of over 1.5 million to the five principal receiving countries of Australia, Canada, New Zealand, South Africa, and Southern Rhodesia for the period 1946 through 1960 at a direct cost to the Treasury of £7.5 million.[51] This figure represented 80 percent of total Commonwealth emigration. The peak year was undoubtedly 1957, when 175,892 people departed Britain to take up permanent residence in one of the five principal receiving countries.[52]

Throughout the period a substantial in-migration of British subjects also occurred. In the early postwar years, this movement consisted predominantly of "failed" "British stock" emigrants, dominion migrants coming "to try their luck," and former officers of the imperial civil and military service returning to Britain following colonial independence. As the 1950s progressed, the in-migration increasingly involved West Indians, Indians, and Pakistanis seeking work in the "motherland." In addition, the United Kingdom continued to accept a substantial immigrant flow from the Irish Republic, and other foreign countries, which, combined with British subject inward migration, often nearly balanced emigration. At issue, however, is not the number who left—though it is significant that so many departed—but the reasons behind the government policy that encouraged and facilitated their departure despite per-ceived financial and demographic crises.

Although only about a quarter of all emigrants received direct financial as-sistance, both Labour and Conservative administrations demonstrated their support for "British stock" emigration in a wide variety of ways.[53] From the beginning, the Ministry of Labour was the agency charged with the practical running of the Free and Assisted Passages Schemes. It was initially chosen over the more obvious Commonwealth Relations Office because the cost of ex-servicemen's free passages was to fall on the ministry's vote. Once in place, it remained the competent authority because its employment exchanges pro-vided daily access to likely constituents. The ministry acted as a conduit for would-be emigrants, shepherding them through the notification, interview, and selection process. Employment exchanges stocked application forms and informational booklets for public distribution and displayed promotional posters and literature. The ministry organized publicity and selection tours for all dominion officials in addition to arranging and attending interviews with prospective emigrants. The scale of the ministry's involvement is evident from the figures for 1950 alone and dealing solely with Australia: 50 publicity tours and almost 1,500 days of selection work in about 1,000 different centers, concerning just under 14,000 applicants (exclusive of dependents).[54] In addi-tion to informing as wide a body of people as possible about the advantages of emigration, ministry officials believed that their cooperation was helpful in regulating both occupational and regional areas of recruitment, avoiding publicity tours in, for example, mining areas. This informal leverage existed only in the case of the Australian schemes to which Britain contributed finan-cially. Other dominions were also in receipt of much administrative assistance but were free to recruit at will.

Perhaps nothing illustrates the depth of the Attlee government's initial commitment to imperial migration better than the course of its negotiations with the Australian government. When talks first began, London pressed for certain issues on which it later made concessions to avoid jeopardizing the whole scheme. Initially, London demanded that UK veterans enjoy the same employment preference as Australian soldiers; that the Free Passage Scheme open first as a demonstration of good faith to the armed services; that the assisted migrant contribute fifteen pounds toward the fare to relieve the burden on the UK Treasury; and that migrants be recruited only as individuals, not as occupational groups, in order to lessen the impact of departure on the UK labor market. Canberra had its way on every issue. Australian veterans received privileges above all others; the schemes opened simultaneously so that Australia House would have free choice over the entire UK labor market; the fare was ten pounds to encourage as many people as possible to apply; and bulk recruitment was permitted to better serve Australian industry. In addition to these concessions, London made yet one more—perhaps the most flagrant example of the commitment to emigration. The Australian government wanted to publicize the schemes prior to its parliamentary recess, to begin on 6 March 1946. UK officials, believing that such an announcement might be "inopportune . . . in view of the present Government manpower campaign," pushed for a delay.[55] Despite London's misgivings, Canberra refused to alter the date. The scheme was announced on 6 March in the midst of a UK domestic productivity drive and hard on the heels of the formation of the Foreign Labour Committee, the body charged with the job of importing workers from Europe for Britain's essential industries. It was hardly the most propitious time to announce the sponsored annual departure of over twenty-five thousand citizens. Significantly, officials were not concerned about saving the labor for Britain but merely that the timing might cause some embarrassment for the government.

III

The readiness to overlook the demands of a productivity drive in the midst of a domestic economic crisis and labor shortage points to the significance attached to the policy of imperial migration. As we have seen, the wartime Coalition government under Churchill proposed the redistribution of population as a means of securing postwar influence. This political program remained in place throughout the postwar period and was given public face by a variety of state agencies and representatives. As early as 1949 the *Report of the Royal Commission on Population* credited "the preponderance of British stock in the population of the Dominions" with maintaining "the sense of unity which animates, and is the main connecting link between, the self-governing parts of the British Commonwealth." The commission concluded that "if the sentiment is to be maintained and the political character of the British Empire is to remain what it has been," future population growth in the dominions should stem primarily from "persons of British origin." Furthermore, the commission feared that if imperial migration "were to cease altogether or to drop to insignificant numbers the consequences for Britain's economic future and her place in the world might be serious."[56]

These political arguments in defense of imperial migration were repeated throughout the following decade. The Labour Commonwealth Relations Secretary Patrick Gordon-Walker declared in 1950 that the "solidarity and increasing strength of the Commonwealth depends on the increasing migration of people from this country." Thus, it was the "firm policy" of the government "to facilitate and encourage the outflow of all those people who wish to leave these islands." Gordon-Walker stressed the point: "This is not just a formal policy which we state and re-state. We have in fact been carrying it out with vigour."[57] A 1950 Cabinet memo, prepared jointly by the Ministry of Labour and Commonwealth Relations Office, reiterated these themes, asserting that the government's policy "has been not merely to place no obstacles in the way of independent migration but to encourage and assist Commonwealth migration because . . . the important and long-term advantages of interchange and better distribution of population within the British Commonwealth . . . considerably . . . outweigh the relatively small loss of manpower to this country." The memo pushed the argument a stage further by suggesting that to permit the percentage of "British stock" population in the dominions to diminish could affect Britain's "future strength, influence and safety in ways that cannot be forecast."[58] The Ministry of Labour emphasized the need to have Australia "retain enough of the British tradition to want to defend us if the UK gets into trouble."[59] In 1951 Dame Mary Smieton of the Ministry of Labour emphasized in a public speech that it was the United Kingdom's responsibility to dispatch "men and women who will carry to these Commonwealth countries our own particular traditions." Smieton, depicting the migrants as so many mules of culture, declared that they "will all help to carry with them British traditions and British ways of life."[60] A year later, the ministry and the Commonwealth Relations Office remained committed to imperial migration: "Never has the need on social, economic and strategic grounds for the greater solidarity of the British people throughout the Commonwealth been greater than it is today. Moreover, it is recognized by the Government that, even at some loss to the UK in terms of manpower, it is in this country's wider interests to maintain the British connection in a society of nations from which this country derives much of its practical influence in the affairs of the world."[61]

When Churchill replaced Attlee as Prime Minister in October 1951, the commitment to imperial migration remained unchanged. Advocating the renewal of the Empire Settlement Act in 1952, the Conservative Commonwealth Relations Secretary Lord Salisbury stated his belief that the exchange of migrants within the Commonwealth represented "a transfusion of blood which strengthens the whole" and against which the "comparatively small loss in manpower was as nothing."[62] In 1954 an interdepartmental committee justified government policy "to encourage migration as a means of strengthening the bonds of the various parts of the Commonwealth and Empire." The committee emphasized that "whatever the demographic, economic and strategic arguments may suggest, we feel that it is a continuing United Kingdom interest to ensure that the British character of the Commonwealth is preserved." Migration was essential, since, without it, the proportion of dominion populations "having direct personal links with the Mother Country is bound to diminish." As a result, the committee unequivocally recommended in favor of "refresh[ing] . . . the life blood of the 'old' Commonwealth countries . . . with new settlers from this country."[63] Two years later, in 1956, the same committee reiterated its belief "that the British stock of the new countries should be constantly replenished and fortified" because "the closer these ties, the better disposed will their governments be toward supporting and co-operating with United Kingdom policy in every field—foreign, economic, financial, military, etc.—and the more inclined will their peoples be to understand the British outlook, to buy British goods and services, to visit Britain, and themselves to propound the British point of view."[64] For its part, in anticipation of the expiration of the Empire Settlement Act in 1957, the Commonwealth Relations Office believed that "the nationalist upsurge in Asia" made Australian military and industrial potential all the more critical in supporting British power in the Pacific and Far East. Furthermore, a powerful Commonwealth containing "strong British communities" would provide a counterbalance to Moscow and Washington.[65] The same year, Commonwealth Relations Secretary Sir Alec Douglas-Home urged the Cabinet to pursue renewal of the Empire Settlement Act because "a strong Australia continuing to be predominantly of British stock is of great strategic and economic importance to us."[66] Speaking to the House of Commons, Home wanted to leave no doubt that it was government policy "to encourage a regular flow of UK citizens to make their lives in . . . other Commonwealth countries."[67] In 1958 while in Australia, Prime Minister Macmillan emphasized his commitment to helping Australia "remain British in blood and in tradition."[68] Four years later, a third interdepartmental committee drew attention to the potential of "British stock" to influence political developments in the dominions "as voters, Members of Parliament and as Ministers."[69]

Behind all these statements lay the general conviction that an empire heavily British in stock would remain eternally loyal to the "mother country." Historically, the strategy was an old one. Cromwell's venture into Ireland, Europe's settlement of the Americas, Tsarist Russia's expansion into Asia and Siberia, the United States' manifest destiny, Germany's lebensraum—all relied for their success on the physical plantation of frontier folk and pioneers. Recognizing the limits of formal political control over dominion governments, or

The *Himalaya* and its cargo of British stock emigrants just departing Tilbury Landing Stage for Australia and New Zealand, 1957. (The Museum of London, Museum in Docklands Project, Library and Archive.)

even formal political influence, both Labour and Conservative administrations placed their bets on a revitalized imperial strategy to sustain British global influence. In an age of superpowers, an isolated poverty-stricken European island was very little, but an empire fully deserved a permanent seat on the United Nations Security Council and could legitimately command respect for its international position. This version of colonization was to create Australians who, though formally independent citizens of Australia, would yet admit and practice a sympathy for Britain and British policies. Likewise, it was designed to produce a New Zealand government that, though representing itself at the United Nations, would be the delegate of recently immigrated or -descended British stock from the United Kingdom. Though physically distant, these component parts of the empire were to be integrated with the "mother country" through race, blood, and nation, mediated by the new, fast means of telecommunication and transport. The metaphor of the imperial family ruled, and the rhetoric of politicians from both major parties resounded with references to "kith and kin," "blood," and "family." Such language suggested both strength—for what could be stronger than a family constantly replenishing and extending itself?—and intimacy—for what could be more intimate than a family?

As exclusive as the rhetoric of family was, however, the practice of imperial migration was yet more exclusive. It is clear from the public record that the governing elites of the participating Commonwealth countries all understood the British family to consist solely of blood relatives and not to include those whose membership in the empire was perceived in purely political terms. It was to the restricted community of white-skinned British stock that London looked for the renewal of Britain's imperial fortunes. Thus, despite the use of universal language, the principle and practice of imperial migration, like the discussions surrounding the 1948 British Nationality Act, rested on competing, defensive definitions of Britishness. On the one hand, the readiness to transfer population from one part of the empire to another stemmed from a belief in the imperial nationality and a confidence that Britishness could span the continents. On the other hand, the practical definition suggested a narrower interpretation of Britishness which reflected the racialization of the imperial population and subsequent creation of a racial hierarchy. UK policy makers made few overt references to the skin color of those whose emigration they sponsored, but not because of color blindness. Rather, it was simply assumed that UK residents would be white, and therefore the job of discriminating at the door was left to dominion authorities. UK officials proved wholly capable of cooperating in these restrictions, however, confident of two things: first, that true "British ways" could be carried only by true Britons and, second, that true Britons were white Britons.

The New Zealand government originally wanted to include a statement on its application form specifying that only applicants "wholly of European race" would be eligible. In discussion, London suggested that such an "official recognition of a colour bar might be embarrassing" and persuaded Wellington to exchange such open discrimination for a subtler form, commenting that "the rejection of a coloured applicant after interview without any reason being given was not open to the same objections."[70] By the mid-1950s Wellington was trying to find a less obvious form of discrimination and opted to exclude those who were not "readily assimilable to the New Zealand way of life." Despite the change of language, the intent was still to differentiate between black and white members of the British Empire.[71]

Southern Rhodesia also favored immigration of the "right type" in order "to build up a large white population."[72] Indeed, as UK officials noted, Southern Rhodesia needed immigrant labor only because, notwithstanding their status as British subjects, Salisbury did not permit Africans to perform skilled work in areas of European settlement.[73] South Africa shaped its immigration policy by excluding immigrants of unsuitable "standards or habits of life."[74] The Canadian government sought immigrants who would not alter the nation's "fundamental character" and applied flexible but absolute control against any "unsuitable" applicants. On the assumption that the fundamental character was white European, Canada overtly discriminated against "Asiatics" and covertly denied admission to Africans and West Indians.[75] For its part, Australia "broadly speaking" had few restrictions for its Free Passage Scheme, insisting only that "the men should be of sound health and good character." Australian officials were confident, however, that London would "appreciate that only white British servicemen will be acceptable as migrants." Despite the fact that Indian servicemen had earned a resettlement bonus as much as their white colleagues, London appreciated Canberra's difficulty very well. So well, in fact, that a separate agreement was signed in order that Poles who had served under British direction during the last stages of war and were currently living in Britain would be eligible for emigration, but West Indians who had constituted part of the imperial forces throughout the conflict would be ineligible.[76] Discrimination against British servicemen from India was but one part of the larger "white Australia" immigration policy. Although this policy did not appear in print in any statute, all political parties since the turn of the century (except the Communists) had accepted the practice of excluding "undesirables" by means of dictation and literacy tests. In 1951 at the Australian Citizenship Convention, the Australian Minister for Immigration H. E. Holt spoke openly of the "traditional . . . restriction of Asian immigration" and the need to confine the privileges and opportunities of immigration to whites.[77] Thus, while the details of the migration schemes differed and some dominions chose not to institute any schemes at all, the common element was the limitation of migration opportunities to British stock, defined, despite the use of language common to all residents of the empire, as white residents of the United Kingdom.

As British stock, these emigrants were entrusted with the responsibility of maintaining the Britishness of the imperial community. Significantly, although leaving the United Kingdom at a time of economic hardship, they were regarded as favored children undertaking the work of empire rather than rats leaving a sinking ship.[78] However startling the governing elite's absolute conviction that allegiance to Britain would survive transplantation into a new society, a sense of the empire's vulnerability is detectable. Policy makers believed that the nationality would survive because the plantation was to a British community, but unless the plantations occurred, the community would soon no longer be British. Thus, as strong as Britishness appeared to be, policy makers' fears for its purity and security revealed their belief that it was precarious and fragile.

The belief that the dominions were currently British stemmed from a particular reading of their demographic makeup. In reality, the dominions housed a great many non-British people. In Australia and New Zealand the most significant non-British ethnic groups were the Aborigine and Maori; Canada and South Africa, in addition to aboriginal populations of Native Americans or Africans, had competing European immigrant populations. As challenging as these alternative populations were, however, they were of long standing and had in some ways been accepted by London. A more recent threat to the perceived Britishness of the dominions was the millions of displaced persons (DPs) currently in refugee camps in Germany and Austria awaiting resettlement elsewhere.

As we shall see in the next chapter, the Attlee government quickly realized the potential economic value of these people and instituted schemes designed to bring them over to Britain. To the horror of London, however, Canberra and Wellington, notwithstanding their stated preference for "British stock," began to do the same, and by 1950 both faced pressure from the International Labour Office to absorb additional "surplus labour" from Europe.[79] Gwyllim Myrddin-Evans, Parliamentary Under Secretary at the Ministry of Labour believed it would be "disastrous" if Australia recruited from among refugees and therefore urged that "in the matter of providing suitable migrants" Australia be given "all the help we possibly can."[80] Accordingly, the ministry offered the Dominions Office its "strongest support . . . since we are so completely convinced of the desirability of getting Australia to look to Great Britain rather than to some foreign country for her immigrants."[81] Ministry of Labour officials referred to "the continental surplus" as "competition" to the United Kingdom's efforts to keep the dominions 100 percent British, particularly inasmuch as the transport and settlement of British migrants cost three times as much as that of continental migrants.[82] Specifically, ministry officials feared that even if Australia rejected the "Italians and the swarthier races," it might well accept considerable numbers of Germans or Dutch.[83] Similar sentiments came from officers in the field. W. J. Garnett, Assistant High Commissioner to Australia, declared in 1950 that "experience" had shown "that the nearer we are racially to a Dominion the more reliance we can place on their whole-hearted co-operation in an emergency." It would thus be "politically suicidal" to allow Australia to follow Canada with its growing preponderance of "alien stock."[84] Less poetically, the Interdepartmental Committee on Migration Policy, while believing that a limited amount of "foreign blood" would not do irreparable harm, advocated continued imperial migration to maintain the dominions' British character.[85]

The availability of a competing population source for the dominions helped shape migration policy in the early postwar years. As we shall see in the next chapter, the principal reason behind the recruitment of European refugees was the domestic postwar labor crisis. A secondary factor, however, was a determination to maintain the dominions as British territories through a re-fashioned version of the triangular trade: continental aliens were brought to Britain so that they would not go to Australia, and their in-migration facili-tated the out-migration of UK residents to the dominions. In this way the burden of assimilation "into the British way of life fell upon the Home Coun-try," which was fortunate, since "we can absorb a larger number of foreigners into a population of 50 million more easily and safely than can Common-wealth countries with smaller populations." As a result the Commonwealth's "British characteristics" would not be diluted, while the United Kingdom would keep its "reservoir full."[86] This "import-export" policy was first sug-gested by the Royal Commission on Population, which acknowledged the "risks," yet recommended a selective immigration policy to enable the United Kingdom to meet at least some of the dominions' demographic needs. Still aiming "at a balance between the intake from the continent and the export to Australia over a period of time," one Ministry of Labour official suggested that the ministry should recruit individuals from abroad, train them as build-ing workers, and then send them, or at least some of them, out to Australia. Though the suggestion was not implemented for fear of public reaction, it reveals the degree to which UK migration policy was shaped by the perceived competition offered by European refugees.[87]

By the 1950s officials shifted their fear of displaced persons to a fear of so-called Asiatics. If displaced persons were a threat that could be tamed by rerouting them to Britain, "Asiatics" could be dealt with only by preventing their admission into the empire in the first place. The Royal Commission on Population had early on drawn attention to the allegedly accelerating birthrate of "Orientals" as a threat to "Western values, ideas and culture."[88] A year later, in July 1950, Assistant High Commissioner Garnett suggested that it was changes in the Far East which were responsible for the Australian govern-ment's pursuit of immigrants.[89] The image of "Asiatics" crowding the borders of the empire was a recurrent theme in postwar parliamentary debates on emigration.[90] Officers in the field, such as Stephen Holmes, the UK High Commissioner to Australia, fed these fears with talk of a world population "unbalanced" between "Asiatics" and whites. According to Holmes, there was little point in allowing Australia to become a repository for a "polyglot collec-tion of people, the surplus of uncontrolled breeding elsewhere."[91] Likewise, the Interdepartmental Committee on Migration Policy suggested in 1956 that the "nationalist upsurge in Asia" was one good reason to maintain a popula-tion of "British-minded Australians."[92]

These perspectives reflect the perception of separate spheres of nationality.

The strongest community of Britishness, as one might expect, was based in the United Kingdom. This domestic community was capable of assimilating aliens and dispatching residents while maintaining its identity. Next in line was the familial imperial community of Britishness, which, with its roots firmly anchored in the United Kingdom, could sustain itself so long as it was constantly replenished with fresh "blood." UK policy makers clearly considered the dominions to be nations in transition, under construction. It was essential that they be constructed with British materials. At the outer perimeter of Britishness were those who held British nationality in law but whose allegiance was suspect. Included in this group were aliens migrating directly from their native land, whether continental Europe or Asia, to the dominions, where their alien allegiances and nationalities would pollute the community of imperial Britishness. Thus, London's desire to use the dominions as a source of British international strength was complicated both by the competition provided by political, nonfamilial Britons and by the restricted understanding of British stock to mean only white-skinned subjects originally hailing from the United Kingdom. Continually providing the material deemed necessary to sustain the familial imperial community was an arduous task, all the more so just after the war when Britain faced its greatest economic and financial crises of the century.

IV

From the outset, the needs of the imperial migration program conflicted with the needs of domestic economic recovery. The year's delay in operation of the Australian Assisted Passage Scheme owing to a shortage of available shipping space inspired private expressions of gratitude from Ministry of Labour officials for the consequent relief for the UK labor market.[93] In early 1947 some ministry officials resented Southern Rhodesia's request for seven hundred building workers and even hoped that they might not be found.[94] Three years later, the Ministry of Labour informed Salisbury that while the UK government viewed Southern Rhodesia's needs "sympathetically," Britain had its "own difficulties," likely to be intensified by the rearmament program of the Korean War, and would "prefer, for obvious reasons, that emigration schemes should be so designed that they will take a reasonable cross-section of the population as regards matters such as age and industrial skill."[95] More forthrightly still, one civil servant pointed out that the annual demographic and material loss of seventy thousand people of "British stock" would have "a cumulative effect in diminishing the economic resources of this country." He continued: "If anything is certain it is that we cannot possibly afford to lose large numbers of highly skilled work people, even to Australia."

Writing to Attlee, another permanent official declared the policy of assisted migration to be "suicidal."[96] Despite his wartime approval of imperial migration, similar sentiments came from former Prime Minister Churchill. During a party political broadcast Churchill used the large number of potential migrants in 1947 as a stick with which to beat Labour, blaming "two years of Socialist rule" for the "half-a-million of our . . . most lively and active citizens in the prime of life" who had applied to emigrate since the war. Churchill called on these people to "stay here and fight it out," for "we cannot spare you . . . at a time when we are scouring Europe for 20,000 or 30,000 or more of the unfortunate displaced persons of the great war to come in and swell our labour force."[97] There is no record of Attlee's response to Churchill's broadcast but despite his written agreement with the fears expressed by his civil servants, Attlee's government continued to advocate the virtues of imperial migration.[98]

The conflict of interest posed by the emigration schemes is highlighted by a comparison of the labor demands of Australia House and the Foreign Labour Committee. Both sought recruits from the same employment categories: metal industry, textiles, construction, engineering, nursing, and domestic work, among others. Australia's immediate requirements for 1947 were 530 trained or trainee nurses, 737 domestics, 902 building workers, 330 textile operatives, 269 engineers, and 2,632 other workers. The ministry's recognition of a potential public relations fiasco is evident in the decision not to display these and subsequent lists in the public area of local offices "in view of the shortage of labour in this country, particularly in the general sort of labour which the Australian Government seek to attract." Instead, the lists remained behind the counter, and the public section was decorated with posters encouraging people to inquire about the possibilities of imperial migration. Likewise, Australia House was discouraged from advertising in textile areas, for "the government would be very sharply criticised if it was known that British women engaged on textiles were being encouraged to emigrate to Australia when we have been at great pains to import foreign women to fill essential vacancies in wool and cotton." Similarly, the ministry feared public criticism following Australia's placement of newspaper advertisements seeking single men.[99]

A 1950 joint Ministry of Labour–Commonwealth Relations Office memo confirmed the existence of a conflict of interest in its report that of the 53,000 males who emigrated in 1948 over 21,000 came from the skilled mining, building, or engineering trades. In both 1947 and 1948 skilled workers constituted the largest single occupational group.[100] In the period 1946 through 1949 skilled workers constituted 43 percent of all assisted and free passage migrants.[101] In order to control just such "leakage" the Ministry of Labour had previously secured the right to control emigration from certain industries informally, but "in the interests of Commonwealth goodwill," it rarely invoked the sanctions. Instead, the ministry relied on an absence of protests from employers to suggest that emigration did not cause serious problems. By 1950, however, officials reported a "clash of interests" with regard to textile operatives and iron and steel workers and were unsure how the situation would develop once the "post-war reserve of occupationally 'unattached'" labor dried up and Australia became more selective in its recruitment programs.[102] This selectivity manifested itself in Australia's continuing pursuit of skilled labor. A sample survey conducted in 1959 revealed that whereas 52.9 percent of the total work force was skilled, 68.2 percent of emigrants were so classified. In general the survey concluded that emigration drew most heavily on the materially comfortable skilled sector, leaving the very wealthy, professionals, unskilled, and poor underrepresented. The significance of the assisted passage schemes in facilitating the departure of this sector of society may be judged by the estimate that only 25 percent of those receiving an assisted passage could otherwise have afforded the venture.[103]

The age and sex of the emigrants also posed a potential conflict of interest with Britain's own demographic needs. The Royal Commission on Population somewhat gloomily observed that nothing could alter the rising average age of the population: "The number of British young persons reaching working age is abnormally low today, and will remain abnormally low for another decade."[104] Conscious of these demographic difficulties and that there was "no manpower to waste," the Ministry of Labour sought to ensure that emigrants were drawn from a broad cross section of the population. Nevertheless, the emigrant flow did not fully reflect the UK population. A popular image of the emigrant as "a youngish man with a trade at his fingertips, accompanied by a wife who is a good housekeeper and a good mother" suggests both the continuing subsidiary status of female subjects, wherever in the empire they ended up, and the youth of emigrants.[105] Whereas males aged between twenty and thirty-four constituted 23 percent of the general population between 1946 and 1949, they formed 36 percent of emigrants. Even more striking, females aged between twenty and twenty-nine, though they constituted 14 percent of the general population, formed 31 percent of emigrants. Thirteen of every one hundred people in Britain were classed as old-age pensioners in 1949, but in the preceding three-year period, only four of every hundred emigrants were so classed. In general terms, while the volume of emigration between 1946 and 1949 was too small to have had a "marked effect," the consequences "of free and assisted migration were from the demographic viewpoint unfavorable both with regard to age and sex composition." In 1956 individuals aged between fifteen and forty-four constituted 41 percent of the general population but 63 percent of emigrants. Perhaps for this reason, the ministry in 1961 described the preceding fifteen years as a period of "continuing manpower

The popular image of the average emigrant as "a youngish man with a trade at his fingertips, accompanied by a wife who is a good housekeeper and mother," is typified by this portrait of two families on board the *Ormonde* heading for New South Wales. The men expected to take up work in building and engineering, and the women would be expected to position themselves within the reproductive labor force. October 1947. (The Hulton Deutsch Collection.)

shortage" and advocated both an absolute increase in the skilled labor force and the judicious use of existing man (and woman) power.[106]

Conscious that it risked political criticism for imperial migration in the midst of perceived labor and demographic crises, the Attlee government followed the strategy suggested early on by the Ministry of Labour: "In order to forestall criticism on manpower grounds it will be desirable for the parliamentary announcement [of the Australian schemes] to include a statement of the Government's view that the advantages of migration within the British Commonwealth considerably outweigh the relatively small loss of manpower to this country." Accordingly, in explaining the scheme to the House, Dominions Secretary Addison provided a wider imperial context, a reassurance that London could refuse assistance to individuals drawn from essential industries, and the information that shortage of shipping would delay the formal opening until the end of 1946.[107] Speaking in the Commons in late 1947, at a point when the labor shortage had become a recurrent topic in Cabinet discussion, Minister of Labor George Isaacs declared that "the question of emigration must be regarded not solely from the standpoint of our production needs, but also from that of the long-term advantages of the interchange of population within the British Commonwealth." Isaacs had already made his public commitment to emigration as early as December 1946 when, photographed in the *Times* bidding farewell to the first group of sponsored emigrants, he emphasized his belief that although their labor would be missed, they were the first of many Britons who would meet a greater need by going to Australia.[108] In a similar vein, Lord Addison agreed that "the manpower position here was certainly very grave" and Britain could not afford to "lose the pick of our skilled artisans in large numbers," but "at the same time we had to have long views . . . and the Government were aware of the obvious necessity, so far as humanly possible, to increase British stock in the Dominions and other parts of the Commonwealth."[109] These long views included the recognition that the current proportion of "British stock" in the dominion populations was declining and the Britishness of imperial outposts was in need of material replenishment. Likewise, Dame Smieton, of the Ministry of Labour, admitted that "the obvious answer" to Britain's labor crisis was "a complete discouragement of emigration," but she proceeded to persuade her audience of the numerical insignificance of the loss of labor through imperial migration and the greater long-term political value of demographic growth in the dominions.[110] Much the same argument appeared in a 1952 Ministry of Labour review of emigration, which observed that "on a narrow view there might appear to be a clash" between UK and Commonwealth interests, since the Commonwealth sought the "bright and ambitious," the "masters of trades and skills needed in the United Kingdom." Nevertheless, from a wider perspective, the percentage loss of migrants was small, and Britain would actually benefit from the long-term growth of the dominions.[111] Even when dealing directly with dominion authorities, London maintained its stated support for the policy of imperial migration. Thus, a first draft of a prime ministerial reply to an Australian request that the Assisted Passage Scheme be put under way was altered to remove any references to Britain's own labor shortages as a possible inhibiting factor and to emphasize instead the shipping difficulties.[112]

Although policy makers yielded before the apparently larger and more significant policy objectives of imperial migration, the public face of imperial advantage masked private concerns about domestic economic loss. One Ministry of Labour official, for example, "most reluctant to see the bricklayers go," acquiesced because the number was relatively small and because "we are too far committed to raise any objection." Likewise, a colleague "regretted" the departure of molders and boilermakers, particularly since the ministry was currently importing the same from Italy to meet UK shortages. Another ministry official, "loath to see the 123 clothing machinists go, as they are so much needed here," accepted that "cooperation is obviously the primary consideration here and we should not object." In 1950 senior Ministry of Labour officials remarked that while they would offer no general objections to Australia's plans to intensify recruitment of skilled workers," in view of the political desirability of building up in Australia an English-speaking population," yet they hoped that a considerable number of those selected might come from the older age groups to avoid leaving Britain with an undue proportion of elderly people.[113] The variety and extent of these comments reveal that even in the minds of the senior officials most intimately connected with the whole business, enthusiasm was intermingled with reluctance.

In the early postwar years this reluctance focused on the loss of current workers and the potential damage to the reconstruction effort at hand. There was little or no discussion of the opportunity cost of losing citizens for whom the UK had already paid and from whom the dominions would reap all the dividend. Nor did anybody appear to question the validity of emigration per se; what criticism there was seems to have been prompted only by immediate pressures that made departure at the current time a little awkward. This failure to consider indirect costs probably stemmed from a combination of poor accounting skills and the conviction that the dominions and the UK were part of a single imperial family.[114] Ironically, the imperial British nationality, created to facilitate imperial control, now also worked to the advantage of (some) component parts of the empire: within the naturalized imperial community Labour and Tory governments recognized neither competing national economies nor separate demographic treasuries. Thus, despite the fears and anxieties regarding population decline and labor shortage, there was overwhelming consensus that the UK government should "do all that is practicable to assist Australia (and any other Dominion) to build up their population as quickly as possible and to do so from British stock," and that "immediate manpower difficulties should not . . . be allowed to deflect us from this major object of British Commonwealth policy."[115]

V

Despite this firm commitment to imperial objectives, anxiety about sponsored emigration continued throughout the next decade, particularly with regard to Britain's financial contribution to the Australian Assisted

Passage Scheme. As early as the summer of 1950, Labour Commonwealth Relations Secretary Patrick Gordon-Walker asked "whether a subsidy to encourage people to leave this country might not be an outmoded policy dating from the inter-war years, when we tried to get rid of unemployment by physically moving the unemployed from this country to other countries."[116] An interdepartmental committee on future migration policy also questioned the efficiency of subsidies that might funnel migration toward Australia at the expense of other dominions, such as Canada, where the demographic and political weight of French Canadians posed a greater immediate threat to the British character of the nation. Divided as to the advisability of renewing Britain's financial commitment to the Australian scheme, the committee discussed the "quixotic" behavior of the UK government in spending "large sums of public money on helping some of the most productive elements in this country to leave it."[117] In a similar vein, as a result of the immediate burden of rearmament for the Korean War and in response to the Chancellor's call to cut all expenditure not "absolutely essential," Gordon-Walker in December 1950 advised the government to withdraw its financial contribution to the Assisted Passages Scheme when it expired the following year and to demonstrate its commitment to migration in other ways.[118] Intense interdepartmental debates followed his proposal. Minister of Labour Isaacs disagreed with Gordon-Walker, maintaining that financial participation concretely illustrated the United Kingdom's commitment to imperial migration and, in addition, secured the Ministry of Labour's right to be consulted about regional and occupational areas of recruitment. Above all, Isaacs reiterated the "paramount" consideration that "on all grounds—social, economic, political and defence—it is desirable to maintain so far as possible the present preponderance of British stock in Australia."[119] The Cabinet compromised by renewing the scheme for the short term of six months, deferring a long-term decision pending discussions with the Australian Prime Minister R. G. Menzies.[120]

Six months later Gordon-Walker again brought the issue before the Cabinet, and once more he suggested termination of the UK financial contribution on the grounds of both fiscal expediency and long-term policy, asking whether it was "any longer appropriate to pay people to emigrate." Recognizing that "the strength and solidarity of the Commonwealth" depended on the "outflow of people from this country," however, the Commonwealth Relations Secretary stressed that his personal commitment and the "firm policy" of the government remained to "facilitate and encourage migration from the United Kingdom to other Commonwealth countries."[121] Despite the Cabinet's approval, Gordon-Walker subsequently amended his proposal by suggesting a financial contribution of £250,000 following representations from Australia House that total withdrawal of the UK subsidy "would inevitably be construed in both countries, whatever might be publicly stated, as meaning that

the United Kingdom government were no longer in favour of emigration."
He also called for a public statement that the Empire Settlement Act, due to
expire in 1952, would be renewed for two more years only.[122] The Ministry
of Labour again opposed the Commonwealth Office's proposal and reminded
the Cabinet that the original agreements were signed *"by a Labour Government"* and represented "a practical token of our desire that those who wish to
do so should have a chance of advancement within the Commonwealth and
so maintain the British connection in a society of nations from which this
country derives much of its practical influence in the affairs of the world." The
new Labour Minister, Alfred Robens, took particular exception to the use of
the phrase "paying our people to emigrate," fearing that it would offend the
Australian government and those who had emigrated, "some of the best of
our stock." Recognizing the fiscal limitations of the UK budget, however, the
ministry was willing to accept an annual ceiling of £500,000—a significant
reduction from the existing cap of £1.5 million and the previous year's expenditure of £900,000—but called for an "open mind" on the continuation of the
Empire Settlement Act.[123] Cabinet ministers discussed the matter at length,
eventually concluding in favor of the Ministry of Labour. Notwithstanding
the anomaly of financing emigration at a time of labor shortage, they placed
greater emphasis on "the importance of preserving, in the population of Australia and other Commonwealth countries, a due proportion of people of
Anglo-Saxon stock."[124] Thus, the Attlee administration ended as it had begun.
Conscious of the contradictions behind the migration of "British stock," Labour nevertheless implemented a vision of a universal imperial nationality that
could be used to support pretensions to great-power status.

Behind the Cabinet's discussion of migration in 1950–1951 lay an interdepartmental committee established to review migration policy. This was but
the first of several reviews undertaken throughout the 1950s, a decade of inde-
cision as the Conservative government that succeeded Attlee attempted to
reconcile its belief that the United Kingdom derived much political benefit
from imperial migration with its fear that Britain, by paying to export its
finest asset, was acting contrary to its own economic needs. With each review,
however, came the same conclusions: the long-term Commonwealth benefits
surely outweighed the short-term domestic cost. Nevertheless, also with each
review came a slow but steady weakening of conviction as each recommendation made slightly more of the costs and slightly less of the benefits. As the
decade progressed, the debate shifted ground. If in 1947 the fear was for the
direct loss of skilled labor and the potential immediate dangers to the UK
economy, by 1952 attention began to turn to the indirect costs—the amount
of capital invested by Britain in emigrants whose dividends were to be reaped
by Australia. By 1957 the debate had assumed the image of the "brain drain"
and captured both parliamentary and popular imagination amidst fears that

all of Britain's best and brightest were fleeing the country in search of better (and warmer) climes.

Within months of taking office, the Conservative Commonwealth Relations Secretary Lord Ismay "reluctantly" suggested that, in light of the government's economy drive, Britain's recently agreed £500,000 contribution to the Australian scheme should be withdrawn or at least reduced. Ismay said it was difficult to justify spending large sums of public money on helping "some of the most productive elements in the country to leave." In his statement he neatly summarized the dilemma facing Britain: "To put it shortly, one can agree that the underpopulated areas of the Commonwealth require a blood transfusion which can best be supplied from this densely populated island; but there seems no reason why part of the cost of the operation should be paid by the impoverished donor." Ismay was particularly concerned by Canberra's announcement that, notwithstanding informal understandings with the Ministry of Labour, it would shortly be recruiting workers from occupations previously considered off limits, such as coal mining. In spite of this apparent lapse of good faith, Ismay recommended the renewal of the Empire Settlement Act in order to avoid adverse publicity and to leave open the possibility of resumption in better circumstances.[125]

Debate on Ismay's suggestion lasted for another six months. Australia urged Britain to continue its contribution as a public sign of commitment to imperial migration. Within the United Kingdom departments were again divided on the merits of paying Australia to take that which it most desperately wanted anyway. In supporting Canberra and stressing the need to strengthen the Commonwealth at "an important strategic point," the Ministry of Labour placed increasing emphasis on the rights given them by participation in a joint scheme to monitor departing citizens' skills and demographic profile. In addition, Walter Monckton, as Minister of Labour, pointed out the "unfortunate political impression" that might be created by "a Conservative government . . . singling out the more enterprising elements of the less well-to-do classes in inflicting this economy." Also supporting Canberra was the UK High Commissioner to Australia who claimed that the withdrawal of the UK contribution would cause dismay and provoke criticism of Britain within Australia. Despite this support, the Chancellor of the Exchequer, R. A. "Rab" Butler, and the rest of the Cabinet initially agreed with Ismay, maintaining that cooperation between Australia and Britain must rest on "general amicability," not financial subvention. After further protests from Canberra, however, London agreed to continue contributing, though at a much reduced rate of £150,000—a sum equal to just over 2 percent of the costs of the whole scheme.[126] The Conservative Cabinet further confirmed its commitment to imperial migration by renewing the Empire Settlement Act upon its expiry in 1952. It is an indication of the ambiguity surrounding the issue, however, that the act was renewed for only five years in order to give the government time to "reconsider its entire attitude towards Commonwealth migration."[127]

As a part of this process of reconsideration, the Churchill government in 1953 reconvened the Oversea Migration Board (OMB), consisting primarily of pro-emigration MPs, and created the Interdepartmental Committee on Migration Expenditure, a formalization of the first interdepartmental committee of 1950. Perhaps nothing better illustrates the departmental differences and increasing ambiguity surrounding imperial migration than these two bodies. Believing that the Commonwealth Relations Office (CRO) was "oblivious" to the "important part which migration can play in forging new links" between the UK and Commonwealth countries, the Ministry of Labour hoped that the OMB would "help stiffen opinion in favor of imperial migration" and help the CRO "formulate a more far-sighted Commonwealth migration policy." For its part, the CRO was initially lukewarm in its support for the OMB; one official later explained that it was created to serve as a " 'safety valve' for those with fanciful and theoretical ideas about mass migration." In the event, the reports of both bodies followed much the same pattern. The OMB proclaimed "the migration tradition" had been "re-established," while the committee of officials declared in favor of continued financial and other support for imperial migration. While supporting migration, however, both reports drew attention to the indirect costs involved. Dismissing Britain's direct financial contribution to the Australian scheme as of relatively minor significance, the OMB focused instead on the "invisible contribution" of "human beings who leave this country and go to Australia to create wealth there." In light of this "severe loss," especially at a time of economic hardship in Britain, the OMB recognized that it could appear "quixotic to assist the departure of men and women whose skills are needed to redress the economic balance in this country."[128] Likewise, the official committee recognized that "the old picture of a mother country and her children has been replaced by a new one" of independent nations capable of looking after their own affairs.[129] Two years later, the interdepartmental committee, though again recommending in favor of imperial migration, added a cautionary observation on the demographic and economic costs of losing 100,000 people per year from a declining and aging population and advised London to rethink its future financial contribution to this process.[130] By this time, 1956, the Commonwealth Relations Office was recommending continued financial support, primarily because withdrawing the subsidy would provoke greater "political and psychological disadvantages" than were justified by the small financial saving. Indeed, G. E. B. Shannon, a CRO official closely connected with imperial migration, went so far as to admit that had the CRO been "starting with a clean sheet," it would be unlikely in current circumstances to recommend a measure on the lines of the Empire Settlement Act.[131] Significantly, the CRO was not objecting to the policy of populating the empire; it was merely suggesting that in 1956 it would not offer to pay for it.

By the mid-1950s, the growth of the technologically oriented nuclear state, with its widespread requirements for highly trained scientific and technical personnel, had turned a general awareness of labor shortage into a specific fear about the departure of the "cream of our highly educated scientists." This so-called brain drain constituted the focus of parliamentary questions on emigration, as MPs repeatedly asked for facts and figures on the number of departing scientists, university graduates, and other technically qualified individuals. The press joined in with stories decrying the departure of people whom in a "scientific age" Britain could not afford to lose.[132] These fears appear to have been reflected in government policy, for in 1958 the Civil Service Commission and Atomic Energy Authority began offering research grants in an attempt to lure British scientists back from North America.[133] Prime Minister Macmillan's response to parliamentary questions was to demonstrate his government's efforts to encourage British scientists to return and to remind the House that half of British emigrants were settled in the dominions and thus represented Britain's contribution to Commonwealth development.[134]

This new emphasis on the alleged quality of departing emigrants was echoed in a 1961 Cabinet review of long-term UK emigration policy. Noting that the majority of emigrants were professional or skilled workers of which there was a shortage in Britain, this study recorded "a growing competition for skill between the sending and receiving countries," which, the Cabinet concluded, "was likely to become more and more damaging to [the] economy." The official interdepartmental review committee also commented on the political difficulties of asking the UK population to increase industrial productivity and technical proficiency while the government was encouraging emigration. Although the committee recommended renewal of the Empire Settlement Act for fear of the political consequences of allowing it to lapse, it advised that Britain should shape "her future emigration policy primarily in the light of her own interests." In strict order, these interests were to "maintain a buoyant economy; and to maintain and develop her links with the other countries of the Commonwealth."[135] The Macmillan Cabinet did renew the act for the now-customary period of five years, but with the caution that certain sectors of the economy might have to be protected.[136] Further complicating reviews of migration policy by the early 1960s were the comparisons made by many people between those whom Britain exported and those whom it imported. MPs, some of them members of the OMB, questioned whether in replacing "a portion of our best citizens" with 100,000 West Indians, Britain was "making a good bargain." In a similar vein, the UK High Commissioner for Australia wondered whether Canberra, apparently so eager to receive more British subjects, "would like a number of the West Indians who at the moment seemed to wish to come to the UK."[137]

These comments, together with the extracts from official reviews, reflect the political elite's continuing struggle with the competing demands of empire and domestic reconstruction. By the end of the fifteen-year postwar period, the balance was increasingly weighted in favor of domestic concerns. This maturity of opinion about the dubious benefits of imperial migration correlates with the much more famous "Wind of Change" that blew through external imperial policy in the early 1960s. This correlation makes clear that imperial migration was a tool of imperial policy. For just as policy makers began to question the long-term benefits of maintaining the British Empire/Commonwealth in the idealized form of the immediate postwar years, so did they adjust their plans for imperial migration by recognizing that it should be shaped by the primary interests of the United Kingdom. In adopting this position, the UK authorities were doing no more than the dominion governments had done throughout the postwar era.

VI

As we have seen, the Attlee government believed it necessary "to encourage and assist migration because of the importance and long-term advantages (including the interests of Commonwealth defence) of interchange and better distribution of population within the British Commonwealth."[138] Superficially, the dominions appeared to believe the same rhetoric. H. E. Holt, the Australian Minister for Immigration, saw two imperatives for Australian development in 1950: "increasing the annual intake of immigrants to the highest level possible" and "ensuring that British immigration is first and foremost."[139] In spite of the similar language, however, closer examination suggests that Australia sought British migrants because it wanted to stay white, retain a homogeneous population, and promote social and political stability. This self-interest had been evident as early as 1945 when a previous Minister of Immigration emphasized that while he would prefer immigrants from Britain, he would also recruit Poles, Czechs, Yugoslavs, Latvians, Estonians, Lithuanians, Norwegians, Swedes, Swiss, Danes, and Dutch.[140] This mixing of migrants was particularly offensive to the Ministry of Labour when it involved the "apparent equation of British workers with displaced persons" and a refusal to house each group individually.[141] Canberra's readiness to augment the population any (European) way possible contrasts with London's determination that non-British Europeans should not go to Australia. The line of difference is perhaps a fine one, but it is worth pointing out nonetheless: Canberra wanted a strong Australia and preferred "British stock" emigrants but would take any Europeans rather than risk domestic population decline: London wanted a strong Commonwealth and would send "British stock" emigrants even at substantial domestic cost in pursuit of that goal. In general, Canberra appears to have shown little sympathy for Britain's financial and demographic crises and to have been willing to exploit London's fears about alien stock by continually urging Britain to send yet more emigrants and contribute yet more money.[142] And although Australia had promised to recruit a cross section of the population, those it accepted were drawn from the most economically productive sectors of UK society. As a result of the policy whereby "the fit single man or woman is practically always preferred to the family man," 55 percent of Australia's immigrants could immediately be transferred to a work force currently constituting only 42 percent of the total population.

Australia was not alone in its pursuit of national self-interest. Other dominions initially resisted agreements until sure of their economic futures and, once they began participating, recruited from among the most skilled and productive sectors of UK society and imposed individual restrictions on the kind of "British stock" they would accept. Of 100,000 males emigrating in 1946 and 1947, 40,000 were aged between eighteen and forty-four. Only 17,000 were over forty-five years old. Similarly, of 191,000 emigrating females, 121,000 fell between eighteen and forty-four, with 30,000 aged forty-five or older.[143] New Zealand recruited largely single men and women, particularly skilled construction and farm workers "from whom an early return could be expected."[144] Not amenable to Ministry of Labour requests that their offtake be subject to joint regulation, Canada's initial needs favored "young, healthy people," preferably unmarried and with an "acceptable level of education." By 1960 Canada sought only "skilled workers and professional people."[145] Throughout the 1950s Canadian authorities called for more British immigrants for Canada, "tacitly assum[ing] that the United Kingdom should be only too happy to allow Canada to have this, the most valuable of her exports, entirely freely."[146] In 1951 the Canadian government requested the abolition of currency restrictions in order to stimulate emigration without any apparent consideration for the precarious UK financial situation that had necessitated the restrictions in the first place.[147] Southern Rhodesia opened and closed schemes for British settlers according to its interpretation of what best suited Southern Rhodesia. It targeted skilled and professional workers with sufficient capital to set up in a new country and "who could be immediately productive assets."[148] Stepping up its search for "the best brains we can get . . . the cream of some of the finest human material the UK has to offer" and making clear that "escapists and complainers" would not be welcomed, the government of Rhodesia and Nyasaland (formerly Southern Rhodesia) initiated a loan scheme for former officers of the British army who could arrive with a cash lump sum of £4,000 to £6,000.[149] And for all dominions, migrants tended to come from the healthiest sectors of the population, since all applicants had to pass a medical exam.

In spite of the significant transfer of population between the United Kingdom and the "outposts of Empire," the cumulative picture painted by fifteen years' correspondence is that whatever Britain did, it could never do enough. Since 1945 Britain had directly spent £7 million, in addition to administrative assistance, to send over 1.5 million people to the dominions. All this was done in order to maintain the Britishness of the empire and to sustain imperial links, and yet in the postwar period Britain provided only 34 percent of the 4.43 million new settlers to Australia, Canada, New Zealand, South Africa, and Rhodesia. At just over one-third, this percentage compares unfavorably with the period between 1901 and 1930, when British stock had constituted between 80 percent and 88 percent of immigrants entering Australia alone. Rising dominion birthrates and the existence of alternative migrant sources with access to cheap transportation combined to make Britain's self-appointed task of keeping the empire wholly British near impossible.[150] It seemed that no matter how many were sent, the dominions would always want more. After all, the export of over a million and a half citizens in just one decade is a sizable contribution to population growth; yet it was not even enough to keep the British stock in the dominions at 50 percent.

Placing these demands against the United Kingdom's postwar economic and demographic crises emphasizes the contradictory viewpoints that the UK and the dominions brought to imperial migration. For the British, the schemes revolved around the "question of the best distribution of the British population within the Commonwealth." For the Australians (and other dominions in turn) the schemes were intended to help in "the future development and security of Australia."[151] Britain did not act altruistically for the greater good of Commonwealth members. Both Labour and Conservative administrations believed the foundation of Britain's continued international prestige was a united empire/commonwealth. They overestimated the extent to which the dominions would share this view. In the long run this divergence of interests was to Britain's disadvantage, inasmuch as the gift of money and migrants was much more active, and costly, than the dominions' gift of political weight. By 1956, the fiasco of Suez, it became increasingly obvious that Britain was not the equal of the United States or the USSR and that imperial pretensions to power could not make it so. The dominions, meanwhile, retained all the permanent benefits of immigrant population growth.

VII

Throughout the debates on imperial migration, first Labour and then Conservative ministers and their officials feared public criticism for encouraging migration during a financial and demographic crisis. In the event, in the early postwar years, what criticism there was came from parliamentarians and journalists convinced that the United Kingdom should do *more* to populate the dominions. Conservative MPs and peers spoke of Britain's reliance on the Commonwealth as a source of strength and gave their wholehearted approval to the sending of emigrants as a means of securing that strength. These observations put Labour Commonwealth Relations Secretary Gordon-Walker very much on the defensive as he explained that limitations of cost and housing restricted the number of emigrants the dominions could absorb. While condemning as "madness" the apparent desire of some MPs to run a nineteenth-century migration policy with a twentieth-century population, the CRO Secretary reiterated his commitment to a steady emigrant flow with his assurance that the government did "not regard a person who goes to the Commonwealth as a loss in any sense."[152] In the early postwar years, the press reflected and encouraged these pro-emigration sentiments, calling on the government to fly emigrants to dominions "ready, even eager to welcome settlers of British blood." In 1947 identifying the "expansion of the Dominions within the British way of life and the maintenance of a balanced labour force in the Mother Country" as essential "requirements of Empire and World prosperity," the *Times* called on the government to encourage larger families in order to facilitate emigration.[153] In the most practical way possible, many UK residents showed themselves equally eager to support imperial migration.

Travel agents' stock of Ministry of Labour–issued leaflets describing the possibilities for imperial migration were "completely exhausted" within days of receipt.[154] Within two months of the Australian Assisted Passage Scheme's opening, Australia House held over 96,000 applications on file, representing 240,000 people. Within six months this total had almost doubled to 400,000.[155] In consultation with dominion governments, Ministry of Labour officials estimated in 1949 that 173,000 breadwinners had expressed serious interest in emigrating. Adding a cautious 1.25 dependents per breadwinner, the ministry suggested a total possible emigrant population of 605,000.[156] In the first quarter of 1957 alone, Australia House received 35,000 letters of application, and in January 1957, Canada House was conducting 6,000 medical exams per week.[157] Although the number of actual emigrants would always be less than the number of potential ones, it still seems remarkable that so many were attracted by the idea of leaving Britain during a period generally renowned for the creation of the welfare state and increasing material well-being.

A sample survey conducted in 1959, together with informal questionnaires compiled by contemporary newspapers, suggests a variety of reasons behind the postwar emigration boom. In the early years, male emigrants were apparently influenced by wartime service abroad, and all emigrants were affected by the continuing food shortages, rationing, and labor controls within Britain.

Something of the 1957 rush for Canada may be seen in this picture of would-be emigrants waiting at the Canadian Immigration Office in Mayfair, January 1957. (The Hulton Deutsch Collection.)

By the mid-1950s emigration appears to have been fueled by popular anger at rising taxes, frustration with continued austerity, and despair over the disaster of Suez. More positively, many were inspired by the encouragement of friends and relatives already in place, and others spoke of the desire to provide a better life for themselves and their children—a life persuasively suggested by the advertisements on display in every labour exchange office.[158] This collection of motives suggests that despite the Ministry of Labour's perception of emigrants as mules of British culture constituting strong links in the imperial chain, emigrants themselves conceived of their departure as an economic move. That is not to say that they did not also, if unconsciously, fulfill the roles prescribed for them by London. Still, it is a fitting summary of the distance between the metropolitan center and the outposts of empire that while the emigrants and the dominion governments looked primarily for the economic benefits of migration, London continued to hope for political advantage. It seems most likely that despite all the political rhetoric, these were no less economic migrants than their compatriots of the nineteenth century, or indeed their "replacements" of the twentieth.

As they were working to facilitate the imperial migration of British stock, Ministry of Labour officers were working just as hard to attract residents of continental refugee camps to Britain. Curiously, although the British stock emigrants were expected to retain their nationality, these continental recruits, undergoing a similar transplantation, were supposed to lose their former allegiances and to assimilate into the "British way of life." Thus, according to the postwar politics of citizenship, departing UK residents would ever be British while incoming alien refugees would soon become British.

CHAPTER 3

Recruiting Potential Britons

Although it is usually not presented as an immigrant country, the land now known as the United Kingdom has in fact played host to a great many foreign migrants. Indeed, taking historian V. G. Kiernan at his word, one might posit that all the inhabitants trace their origins to some other place.[1] Certainly, the historical record reports successive invasions by Celts, Romans, Angles, Saxons, Jutes, Vikings, and perhaps most famous of all, the Normans in 1066. The transformation of alien invader William of Normandy into the popularly recognized progenitor of the English monarchy stands perhaps as one of the first reconstructions of national identity in Britain. William was demonstrably French, his army defeated the King of England on the field of battle, and he quickly replaced many of the Anglo-Saxon elite with his own nobles. He subsequently cataloged much of England's natural wealth to make sure that he received all he was due as king. Despite the manner of his invasion and subsequent accumulation of wealth, history has converted this most alien of men into the most British of kings.[2] The success of this transformation and the purposes to which it has been put—suggesting continuity at the center of the state and providing an allegedly common focus—reveal how nationality and migration can be manipulated. Clearly, the state is able, in pursuit of larger objectives, to alter the status of individuals by transforming alien immigrants into resident subjects. After World War II, the larger objective was economic recovery and the individuals were 345,000 European aliens recruited for work and life in Britain. This chapter examines how these aliens were recruited and transformed from foreign immigrants into potential British subjects.

Successful recruitment depended on the cooperation of several government departments and continued throughout the tenure of the Attlee government. Having gone to considerable trouble to import these aliens, Labour went to an equal degree of trouble to retain them. The government was motivated partly by a desire to secure full economic value from their recruits—upsets in the workplace would only disrupt production and thereby nullify the original intent of hiring additional labor—and partly by larger demographic goals. The apparently declining UK birthrate convinced many within the governing elite that these new laborers could be fitted into Britain's population. Ministers and officials believed that the success of this "insertion" depended on their active intervention, however, and thus they took a number of steps designed to facilitate integration. Officials manipulated public opinion so that it would more readily accept the foreigners and Ministers struck deals with trade unions to ensure that the newcomers found acceptance in the workplace. And the aliens themselves were massaged, receiving lessons in the English language and in British ways in order that they might more quickly "settle down." The intention in both cases was to transform aliens into subjects by clothing them in a discourse of potential Britishness. This discourse itself aided the reconstructive process by giving aliens a category within which to live their lives in Britain and through which they might more quickly become British. Critical to this reconstruction was the demographic acceptability of aliens. Selection of the 345,000 postwar immigrants was guided by the consciousness that recruiting for the labor market in the short term was tantamount to recruiting for the population of Britain in the long term.

I

Migration has a long history as a political tool in Britain, and many groups have successively been welcomed or discouraged according to their perceived value. Norman Kings, for example, encouraged the settlement of Jewish merchants as a means of promoting trade and industry within the realm. Two hundred years later, when heavy taxation and religious discrimination had lessened the financial contributions of this group, Edward I initiated a series of pogroms designed to expedite their departure. In the sixteenth and seventeenth centuries, valued commercial and artisanal skills, together with a common religion, helped Protestants from Holland and France find refuge in England. In the late eighteenth century, against the background of the French Revolution, the British government enacted legislation to prevent the immigration of radicals and subversives. In the nineteenth century, partly in response to a growing perception that immigration was a valuable means of augmenting the population with skilled workers, the British government simplified the process by which an immigrant might become a subject. A successful application, however, depended upon whether the Home Office believed the immigrant's presence in Britain was likely to be "conducive to the public good."

In 1905 the state enacted the most wide-ranging intervention in the field of immigration up to that time. The Aliens Act of that year empowered landing officers to prohibit the immigration of certain aliens traveling on certain ships, provided for the registration of all aliens within Britain, and imposed restrictions on aliens' freedom of movement. The act was a clear response to the immigration of approximately 120,000 East European Jews fleeing Russian persecution between 1875 and 1914. The vast majority settled in the East End of London and soon became a target for anti-alien, anti-Semitic prejudice. Despite the findings of a select committee and a royal commission that the immigrants did not place undue burdens upon society, Arthur Balfour's Conservative government enacted a clear piece of demographic engineering. The Aliens Act sought to exclude immigrants perceived as incapable of supporting themselves or their dependents and was directed only at immigrants arriving on ships carrying twenty or more passengers—thus reaching the steerage class in which most Jewish immigrants traveled. Though revealing government prejudices, the act was significant less for the actual numbers controlled than for the breach of the principle of freedom of entry.[3]

The outbreak of war in 1914 stimulated Herbert Asquith's Liberal government to surround the United Kingdom with an even stronger wall of legislative protection. The Aliens Restriction Act of 1914 dramatically enlarged the authority of the Home Secretary to prohibit entry and enforce registration and deportation of aliens. The scope of these increased powers has been described as "the great turning-point in the history of British immigration control," representing a shift "from the historic presumption that an alien could come and go freely unless there was a specific reason to exclude him, to the new presumption that an alien had no claim to be received, or to remain, but could enter only as the interest of the state—as defined by the state authorities—dictated."[4] Though inspired by war, the provisions of the act were renewed annually from 1919 through to 1971. As this brief review demonstrates, the history of alien immigration into the United Kingdom is largely the history of discretionary control, with organs of the state seeking to shape the demographic makeup of Britain by controlling which individuals should have access, first, to British soil and, second, to British nationality.

Reflecting the general downturn in the international economy, immigration to Britain, indeed migration anywhere, was seriously curtailed during the interwar period. It picked up only as refugees attempted to flee the growth of fascism in Central Europe. A combination of anti-Semitism and unemployment ensured that only 11,000 Jewish refugees entered Britain between 1933 and November 1938. In the following nine months, however, as Britain geared up for war and Anglo-Jewish groups exerted pressure, a window of generosity enabled 44,000 Jewish refugees to be admitted. Many of these people were subsequently interned during the invasion panic of spring 1940, but were later released as the atmosphere in Britain became less hostile and industry demanded ever more labor to wage total war.[5] Some of these labor demands were met by the 334,000 German and Italian prisoners of war who were employed in essential areas such as agriculture.[6] In addition to involuntary labor produced by war, the UK economy, as we shall see in greater detail in the next chapter, also made significant use of Irish workers. Thus, it was with help from refugees, enemy aliens, and neutrals that the United Kingdom secured its share in the victory of World War II. Winning the peace would demand just as varied a work force.

II

Within just a few months of taking office in July 1945, the Attlee government confronted a labor shortage in the industries deemed essential for postwar reconstruction and recovery: agriculture, coal mining, textiles, construction, foundry work, health services, and institutional domestic service. In an attempt to meet these shortages, the government quickly arranged to import an additional 118,000 prisoners of war from the United States and Canada, launched a domestic productivity drive, urged women to return to work, and in October 1947 instituted a Control of Engagement Order.[7] By December 1947, the total UK working population had increased by 600,000 over the mid-1939 figure. As dramatic as this increase was, however, it was achieved only gradually, and throughout its first year of office the Attlee government faced "acute" labor shortages in the "essential" industries. Consequently, the administration expanded its search for additional labor. Concrete form was given to this search with the appointment in February 1946 of the Foreign Labour Committee (FLC) to "examine, in the light of the existing manpower shortages, the possibility of making increased use of foreign labor, particularly in essential industries which are now finding special difficulty in recruiting labour."[8] Manifesting the importance attached to the issue, seven members of the Cabinet were appointed: Lord Privy Seal Arthur Greenwood, Home Secretary Chuter Ede, Minister of Labor George Isaacs, Minister of Agriculture and Fisheries Tom Williams, Minister of Fuel and Power Emanuel Shinwell, and Secretary of State for Scotland Joseph Westwood. Appointed initially to find short-term solutions to Britain's labor shortage, the committee soon became responsible for Britain's de facto resettlement scheme for refugees and other "displaced persons" and ultimately assumed responsibility for the transformation of aliens into Britons.

The first alien group to be examined by the FLC were Polish veterans. Constituted as a national unit, the Poles had fought under British direction during the war. Afterward, when Britain transferred recognition from the London government-in-exile to the Communist government in Warsaw, Churchill promised that no Poles or their dependents would be forced to return home against their will. In the spring of 1946 the majority of Poles were still in military formation in camps either in Britain or on the Continent and were the financial responsibility of Britain. It was only as they were reviewing the costs of sustaining this force of "unemployed soldiers" that ministers hit upon the notion of killing two birds with one stone: lessening the country's financial burden and ameliorating the labor shortage by employing the Poles in Britain.[9] Initially this was to be a temporary measure until the Poles had either voluntarily returned home or emigrated to a third country. Within a few months, however, as the labor shortage worsened, the FLC began to view the Polish soldiers as potentially permanent replacements.[10] Ministers proposed the creation of a transitional body designed to facilitate the Poles' entry into UK society and the labor market and to provide a forum where Poles "could be controlled, maintained and educated pending their . . . reabsorption as civilians."[11] As a result, in May 1946 the government announced the formation of the Polish Resettlement Corps, a noncombatant military unit under the administration of the War Office, in which Polish veterans were encouraged to enroll by the promise of resettlement and the receipt of a stipend. Once in the corps, formally established in September 1946, veterans were guided into civilian employment by Ministry of Labour officers. To complement the corps the government introduced the Polish Resettlement Act in February 1947, which made financial provision for pensions and other welfare benefits aimed at easing the transition of Polish veterans and their families into British society.

Within two years of its inception, 114,000 men and women (but mostly men) had enrolled in the corps. Approximately 67,000 had gone into civilian employment, 16,000 had opted to return to Poland or to emigrate to a third country, and 29,000 still remained to be settled. By April 1949 only 1,000 corps members remained unplaced and by the end of the year, between 120,000 and 125,500 former members of the Polish armed forces and their dependents were living in Britain and were expected to remain permanently.[12] The official cost of the Polish resettlement exercise was given as £14.6 million covering the period from July 1945 through January 1950.[13] Given the industry-specific labor shortages, the Ministry of Labour was eager to direct as many Poles as possible into the "essential" industries, but under the terms of the Poles' initial admission to the United Kingdom, it was unable to compel such work. As a result, although the government had over 90,000 individuals available for work, by April 1949 only 27,217 had entered the "essential" industries of construction, agriculture, and coal mining, and a mere 13,750 had entered the textiles, brickmaking, foundries, and general engineering industries.[14] Thus, while the Polish army constituted a useful addition to Britain's resources, it could not be relied upon to satisfy the critical labor gaps, which appeared to be worsening.

At the FLC's first meeting in March 1946, ministers identified a labor shortage of one million and admitted that "all the evidence suggests that there is little hope of restoring the balance between requirements and supply for some time to come."[15] Particularly hard hit were hospitals, sanitoriums, and other institutions short of domestic workers. To help relieve this specific shortage, the FLC agreed upon a limited recruitment of 1,000 "Baltic" women drawn from Latvia, Lithuania, and Estonia. By the time the scheme, named Balt Cygnet, was folded into larger programs, it had exceeded its original goal by 1,575.[16] In September 1946 the impending repatriation of German prisoners of war prompted the Cabinet to confirm that "the general policy should be to make increased use of Poles and other free foreign labour throughout 1947 and 1948."[17] Just a month later, the FLC received further depressing news as early reports from the Royal Commission on Population projected a 0.6 percent drop in the working-age population by 1959. Discussing what measures might be adopted to reverse this trend, the FLC noted that an increase in the birthrate would only increase Britain's economic dependency since it would be many years before the new additions could be expected to make any economic contribution.[18] These conclusions fostered an ideal climate in which the idea of permanent alien immigration might grow.

Evidence that it had grown came in January 1947, in the midst of the fuel crisis, as the *Economic Survey* identified three major problems facing the country: a shortage of power, a shortage of total labor, and a maldistribution of available labor. Recognizing foreign labor as "the only substantial additional source of man-power which is open to us," the survey claimed that the "old arguments against foreign labor are no longer valid" and that there was "no danger for years to come that foreign labor will rob British workers of their jobs." The survey advocated the extension of schemes for the recruitment of foreign workers on the grounds that the "need to increase the working population is not temporary; it is a permanent feature of our national life."[19] The combination of these gloomy forecasts, the refusal to reduce troop numbers, success with early alien recruits (Poles and Balt Cygnet), and a continuing perception that Britain was "trying to do too many things at once" with too little labor persuaded the Cabinet in late January 1947 to initiate "a much larger recruitment of suitable displaced persons." It was from this point that the Attlee government swung all its weight "as a matter of urgency" in search of additional sources of "free foreign labor" to fill the pressing gaps in Britain.[20] Significantly, this option was chosen in preference to a reduction in the

ALIEN IDENTITY CERTIFICATE
DOWÓD OSOBISTY OBCOKRAJOWCA

POLISH RESETTLEMENT CORPS AND A.T.S. POLISH RESETTLEMENT SECTION. RELEGATION TO
THE UNEMPLOYED LIST OR TO THE RESERVE FOR EMPLOYMENT APPROVED BY THE MINISTRY
OF LABOUR AND NATIONAL SERVICE

POLSKI KORPUS PRZYSPOSOBIENIA I ROZMIESZCZENIA ORAZ POLSKA SEKCJA PRZYSPOSOBIENIA
I ROZMIESZCZENIA (A.T.S.). PRZENIESIENIE NA LISTĘ, NIEZATRUDNIONYCH LUB DO REZERWY
CELEM PODJĘCIA ZATRUDNIENIA ZATWIERDZONEGO PRZEZ MINISTRY OF LABOUR AND
NATIONAL SERVICE

Number/ Numer ewidencyjny	Rank/Stopień	Name (Block Capitals)/Nazwisko (litery drukowane)	
3 0 0 2 0 1 5 2	Pte	M A R E S C H J e r z y	

Date of Birth Data urodzenia	Height/Wzrost	Colour of hair/Kolor włosów	Colour of eyes/Kolor oczu
26. 7. 23.	5 ft. stóp 5½ ins. cali	d a r k	b r o w n

Complexion/Cera	Marks or scars/Znaki szczególne
-/-	-/-

Address to which proceeding/Adres miejsca przeznaczenia

c/o   e m p l o y e r

Occupation/Zawód	Employer (name and address)/Pracodawca (nazwisko i adres)
Student	School of Foreign Trade & Port Administration, Stukely Street, L O N D O N, W.C.2.

Ministry of Labour occupational Classification No. (if known) Numer zawodowej klasyfikacji Ministry of Labour (jeśli znany)	Date of relegation for an indefinite period Data przeniesienia
	5 MAY 1948

Local Office of the Ministry of Labour and National Service
at which he/she will report
Miejscowy Urząd Ministry of Labour and National Service **Kings Cross**, L O N D O N
do którego winien/a się zgłosić

A. I CERTIFY that the above named alien has been relegated from military service to the Unemployed List/Class "W"
Royal Army Reserve*. He/She has been instructed to report to the Police on his/her arrival in
Grays Inn Rd., High Holborn, London, W.C.2. hereafter to the local office of the Ministry of Labour and National
Service.

STWIERDZAM, że wyżej wymieniony obcokrajowiec został przeniesiony ze służby wojskowej na Listę
Niezatrudnionych/do Rezerwy.* Został/a on/a pouczony/a, że z chwilą przybycia Grays Inn Road, High Holborn, W.C.2.
ma się zgłosić do Urzędu Policyjnego, a następnie do miejscowego Urzędu Ministry of Labour and National Service.

Date/Data	Signature of Officer Commanding Podpis Dowódcy Oddziału
5 MAY 1948	

B. I understand that, with my consent, I have been relegated to the Unemployed List/Reserve*. from the Polish
Resettlement Corps/A.T.S. Polish Resettlement Section* in order that I may take up work with the employer specified
above or such further work as may be approved by the Ministry of Labour and National Service. I understand
that if I fail to take up such work or if I change this work without the permission of the Ministry of Labour and
National Service, I shall be liable to be recalled, and, if recalled, any pay or allowances in lieu of leave which I may
be given when I am again relegated to the Unemployed List/Reserve* will be deducted from the amount of any
financial benefit due to me on final relinquishment of my commission/discharge*. I also understand that I shall
not be entitled to another civilian outfit or cash grant in lieu, or a further issue of supplementary clothing coupons.

Jest mi wiadome, że za moją zgodą zostałem przeniesiony z Polskiego Korpusu Przysposobienia i Rozmieszczenia/
Polskiej Sekcji Przysposobienia i Rozmieszczenia (A.T.S.)*/na Listę Niezatrudnionych/do Rezerwy* celem
rozpoczęcia pracy u wyżej wskazanego pracodawcy lub też takiego dalszego zatrudnienia, które zatwierdzi Ministry
of Labour and National Service. Jest mi również wiadome, że, w wypadku niepodjęcia przezemnie takiej pracy lub
zmiany zatrudnienia bez zgody Ministry of Labour and National Service, mogę zostać odwołany i że w razie odwołania
żołd i należności pobrane zamiast urlopu, które mogą mi być następnie wypłacone w związku z ponownym
przeniesieniem na Listę Niezatrudnionych/do Rezerwy*, zostaną potrącone z sumy należności, przyznanych mi w
związku ze złożeniem stopnia oficerskiego/demobilizacji. *Wiadomo mi również, że nie będę uprawniony do dalszego
wyposażenia cywilnego lub otrzymania równowartości w gotówce, ani do dalszego otrzymania dodatkowych
kuponów odzieżowych.

Date Data	Signature Podpis
5 MAY 1948	J. Maresch
	Counter signature of an officer Kontrasygnata oficera

* Delete whichever is not applicable/* niepotrzebne skreślić   P.T.O./ODWRÓCIĆ

The alien identity certificate issued to Jerzy Maresch on his demobilization from the
Polish Resettlement Corps, 1948. Note the bilingualism of the form, representative
of the government's efforts to accommodate Poles in Britain. (Courtesy of Eugenia
Maresch, Polish Social and Cultural Association Ltd., the Polish Library.)

absolute size of the armed forces and in the number of troops posted abroad. For the majority in the Attlee Cabinet, just as in the encouragement of imperial migration, Britain's domestic economic reconstruction played second fiddle to the maintenance of international preeminence.

Labour found the potential workers it was looking for in the displaced persons camps in continental Europe run by the United Nations Relief and Rehabilitation Administration (UNRRA). Among the DPs were individuals brought to Central Europe as forced labor by the Nazis, uprooted families, ex-prisoners of war, Jews and other concentration camp inmates, and other groups. In the early summer of 1945, approximately 7 million people were "on the move" in Western Europe; by July 3.2 million had "moved" home; and by September only 1.8 million remained to be settled. At this point, the policy of the Allies focused on repatriation, forcibly where necessary in the case of Soviet citizens, who feared that their wartime activities would bring them imprisonment or death upon returning home. As the cold war began to take shape, as the number of DPs rejecting voluntary repatriation and resisting forcible removal grew, as the number of new refugees swelled, with Eastern European Jews fleeing anti-Semitism still rife in Poland and elsewhere, UNRRA began to look anew at the refugee problem. Two years after the end of the war, UNRRA was running 762 DP camps, an increase of over 500 on the 1945 figure.[21] Clearly, these refugees represented a long-term problem, requiring a permanent solution. At the same time, the Attlee government was finding "increasing difficulty" in making its financial contribution to the camps' upkeep.[22] These financial problems, together with the Cabinet's decision to look farther afield for fresh foreign labor coincided with the realization of camp officials and UNRRA administrators that large numbers of displaced persons were in search of a new homeland. The timing could not have been more fortuitous for Britain.

UK officials were extremely enthusiastic about this "free foreign labour." FLC chairman and Lord Privy Seal Arthur Greenwood demonstrated his commitment with the declaration that "we must plan for a large-scale movement if foreign labour is to make a contribution commensurate with the size of the manpower deficit facing us." In reply George Isaacs, Minister of Labour, reported that "for the present we are aiming to get as many suitable volunteers as we can absorb into employment here." Isaacs's haste was in part attributable to his desire that "this huge labor pool should be tapped, and should be tapped quickly" before other countries "steal a march on us." Still the pace was not quick enough for some Cabinet members who, fearful that the "cream" of the refugee crop would be "skimmed off," urged a yet more energetic pursuit of foreign labor.[23]

Throughout the life of the Foreign Labour Committee, the Home Office maintained its wariness of aliens while the Ministry of Labour consistently worked to facilitate the aliens' immigration. Home Office officials worried, for example, that stateless or otherwise "unacceptable" DPs would become a drain upon Britain's resources. To mollify the Home Office and to secure the aliens' entry, the Ministry of Labour accordingly arranged that DPs would be subject to deportation for twelve months after arrival and would be readmitted to their prior camp on such a recommendation. Similarly the Home Office feared that DPs would bring with them an "army of dependents" for whom the British government would ultimately become responsible. The Ministry of Labour reassured the Home Office that adult dependents were subject to the same landing conditions as the DP and the number of eligible nonworking dependents was to be strictly limited.[24] Through such negotiations as these, the FLC succeeded in gaining Home Office compliance in the operation of a number of recruitment schemes.

The most significant was "Westward Ho!" which brought in over 78,500 workers and dependents. Westward Ho! was aimed at men aged between eighteen and fifty-four and women aged eighteen to forty-nine. Among the nationalities recruited were Estonian, Latvian, Lithuanian, Polish, Ukrainian, Rumanian, Bulgarian, and Yugoslavian. Male volunteers were recruited primarily for mining, agriculture, clay pits, and steel. Initially it was they who formed the bulk of recruitment (almost three-quarters of recruits were male in July 1947), but by the fall of 1947 it was women who were wanted. There was a female labor deficiency of between 30,000 and 40,000 in the textile industry alone. Women were also wanted for agriculture, ceramics, wool and hosiery, wholesale clothing, boot and shoe manufacture, domestic work, and in nursing and midwifery.[25]

By April 1947 enthusiastic Ministry of Labour officials prophesied that four thousand foreigners per week would soon be entering Britain. By May the Ministry had thirty-three people working in Germany and Austria under the direction of a special foreign labor branch. By July, with only 17,600 foreigners actually in Britain, the Ministry of Labour was already extending its recruitment area to include the American zones in Germany and Austria and was prepared to go farther if necessary. The age and dependency qualifications were to be relaxed to attract more women, and the ministry was ready to provide English classes inside the camps in order to attract more volunteers.[26]

Westward Ho! was brought to the attention of the DPs by leaflet distribution, presentations, and visits by refugees already in place. All volunteers underwent an interview to assess industrial and personal potential and, if selected, a medical exam. Success at this stage led to a regional collecting center where a percentage check of medical examinations was held. Generally, 15 percent failed these medical tests, and the remainder moved to a transit camp and yet another medical exam combined with a security check.[27] Transit accommodation in Germany and Britain was arranged for up to six thousand

European Volunteer Workers from "the Baltic States" queuing for their medical tests in a displaced persons camp in Hertfordshire, September 1947. (The Hulton Deutsch Collection.)

workers per week (staying an average of two nights) where each volunteer received food, clothing (if necessary), and a small cash grant. A desperate shortage of accommodation in Britain meant that the majority of recruits were housed in government hostels or camps upon being placed in employment. The administration of the scheme depended on the coordination of several government departments ranging from the Home and Foreign Offices, the Ministries of Labour, Transport, and Health, through the National Service Hostels and the National Assistance Board. At its smoothest, the whole process from interview to placement could be completed within a month.

Eager to draw on all the labor it thought Britain might need, and with Cabinet approval, the FLC did not recruit workers for specific jobs but rather took people on the basis of general qualifications, leaving job assignments until arrival in Britain. The system ensured that a steady stream of recruits kept flowing and that a series of "holding pools" was established in Britain for volunteers broadly suitable for work in the essential industries. Though concentrating on manual trades, officers were instructed to be "on the look out" for workers with "outstanding . . . professional or technical" skills. No ceiling was placed on the total number to be recruited, but since the British occupation zones included the more industrialized parts of Germany, with their resultingly high number of refugees, officials anticipated a fertile field of available labor. Although all costs were paid by the government, UK employers were encouraged to visit the British camps to recruit their own labor directly. By the end of 1947 there were 91,000 foreigners *working* in Britain. Just over half of these were Poles; the rest were refugees. By July 1948 the total number had risen to 163,000 working aliens recruited through official schemes and 50,000 working on individual work permits.[28]

Work permits came to figure prominently in postwar immigration. They had been discontinued during wartime, but in its pursuit of as much foreign labor as possible, the Attlee government not only restarted the scheme but distributed permits generously. Work permits facilitated the immigration of nonrefugees who would not otherwise have come within the scope of official recruitment. The majority of permits were issued for domestic service. In the first three months of 1947 alone, for example, 5,244 permits were issued for private domestic workers and officials estimated an annual distribution for this purpose of 20,000.[29] Aliens thus recruited were subject to many of the same obligations as displaced persons. They could work only for the named employer, could not change jobs or occupation without the ministry's permission, and had to register with the police.[30] Though it brought in significant numbers of aliens, the work-permit system troubled some officials at the Ministry of Labour, who suspected that many permit applicants were defeating the purpose of recruitment schemes by working as the (luxury) fourth servant in a large household rather than the (essential) domestic servant in a hardship household such as a farm or doctor's surgery.[31]

Partly to stop this leakage and partly to encourage employers to apply for permits, the Ministry of Labour assumed a more active role in the permit system in August 1949 by simplifying the application process and acting as a mediator between prospective employers and employees. This so-called Private Domestic Worker Scheme, launched publicly on 1 January 1950, was intended to become the primary source of foreign servants. Although the Ministry of Labour claimed a limited responsibility for its scheme, billing itself as a referral service only, officials did try to stimulate interest among employers by placing advertisements in the major English newspapers which publicized the possibilities of recruiting domestic labor from abroad.[32] Overall the work permit system netted a sizable contribution to Britain's labor resources. Between May 1946 and the end of December 1950, close to 93,000 work permits were issued for domestic service alone, and by April 1950 aliens with permits were arriving at an annual rate of 35,000.[33] The generous distribution of work permits continued through the Churchill administration with 265,230 permits issued between 1947 and 1954 and two-thirds of recipients entering domestic service.[34]

Even these rates of admission did not meet all the identified deficiencies within the labor force, and the Attlee administration continued to search for additional foreign labor. By late 1947 the industries experiencing the greatest shortage of labor and those critical to the achievement of export targets were those traditionally staffed by women.[35] Officials deemed the recruitment of women particularly troublesome since the majority of available refugees had families and were unwilling to travel without their dependents. Having "combed the ordinary DP population to exhaustion for single women," officials were greatly relieved to come upon a pool of Sudeten women in 1948. To attract them to Britain, the Ministry of Labour arranged for magazines favorably depicting the British way of life to be sent to the camps along with enthusiastic letters and visits from DPs already in place. Over the course of the ensuing year, high expectations for Sudetens were deflated as officers in the field found that there would be "nowhere near" the hoped-for 3,000 available and reported somewhat gloomily, "We may be able to nurse the recruitment along to a total of 800 to 1,000."[36]

Still searching in late 1948 for "a field of single women . . . to tap," the FLC broadened its recruitment area to include nonrefugee but unemployed labor in Austria, Germany, and Italy.[37] They launched three additional bulk recruitment schemes in the summer of 1948: "Blue Danube" for Austrian women to work in nursing and textiles; "North Sea" for German women to enter domestic service, industrial work, and nursing and an "Official Italian Scheme" for women to work in textiles and other industries. These three schemes netted a total of 13,600 women over two years at a cost of £14 each. Although subject to the same landing conditions as all other alien recruits, these women were initially hired for only two years but eligible for resettlement if they chose to stay within their original industry.[38]

Anticipating labor demands for the year ending June 1949, Ministry of Labour officials estimated that the economy could employ sixty thousand foreign laborers divided equally between men and women. Preference would be given to skilled workers, but the ministry was prepared to train unskilled workers and guaranteed accommodations for all.[39] Although ministry officials later downgraded this estimate for the year ending September 1949 to only 22,500 and framed Britain's economic problems in terms of productivity increases rather than absolute labor increases the estimate still suggests a hungry labor market.[40] A short time later, as the defense industries fighting the Korean War began to consume male workers, the labor market became even leaner and the Ministry of Labour once again sent UK employers to Europe in search of males.

Particularly hard hit by the labor shortage was the National Coal Board (NCB), which, in consultation with the Ministry of Labour, Ministry of Fuel and Power, Home and Foreign Offices, and the Treasury, launched a scheme in March 1951 for the recruitment of Italian males aged between eighteen and thirty-one. This "Italians for coal mining" scheme was a little different from previous recruitment efforts since the potential workers were unemployed, not refugees, and were recruited for one specific industry. It marked the beginning of a shift on the part of the Ministry of Labour toward employer-sponsored schemes. Drawing almost exclusively on Italian labor, the schemes represented a partnership between the state and industries such as iron ore mining, coal mining, railway construction, tinplating, brickmaking, foundries, and stone quarrying. From the Ministry of Labour point of view, employer-sponsored schemes were attractive because incoming aliens were bound by the same landing conditions as DPs and thus could not migrate away from the essential industries for which they had been recruited. The Home Office approved of the schemes because government responsibility and expense were limited, but the aliens were still subject to medicals, "vetting," and other tests of acceptability. And from the employers' perspective, the recruited labor more closely matched the prospective job.[41] Under the schemes the Ministry of Labour attaché at the British Embassy in Rome made presentations to facilitate recruitment, and selection of workers was the responsibility of the employer. Despite its intentions to serve as mediator only, as in the case of the Private Domestic Worker Scheme, the Ministry generally became more involved than it had originally planned. By April 1951 it had committed to selecting recruits, providing transit to England with accompanying guides and aides, ensuring accommodation in London and arranging for tea and buns in Folkestone.[42] The provision of these last amenities, which may be considered a small luxury in austerity Britain, reveals much about the level of official interest in acquiring recruits.

The schemes enjoyed varied success. In March 1951 just under 700 Italians were recruited for work as bricklayers. To help the men settle in Britain, the company also recruited four Italian cooks.[43] Other schemes progressed less smoothly. The NCB and the Ministry of Labour quickly achieved their objective of an inward flow of 60 Italians per week. Just as quickly, however, and with only 1,300 Italians working in mines, problems began to appear as local mining unions refused to accept further foreign labor. A backlog of Italians already in Britain soon developed, and despite much government pressure, the scheme was canceled in May 1952, and the Ministry of Labour assumed responsibility for those 1,100 Italians who had been unable to secure work in the mines. The abrupt termination of the scheme and the apparent default

Front cover of the joint National Coal Board/Ministry of Labour leaflet issued to attract Italian coal miners to Britain, 1951. Note the bilingualism of the text and the suggestion of a pleasant employment atmosphere. (Public Record Office, Kew Document Reference: LAB13/817.)

on NCB contracts prompted a protest from the Italian government, which demanded compensation for its citizens. Rather than face a court case, the ministry urged the NCB to pay.[44] Equally troublesome was the recruitment of Italians for work with British Railways. Hopeful of attracting 7,000 men, British Railways launched a full-scale recruitment scheme in August 1951. After only six months' operation and the placement of just 724 men, BR, like the NCB before it, canceled the scheme following the trade union's refusal to accept Italians.[45] With these experiences very much in mind, and seeking to avoid further compensation claims, the Ministry of Labour advised employers that future contracts should provide no guarantee of employment.[46] As a result, the majority of subsequent Italian recruits entered by means of the work-permit system, albeit with varying levels of official support. In 1955, 2,300 Italians were recruited for tinplate and brickmaking industries, and 1,100 foreigners entered the agricultural labor force. By the end of that year, Britain had recruited 9,000 Italians through special schemes and distributed 4,500 additional work permits.[47] Work permits continued to be issued throughout the 1950s at an average annual rate of 35,000. As the decade progressed, however, increasing numbers of aliens came only for short periods with the apparent intention of returning home upon completion of a one- or two-year contract.[48]

By focusing only on the highly visible Westward Ho! program and ignoring the less-publicized schemes for servants, nurses, and textile workers, the traditional history seriously underestimates the volume and significance of postwar immigration to Britain. The 78,500 European Volunteer Workers were but one category of foreign workers among many. This most famous recruitment *was* relatively short-lived, lasting only about two years, but hundreds of thousands of workers arrived both before and after its existence.[49] A conservative tally of the total number of aliens recruited under the Attlee government yields around 345,000, at a total cost of some £18.1 million.[50] The total recruited consists of 78,500 Westward Ho! volunteers, including 3,500 dependents; 25,000 German, Italian, and Ukrainian prisoners of war accepted for civilian status and permanent residency in Britain; 13,600 German, Austrian, and Italian women recruited under the auspices of the Blue Danube, North Sea, and Official Italian Schemes; and 120,000 former members of the Polish Army and their dependents. By 1952, 110,000 work-permit applicants had been resident in the country for over four years and may be counted among those aliens who planned to make their home in postwar Britain.[51]

III

These 345,000 aliens had a worth beyond their numerical value. From the outset, refugee labor had appealed to the Attlee Cabinet because "within the limits of housing them, they can more readily be directed or steered to particular jobs to help in overcoming industrial 'bottlenecks.' "[52] This expected malleability was made clear to displaced persons while still in Europe. Recruits were informed that "while regard will be paid to their wishes and previous experience, no guarantee can be given that they will be employed in this country in any particular employment. This accords with the specific condition that each volunteer may undertake only employment selected by the Ministry of Labour and may change employment only with the Ministry's consent."[53] These regulations provided officials with the greatest possible freedom in the selection and placement of available labor, together with the option to return "unsuitable" labor. The ready assumption of these powers, together with an unspoken but apparent belief that the refugees should be grateful for their opportunities, suggests that the Attlee government, the civil service, and the administrators of UNRRA, regarded refugee labor as so much portable wealth, a commodity to be sold and distributed by organs of the state for the benefit of the state. Indeed, even before the first batch of recruits had arrived in 1946, the Attlee Cabinet had discussed the economic advantages to be had from a type of worker who "will contribute about twice the amount to the national income that he will receive or consume in the form of wages."[54]

This utilitarian perspective pervaded the instructions given Ministry of Labour recruiting officers who were reminded that the object of Westward Ho! remained to "man up" essential industries, not to resettle DPs in work to their liking. Prospective migrants had to "have full use of their arms, hands and fingers" and "must also be able to stand for lengthy periods without getting tired."[55] Officers were reminded that while "the object is to obtain as many workers as possible . . . obviously it is no use taking women to England who immediately fall sick and become a liability." London instructed officers to accept dependents only in cases where family groups included at least two "normal volunteer workers" and where the mother, or other close relative, though perhaps not capable of work, was "in a reasonably good state of health."[56] Freedom from disease was particularly important as reflected in the number of medicals undergone by potential workers. Having recruited migrants, officials often assessed them in quantifiable terms, stating, for example, that "the quality of labour [from the Sudetens] is as good as anything we have recruited."[57] Even the employer-sponsored schemes borrowed from this discourse with only Italians of "strong physique," "bodily agility," and with "well-developed hands, arms and shoulders" being acceptable for bricklaying work.[58] The Ministry of Labour rejected a request to help relieve the Foreign Office of some its burdens by accepting disabled refugees or married women with children.[59]

Nor, once in Britain, were selected foreigners secure in their placement. Officials resisted International Labour Office proposals which might infringe on the United Kingdom's right to deport refugees who "through ineptitude or general low mental capacity" or because of an "undesirable character" proved useless.[60] In general, the ministry proclaimed its right to deport those whose "presence in Great Britain constitutes a threat to public order and safety (criminals, subversives etc)" and those unable to work "because of some physical/mental problem not immediately identifiable at the medical." Together, the instructions and intentions paint a picture of rifling through the camps' population in search of the best recruits, leaving old people, families, or disabled individuals waiting for some more humanitarian nation. The manner of recruitment did not go unnoticed by contemporaries, who referred to Britain's recognition of "an easy labour market" and claimed that the entire recruitment process had "a whiff of the slave market."[61]

Putting their perception of refugees as contract labor into practice, Ministry of Labour officials employed their regulations to direct the vast majority into the hard-to-recruit-for essential industries such as coal mining, agriculture, construction, textiles, and institutional domestic service. As a result, 70 percent of male DPs were placed in agriculture and mining, and 90 percent of women went into the textile industry and institutional domestic service.[62] The scale of the operation is manifested in the numbers for a single year in just one industry: between June 1947 and June 1948 approximately 51,000 aliens drawn from all sources were placed in agriculture.[63] Critical to this process was the refugees' status as aliens. Britain could not have compelled its own subjects to take up this work without introducing draconian legislation that might well have been resisted and would certainly have undermined the principles of democracy on which the state was allegedly based. Directing aliens into the same jobs, however, went unremarked for the most part and certainly was not challenged as exploitation. Thus, from the outset, discussions about the potential use of foreign labor took place in a context that recognized its vulnerability.[64] The Labour government took advantage both of the DPs' desire to escape camp life, and of the internationally acknowledged customary right of states to decide their own terms of admission, in order to bring in vulnerable and, for that reason, all the more valuable labor to fill gaps in the domestic labor market. Britain thus maintained its image as a liberal democratic country, even as aliens were compelled to accept specific jobs in designated areas and government housing in billets or hostels. The government in effect used nationality and migration as policy tools to help create a community of laborers within Britain whose alien status made it possible to exploit them. Though economic in origin, however, and though open to direction, this group of alien workers was also perceived through a demographic lens.

IV

The use of short-term contracts, the inability to change jobs, and the constant threat of deportation all paint a picture of an oppressed migrant labor group. Focusing upon these terms of engagement, studies of immigration have tended to depict the Attlee administration's continental recruitment drive as purely exploitative.[65] Certainly, officials did impose strict qualifications upon admission and thereby shaped the manner in which aliens could sell their labor power and make an independent life. Nevertheless, there is another layer to the DP experience.

From the outset, despite its use of alienage to extract promises prior to arrival, the Attlee government worked very hard to avoid erecting barriers between these aliens and UK residents. As soon as the government had decided upon the utility of foreign labor in early 1946, it undertook lengthy negotiations with trade unions to ensure workplace acceptance. In June 1946, just three months after the Foreign Labour Committee's inception, Minister of Labour George Isaacs warned Sir Vincent Tewson, General Secretary of the Trades Union Congress, that treating the newcomers as less than British subjects would "run a grave danger of turning the Poles into an underprivileged, discontented emigrant community, which would be dangerous in every kind of way."[66] Heeding his own advice, Isaacs ensured that all alien recruits were eligible for emergency sickness and unemployment benefit prior to their enrollment in regular schemes.[67]

In the beginning, the majority of unions expressed reluctance, fearing that if they acquiesced in the use of alien labor, their particular industry would become a "dumping ground" for all refugees. The tone of subsequent Cabinet debates suggests a determination that trade union intransigence would not be allowed to derail the government's objective. Nye Bevan, for example, facing rejection from the Amalgamated Engineering Union, threatened to bypass the unions entirely by sending the aliens into nonunionized plants. Other members of the Cabinet suggested that "full publicity [be] given to the Union's attitude."[68] By early 1947, with the publication of a joint TUC-government statement asserting the "urgency" of the situation, government officials had convinced the national union leadership of the importance of their goals. They had also secured a smooth entry into the labor force for their alien refugees. The result of government-TUC negotiations was that Poles and displaced persons were employed on the same conditions as resident UK workers. Thus, although vulnerable to state regulations governing their admittance and field of employment, they were not exposed to employer prejudice or discrimination within the labor market. Indeed, their path into the labor force was smoothed by government officers who found them a job and ensured that once employed they were treated exactly the same as UK resident workers. As a result, the jobs they held were guaranteed to offer prevailing wages and conditions and to provide equal access to social insurance, health care, and pensions.[69]

In addition to guaranteeing trade union rates, the government-TUC agreements also stipulated that aliens could be employed only where "British" labor was unavailable and that in the event of a recession, they would be the first to be dismissed.[70] These further qualifications upon aliens' status as free labor could certainly be expected to cancel out the benefits of receiving the prevailing wage. That is, they would have if they had been enforced. Trade union files for the period suggest, however, that in the vast majority of cases, these qualifications were not acted on. Branch complaints that Poles or other "foreigners" had been employed in preference to available British workers were generally dismissed by TUC headquarters. Requesting that the complaining branch recheck its facts or asserting that the majority of DPs were now trade union members and thus could not "indefinitely be regarded as inferior in status to members who were born in this country," TUC officials did nothing to activate the original qualifications upon aliens' employment.[71] Furthermore, they went to considerable trouble to convince complainants of the necessity and value of foreign labor to the UK economy. Taunton and District Trades Council, for example, received a strongly worded assurance from the TUC that the incoming migrants were not Nazis and that Britain could usefully employ an additional one million workers. Thus Taunton's fear of unemployment was misguided.[72] Other TUC responses detailed the economic significance of POW labor and foreign agricultural help both for its own sake and for keeping "British" workers employed and somewhat curtly asked branch officers how they would increase postwar rations without the use of alien labor. Twice the TUC appealed to trade union members' belief in the "ethics of international socialism"; in other cases, TUC officers relied on the impracticality of enforcing the original restrictions as a justification for not doing so.[73] Building on this informal relaxation of rules governing DPs' employment, the TUC and the Ministry of Labour agreed in July 1950 formally to release DPs from all controls after three years' service. Officials on both sides believed it inappropriate that aliens should continue to be regarded as inferior if they were to "become assimilated to British ways of life."[74]

Just as the TUC adopted a relaxed approach to stipulations concerning dismissal and preference, so Ministry of Labour officials employed a flexible approach to the original terms of recruitment. By April 1949 the ministry and the Home Office each seems to have acknowledged that there were limits on the enforcement of the recruits' contracts. A report prepared for a Ministry of Labour regional controllers' meeting noted that the "Westward Ho scheme has become recognized as a resettlement scheme [for] which the British Government takes credit." Officials therefore thought it unlikely that the Home Office would want to validate Eastern European accusations of "slave labour schemes" by enforcing deportation provisions against the "inevitable . . . bad bargains." Indeed, the ministry believed that the threat of deportation could be used only in the most extreme cases. In instances where aliens had left their contracted employer in favor of work with another employer either in the same industry or within the broad field of approved industries, the move went unchallenged. Thus the ministry, while always hoping to contain refugees within the general list of approved industries, acknowledged that the aliens "are not 'slave workers' and must be allowed a reasonable degree of freedom to change from one employment to another."[75]

Unchallenged too were a variety of other means by which aliens escaped the most restrictive parts of their contracts. Recruits who became ill upon arrival in Britain were not deported but sent for treatment to British hospitals, even when the disability was a previously existing condition the alien had concealed. DPs certified by medical examination to be unfit for anything but light work were allowed to take up whatever employment they chose. Aliens petitioning for removal to a place of work close to a relative, even if the relative was a previously unacknowledged spouse, were generally allowed to relocate.[76] Likewise, gross misconduct or unsatisfactory work resulted in relocation to another industry, not deportation. In fact, noting that Scottish agriculture appeared to be suffering a considerable number of such losses, officials wondered how long it would be before all refugees realized that the way out of an inhospitable placement was to secure a behavioral discharge. The means by which 800 aliens gave up their jobs in the tinplate industry is unknown, but it is obvious enough that of 1,200 placed, only 400 remained after three years.[77] In 1949 ministry officials complained of Italians, who more than any other group used a "variety of shifts and devices" to evade immigration restrictions.[78] These complaints suggest that aliens had learned to manipulate the system and to a large extent acted as independent agents in control of their own working lives.

V

The Ministry of Labour wanted to avoid Soviet accusations of "slave labour," but its flexibility was also motivated by a larger goal: the determination that these aliens should become full members of British society. When first confronted with the possibility of recruiting aliens in 1946, the Cabinet looked for demographic acceptability and returnability. Wary of the long-term consequences of a settlement program, ministers advised that "any material increase in the foreign population of this country" be considered very carefully in light of "the demographic issues involved."[79] Following the same train of thought, Home Secretary Ede hoped that "the intake could be limited to entrants from the Western countries, whose traditions and social backgrounds were more nearly equal to our own." Ede also recommended that only individuals "in whose case it would be possible to apply the sanction of deportation" be recruited and warned the Cabinet against conceding any rights to permanent settlement.[80] Questioning the quality of available labor and fearing the difficulties involved in attempting to resettle aliens, ministers debated whether foreigners should be brought to Britain on short "tours of duty" or whether "some classes of workers should be encouraged to make their homes here and add their skills to the common pool."[81] Success with the first batches of workers recruited from Europe and the continuation of the labor shortage appear to have convinced the Cabinet that for selected workers the latter option was preferable. By the spring of 1947 the alien recruitment scheme had taken on the vestiges of a permanent resettlement plan, though policy makers refrained from billing it as such for fear of taking on more commitments than they deemed necessary. By the fall, leaflets issued to DPs openly referred to the possibilities for permanent resettlement, and by the summer of 1948 officials were admitting in internal correspondence that aliens had been accepted on the "reasonable assumption" that "practically all will choose to stay indefinitely."[82]

This assumption was not an accidental policy development. It stemmed from a conscious perception of the long-term demographic potential of both the Poles and the continental refugees. Central to this demographic acceptability was ministers' and officials' conviction that the Poles and other Europeans could become British in both title and substance. Like the debates on imperial migration, the vocabulary of foreign labor recruitment resounded with references to blood and stock. The overall image constructed the foreigners, if not quite as family, then at least as potentially acceptable in-laws. It appeared that the external trappings of Britishness could be acquired so long as the basic building blocks of genetic similarity were in place. Thus in the principal parliamentary debates on foreign labor, government representatives spoke of the "benefits that come from the assimilation of virile, active and industrious people into our stock."[83] The Ministry of Labour described Yugoslav DPs as "a very tough and muscular race," and both Labour and Conservative MPs described the aliens as "first class people" who would "be of great benefit to our stock" and who would replace the "vigorous young blood of our nation" currently being sent to the Commonwealth. With an ordered European immigration policy, claimed one member, Britain's "island population will be refreshed, enriched and strengthened." A Conservative MP hoped that the alien recruits would "feel in every way attracted to the British way of life" and "have a sense of equal citizenship with all the other members of our community." More poetically, a colleague urged that the foreigners should "absorb the British way of life and become one of us." MPs called on the government to override trade union reluctance and popular resistance, so that Britain could receive "the best of the pick" from the camps.[84] For his part, Ede asserted his conviction that the foreigners' "skill and virility" would enable Britain to emerge triumphant from its current trials.[85] In short, the Europeans were deemed to be full of "the spirit and stuff of which we can make Britons."[86]

This perception of demographic acceptability provided the enabling context for the Attlee government to offer these selected aliens all the benefits of membership even though they were outside the formal nationality policy. Thus, Isaacs described the foreign labor schemes as "settlement of a permanent character" of individuals "working their passage to British citizenship."[87] Ede reiterated his absolute determination to see the recruited aliens "assimilated into the British people, to become acquainted with, and to follow, the British way of life."[88] Similar sentiments came from the officials most directly responsible for the foreigners' welfare, whose stated objective was to see them "settle down as satisfactory members of the community."[89] Eighteen months later, a joint government-TUC publication announced as policy that foreigners should be absorbed "into the British way of life and become in due course and to all intents and purposes, fully fledged British citizens."[90] By November 1948 the interested official departments were committed to ensuring the aliens' "ultimate absorption into the British community."[91] European aliens were to be incorporated into the constructed national identity, the domestic community of Britishness, because they did not conflict with the identity as conceived by the policy-making elite. Formal alienage, linguistic, cultural, and political distinctiveness were all held to be of less importance than demographic acceptability as measured by presumed genetic similarity.

Not everybody agreed with this interpretation. During the six years of recruitment, TUC headquarters received an average of one letter a month from the industries and areas directly in receipt of Poles, DPs, and Italians. Members complained of Polish fascism and idleness, antiunion sentiment among the aliens, displacement of "British" workers, and the preferential treatment given to foreigners. Letters hostile to aliens were still being received as late as 1959, and the correspondents frequently specified that the object of their anger was foreign labor, not labor from the Commonwealth.[92] In order to combat this hostility and provide a receptive climate for their recruits, the Attlee government and the officials under its direction engaged in a process of reconstruction designed to transform alien refugees into potential Britons.

As the first barrage in this assault upon the UK population's assumed hostility and wariness, the Foreign Labour Committee decided that upon arrival in Britain, displaced persons were to be known as European Volunteer Workers (EVWs). The linguistic alteration was made so as to prevent "any misconception which might arise amongst ordinary British workers and the public generally" as to the origins of the immigrants.[93] Clearly, ministers hoped that creating a discourse of European kinship and free economic aid would help the resident population accept the aliens. Saddled with the title of "displaced persons," these newcomers might well have appeared unwanted, even useless. By contrast, the much more positive title of European Volunteer Worker created an impression of a hardy citizen offering his or her services to help Britain in its time of need. More generally, officials from a variety of departments agreed that in reference to these workers, the term "foreign," "which was repugnant to the British," should be replaced by the term "European."[94] Likewise, linguistic fashioning recreated former enemy Sudetens into stateless women in order to make the recruits more acceptable to trade unions.[95] And while Poles retained their identity as Poles, the government stimulated "informed publicity" in order to "counteract rumours and uninformed criticism" and create a "better atmosphere" for their employment, while the War Office agreed to present a series of "informative broadcasts" on their behalf.[96] All foreigners were covered by the Ministry of Labour's leaflet *Workers from Abroad* issued to labor exchanges for general distribution. Within a context that presented all foreign labor as positive, the leaflet described the Poles as "gallant men" and DPs as "still possessed of their traditionally purposeful spirit and self-respect."[97]

In addition to playing with language, policy makers used many other means to manipulate public opinion. The Committee for the Education of Public Opinion on Foreign Workers was formed in direct response to popular hostility toward aliens. The startling range of activities in which it involved itself reveals the depth of government concern about the future of its alien recruits. Principal suggestions concerned the propagation of feature articles to women's magazines and local newspapers, which, "if wisely and continuously fed with good information," would be effective means of "shaping public opinion." The BBC agreed to broadcast pro-EVW radio programs and Ukrainian musical concerts and promised to audition foreign artists for general variety shows. By presenting images of hardworking foreigners, these channels were intended to promote acceptance of foreign labor, dispelling myths that idle aliens constituted a burden on the UK economy and were responsible for such evils as the continuation of rationing. The Ministry of Labour even cooperated with an independent organization to produce and distribute a leaflet titled "What the Poles Have Done for You," and it researched the possibility of broadcasting an interview, conducted in a mineshaft, between the radio personality Wilfred Pickles and a Polish miner.

Reconstructing aliens into citizens did not rely exclusively on official initiatives. Immigrants were expected to take an active role in their transformation. Although not spelled out in any formal way, it is clear that there were several stages to the process of becoming British. First, the FLC dispersed foreigners throughout Britain to foster conditions in which former national allegiances might be dropped. Second, aliens were instructed "to make every effort to learn" English through language classes provided free of charge in the camps.

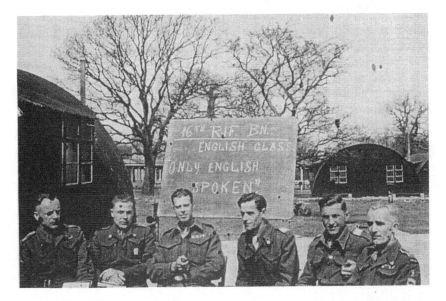

Members of the Polish Resettlement Corps taking a break from class with their English Language Instructor at a PRC camp, 1947. (Courtesy of the Polish Institute and Sikorski Museum, London.)

Third, the aliens were expected to be hardworking, of the right "temperament . . . to be assimilated into the British way of life," and "of good behaviour." Fourth, and perhaps most important, policy makers clearly expected EVWs to naturalize as British subjects, to marry British men and women, and ultimately to produce British children. Sir Harold Wiles, Deputy Permanent Under Secretary at the Ministry of Labour and Chair of the Official Committee on the Employment of Poles, claimed that one of the primary purposes of the foreign labor schemes was to recruit people for "permanent settlement here with a view to their intermarrying and complete absorption into our own working population." During the parliamentary debate, one speaker referred to the declining birthrate and the "unfortunate sociological factor" of "200,000 numerically surplus women" as the "strongest possible ethnographical reasons for having an infusion of vigourous new blood." Encouraging intermarriage between aliens and subjects raised no fears of miscegenation or social problems, as would be the case for British subjects of color. In fact, ministers hoped the foreign labor schemes would "produce a substantial number of women of useful qualifications and of good health who would form a valuable addition to our manpower and a not undesirable element in our population."[98] Thus male aliens were to rectify specific shortages, and female aliens were to boost the general birthrate. In short, at a time of perceived demographic crisis, the United Kingdom could only benefit from an infusion of the right kind of stock, both male and female.

These expectations confirm that in operating recruitment schemes, London was not offering to establish a multicultural society. Foreigners were expected to become British not just in the technical sense of nationality but also in terms of social and cultural norms. Thus, government officials took a consistent interest in the foreigners' welfare. Immediately upon arrival recruits were given a booklet titled *How to Help You Settle in Britain,* followed shortly after by another titled *Contemporary Life in Britain.* The Poles received special funding for education which paid for Polish schools and a university. Although apparently divisive, the money was provided as a temporary measure with the long-term aim of "absorption into our own [British] community."[99] Two years into the recruitment schemes, government officials met with representatives of the various national groups "to consider how the EVWs were settling down in this country, to what extent the present welfare arrangements are meeting their needs, and any new problems which seem likely to develop in the future." That the representatives' "wish-list" consisted of such requests as the observance of national holidays, more organized sports within the hostels, more native-language books in the library, more English lessons, and even a Ukrainian edition of the BBC's popular show *Workers' Playtime* suggests that the aliens' immediate needs were already being met by the government.[100]

The expectation that the aliens' community of potential Britishness would eventually disappear into the larger community of domestic Britishness helps explain the manner of recruitment. The Ministry of Labour and the Home Office were so severe in their selection criteria because they recognized that they were recruiting not just short-term workers but long-term citizens. This context helps explain both the number of medical exams faced by each potential Briton during recruitment and the ministers' insistence that all "newcomers must be readily assimilable."[101] The Attlee government was enlarging the community of domestic Britishness by adding potential Britons to the breeding stock; it was therefore imperative that they recruit only the best material available.

The Attlee government's expectation that the transformation of aliens into Britons would be largely successful reflects a tremendous faith in the assimilatory powers of British nationality and society. Presuming British nationality to be a favored nationality and Britishness to be a privileged status, policy makers assumed that all suitable incoming migrants would eventually become British. This perspective seems diametrically opposed to policy makers' expectations that British stock emigration to the dominions would maintain the Britishness of the empire. Significantly, this apparent acknowledgment of the potential of selected foreigners to become British did not extend to a recognition of the malleability of Britishness. The public record suggests rather that officials and ministers perceived Britishness to be a fixed state which, after several years' residence, certain essentially demographically compatible immigrants could acquire. In truth, of course, any migrant group, even when it is apparently assimilating, changes the nature of the assimilator. Though not recognizing this possibility for continental aliens, the Attlee government and the Conservative administrations that followed appear to have been much more aware of the distinctiveness of the second major source of migrants in the postwar era, a source much closer to "home" and with a much longer history of association.

CHAPTER 4

Neither Subjects nor Aliens but Irish

*T*he role played by Irish migrants in the postwar politics of British citizenship was determined by a combination of three factors. First, on average in the period 1946 through 1962, between 50,000 and 60,000 Irish men and women entered the UK labor market for the first time each year. In the light of the economic crisis and the subsequent desperate search for foreign labor, this steady migrant flow constituted a highly valuable source of labor. It proved sufficiently valuable to provide a reason for ministers and their officials in the Home Office and Ministry of Labour, in the midst of their broader articulation of subjecthood and citizenship in the 1948 British Nationality Act, to construct a unique interpretation of nationality for Irish aliens living in Britain. Described by one observer as "unique in statute law" and "without precedent in legislation dealing with nationality," the Irish provisions of the 1948 British Nationality Act stipulated that the Irish in Britain were to be regarded as neither British subjects nor aliens but as Irish citizens with all the rights of British subjecthood.[1] Second, the Labour government stretched its imagination to construct a separate sphere of nationality for Irish people living in Britain because it believed that not to do so endangered the Commonwealth by undermining larger imperial policy objectives. Third, Labour and later Conservative manipulations of the legal meanings of citizenship were undertaken in an unspoken context of demographic acceptability. Although officials made few references to Irish migrants' skin color, the lengths to which they went to preserve the labor supply and the Commonwealth connection suggest that the Irish passed an unwritten test of potential Britishness measured according to a racialized conception of the world's population. By contrast, as we shall see in Chapters 5 and 6, the West Indies, India and Pakistan, were also useful as members of the Commonwealth and cultivated as independent nation-states, but their residents were not welcome as migrants.

The combination of economic, political, and social utility and acceptability cast the Irish in a positive role in the game of citizenship. That is, throughout the period under review both Labour and Conservative administrations recruited them in pursuit of larger objectives. And yet despite this encouragement, the majority of Irish migrants occupied an ambiguous position within British society. Formally they were neither subjects nor aliens; informally they appear to have been regarded as neither British nor foreign. Instead, in both cases they were simply perceived as Irish, with all the connotations that label carried in Britain. As a result, they faced discrimination and prejudice even as they enjoyed the privileges of subjecthood.

This informal setting apart of the Irish, as well as their unique legal status, ensured that they occupied a separate sphere of nationality within Britain. This separate sphere reflected a community of Britishness based around Irishness. Thus, the Labour government did not seek for the Irish, as they did for continental aliens, their eventual transformation into "real" Britons, nor did they or the Conservatives who succeeded them in office, reject the Irish as they did people of color. Instead, the Irish were allowed to occupy a middle ground, acknowledged to be sufficiently similar to gain entry into the territory, yet identified as sufficiently different to be ever known as Irish. Within the family metaphor so often employed by policy makers in respect to nationality, if British stock emigrants to the dominions were the children of the empire, if "coloured colonials" were friends of the family, and if continental aliens were potential in-laws whose children would be recognized as one's own, the Irish in Britain might be identified as first cousins. Exploring the means by which UK and Irish policy makers articulated this extended family relationship exposes the equivocal position of the Irish, as well as the significance of the racialized interpretation of the world's population which underlay the politics of citizenship in postwar Britain.

I

The origins of Ireland's relationship with England may be said to lie somewhere in the twelfth century with English King Henry II's decision to invade his island neighbor.[2] Succeeding centuries were marked by continuing struggles between those representing government from London and those who fought for an Ireland free of English influence. The battle lines were sometimes blurred as descendants of early Norman "invaders" fought against Tudor control and as descendants of seventeenth-century English "planters" fought against Victorian government. Throughout, but particularly during the reign of Oliver Cromwell, the British government employed migration as a political weapon, encouraging colonists to migrate to Ireland as a means of consolidating British rule over the area. After centuries of such "plantations" and intermittent resistance, the Act of Union in 1801 formally united the two countries as the United Kingdom of Great Britain and Ireland. Many within the majority Catholic population remained estranged from their new country, however, and some regarded the union with England as no better than a colonial yoke.[3] After 122 years of physical and constitutional resistance on the part of Catholic (and some Protestant) Irish nationalists, the English finally conceded that Henry II's invasion had failed. Or at least it had failed in the twenty-six Irish counties that were given independence as the Irish Free State within the British Commonwealth in 1922 and, by the Irish constitution of 1937, became known as Eire. The remaining six counties, all located in the province of Ulster in the northeastern sector of Ireland, the site of the heaviest Protestant settlements, remained part of the renamed United Kingdom of Great Britain and Northern Ireland.

If political colonization proved to be neither wholesale nor permanent, the British were far more successful economically. Geographical proximity, political weakness, and internal divisions combined to ensure that Ireland's agricultural economy assumed an auxiliary status to Britain's industrialized state. As a result, successive UK governments of all political persuasions and many British industries came to regard Ireland as a fertile field of available labor for Britain. Migrants came as temporary workers for the agricultural sector crossing back and forth across the Irish Sea, as permanent members of the industrial work force settling in major conurbations such as Liverpool, Manchester, and London, and as soldiers in the British imperial army. Emigration from all parts of Ireland to Britain continued even after the formation of the Irish Free State and Northern Ireland in 1922. The UK government gave additional stimulus to the flow from Eire by establishing a recruitment office in Dublin during World War II. Shortly after opening, the center was sending around 2,000 people to Britain every week and by the war's end approximately 100,000 citizens of Eire had traveled to the UK mainland to take up employment in essential industries such as coal mining, construction, agriculture, and foundries.[4]

This economic contribution continued after the war. The UK Ministry of Labour retained its Dublin Liaison Office and invested a great deal of energy in recruiting Irish migrants for essential work in Britain. Officially, Irish men could take employment in Britain only on receipt of authorization from the Irish authorities, but since the necessary documents were issued freely and remained valid indefinitely, the system did little to limit the migrant flow. Arriving in Britain, "fit men between 18 and 35" were subject to landing controls (left over from World War II) which enabled the Ministry of Labour "to take advantage of a man's desire to find employment in Great Britain . . . to get him to enter work of vital importance." Exempt from landing controls were professionals such as doctors, dentists, and teachers and all female migrants. Partly because controls were limited, the majority of Irish workers migrated to Britain independently, relying on the resources of friends, family or church to find accommodation and employment.[5] Others availed themselves of the provisions offered by the liaison office in Dublin. Seeking men particularly for coal mining, agriculture, and construction, the UK Ministry of Labour compiled "a pool of available labour" from suitable volunteers. Against this pool, the ministry placed demands from Regional Labour Offices representing requirements from specific employers. Upon matching a potential migrant with a job, the liaison office interviewed him and supplied written details of the precise nature of the employment, the wages and hours, as well as likely accommodation and living costs. Just like continental refugees, Irish migrants underwent a medical exam for both physical and mental fitness. Would-be workers were then provided with travel warrants, food and accommodation vouchers, and even luggage labels—and that just for the journey to Dublin. Upon arrival in the capital migrants were housed and fed and if necessary deloused before being shipped free of charge to Britain where they were met by ministry representatives who provided breakfast and, if the final destination was distant, a day's provisions. Workers were again met at the end of this last stage of the journey and escorted to their lodgings.[6]

Whatever the route, the end result was an annual cross traffic of around one million, with between 50,000 and 60,000 new migrants annually taking up employment in Britain. By 1951 Britain was home to almost three-quarters of a million Irish-born people; ten years later the total had increased to approximately one million. These figures are significant both because Britain had replaced the United States as the primary destination for Irish emigrants and because Irish citizens were consistently the largest national group to enter postwar Britain. In 1959, for example, 64,494 "new" Irish workers migrated to Britain, as compared with 30,842 from the colonies, 35,198 from the Commonwealth, and 46,965 from the rest of the world.[7] To a country in the midst of a decade-long labor shortage sufficiently severe to inspire desperate recruitment of labor from the former enemy, Irish migration offered a welcome respite.

II

The economic value of Irish labor stood Irish migrants in good stead when the Canadian government's 1945 decision to pursue a separate citizenship forced the Attlee administration to reconsider British subjecthood.

The Catholic Women's League was only one institution that tried to arrange accommodation for Irish migrants traveling alone, October 1955. (The Hulton Deutsch Collection.)

In this process, the Home Office expected Ireland to pose the greatest problem.[8] For although Irish nationalists had declared their independence from Britain in 1916, and despite the subsequent achievement of an Irish Free State, British law still recognized Irish citizens, like all other residents of the Commonwealth, as British subjects. This was the case despite a 1935 Irish Citizenship Act that expressly rejected this status for Irish citizens. With the approach of fresh nationality legislation for the entire Commonwealth, however, the Home Office believed that it had little choice but to consider the true nature of the relationship between Irish citizens and the rest of the Commonwealth.[9]

The Labour government was caught between two difficult choices. Continued inactivity risked perpetuating an "anomalous" situation that might cause "friction" with the Eire government and left open the possibility that Eire would, upon joining the United Nations, take the issue into the international arena and thereby embarrass the United Kingdom. And yet the alternative of recognizing the Eire government's renunciation of British subjecthood and acknowledging Irish citizens as aliens in Britain posed a great many problems of its own. First, it would likely provoke "a considerable amount of public discussion as to Eire's position within the Commonwealth" and thus threatened to undermine the strength and unity of the whole Commonwealth. Second, if Irish migrants were reduced to the status of aliens, their need for work permits would not only place a heavy administrative burden on the Ministry of Labour, but, more important, disrupt an extremely valuable labor supply. Third, the classification as aliens and subsequent police registration of the hundreds of thousands of Irish citizens now or in the future living in Britain would not only tax the aliens-control system but would also likely threaten its very credibility. And finally, any attempt to regulate the UK-Irish border would probably prove both costly and inefficient. Avoiding these difficulties by exempting the Irish from some of the standard provisions for aliens was simple enough. Irish migrants could be given unconditional leave to land, a work-permit office could be established in Dublin, and the whole system could be based on co-operation between UK and Irish immigration officers. Following this path, however, would open the UK to challenges from nations with which it had established most-favored-nation treaties. Allowing other nations to claim rights intended only for the Irish would even more seriously undermine the efficiency of aliens control. Faced with these conflicts, the Home Office and the Ministry of Labour, the principal departments concerned, looked for a solution that would take account of Irish law, British practical difficulties, and those Eire citizens who disagreed with the terms of the Irish Citizenship Act and whose loyalty to the United Kingdom had been proven by war or civil service.[10]

The Irish government proved unwilling to reconsider the terms of its 1935 act and declared that Britain's continued assumption of British subjecthood for Irish citizens was "an impertinence." At the same time, Irish representatives meeting to discuss the matter stressed that there was no hostility in their actions, merely the desire to be rid of an "inappropriate" common status.[11] Essentially, there was no room for British subjecthood within an independent Irish identity. The role of Irish officials in these negotiations is interesting since the postwar Irish government, like the British, was playing the game of emigration politics. The Irish politics of emigration may be deconstructed into three parts. First, members of the Irish governing elite felt compelled to denounce publicly what they accepted privately. Second, the economic dependency evidenced by a continuing need for emigration made the pursuit of political independence all the more imperative. Third, through state-sanctioned emigration, Irish migrants were reconstituted as international units of labor.

Simply put, the Irish economy could not provide employment for all its citizens. Twenty-five years after independence, industrial development remained limited; agricultural land remained inequitably distributed, favoring pasture farmers with little need for labor and leaving many citizens holding farms too small to support a family; and population growth, while much reduced from nineteenth-century highs, remained sufficient to produce more people than jobs. Particularly hard hit were the western provinces of Connacht and Munster, areas in which emigrant remittances, government pensions, state benefits, and seasonal wages constituted many people's primary sustenance.[12] From 1945 to 1950, average annual emigration per thousand Irish inhabitants increased from a prewar 6.3 to 8.2 and then to 13.4 by 1955. In addition to drawing primarily upon the residents of the west, this emigration attracted largely young men and women and thus drew away the most potentially productive of Ireland's citizenry.[13]

Official response within Eire policy-making circles to this emigration was ambivalent. On the one hand, wartime officials spoke of emigration as a "safety valve against revolution" and recognized the value of the "resulting inflow of ready money" in relieving distress and maintaining economic activity in the country.[14] On the other hand, Irish administrations of whatever political persuasion could not have been unaware of the irony by which "the very people who flocked from the country in such numbers were the sons and daughters of those who had fought a revolutionary war . . . and on whose behalf the revolutionary war had been fought."[15] And yet the hardest irony to bear perhaps was that balance-of-payment crises, economic stagnation, and rising unemployment made sustained emigration to Britain a necessary feature of the postwar Irish economy. Emigration, "the classic Irish 'solution' to the problem of unemployment," was as vital in the second half of the twentieth century as it had been a hundred years earlier when Ireland lay under "the English yoke."[16]

In the context of Eire's reliance on the UK labor market, the 1935 repudiation of subjecthood and all its rights makes little apparent sense. But perhaps one can speculate that it was the fact of economic dependence which made the proclamation of political independence—manifested in separate nationalities—all the more imperative. Indeed, long before the institution of the Irish Free State in 1922, Irish nationalists had asserted the existence of an Irish identity separate from the governing English culture.[17] After independence, the Irish government continually pressed the boundaries of its relationship with the United Kingdom, emphasizing its separate nationhood even as it remained within the British Commonwealth. In 1924, for example, the Irish Free State government made a point of registering the Anglo-Irish Treaty of 1921 (which had ended the Anglo-Irish War) with the League of Nations despite Britain's protests that a treaty between the United Kingdom and a member of the Commonwealth was not an international treaty. Similarly in 1929, the Irish Free State reserved the right to refer all Anglo-Irish disputes directly to the Permanent Court of International Justice in preference to Commonwealth channels. Cultural and political assertions of identity had converged in the Irish Citizenship Act of 1935 which both defined the body of people known as citizens of Eire and explicitly rejected the status of British subject for such citizens. A year later, the Irish Fianna Fail government, headed by Taoiseach Eamon de Valera, enacted the External Relations Act as a means of ousting the English Crown from Irish domestic affairs while still retaining membership in the Commonwealth.[18] The Irish national identity was further enshrined in 1937 in a new constitution that formally identified the twenty-six counties as Eire and established Catholicism as the preferred religion of the majority. Compounding this litany of perceived affronts to the presumed ties of Commonwealth membership, Eire remained formally neutral during World War II.[19] Yet for all this political autonomy, reliance on the UK labor market to absorb its excess population demonstrated the continued economic dependence of Ireland. Thus, in the context of the long-standing drive for autonomy, Dublin had a difficult game to play: asserting independence from Britain while acquiescing in, even encouraging, the regular and substantial use of Irish labor in the UK market.[20]

For its part, London too was required to exercise some imagination in the management of its Irish relations. The architects of the 1948 British Nationality Act faced a dilemma: making aliens out of the Irish would seriously inconvenience the British; keeping them British subjects would seriously offend the Irish. Officials from the Home, Foreign, and Dominions Offices, the Ministry of Labour, the UK representative to Eire's office, and official representatives of de Valera's Fianna Fail government searched for a compromise. This was found by determining that the Irish government's case was based on the need to reject the *status* of British subject, not the desire to do away with the *rights* of British subjecthood.[21] Separating the status and rights in this way, deeming them distinct, independent characteristics, enabled the Labour government to take the unconventional step of devising a third form of nationality. Hence according to the 1948 British Nationality Act citizens of Eire were neither British subjects nor aliens but Irish citizens with all the rights and duties of British subjecthood. Privileges included the right to enter the country freely, take up any employment available, and vote and stand for Parliament when resident in England; obligations included paying taxes and, after two years' continuous residence, performing national service. This relationship was based on the reciprocal exchange of citizenship rights between members of the Commonwealth and, since the Irish were explicitly not aliens, avoided the possibility of most-favored-nation challenges from foreign countries. Thus, the United Kingdom became perhaps the only country to make no distinction between its own subjects and one group of aliens. Home Secretary Ede recognized the "anomalies" involved in this construction of citizenship but declared: "In attempting to deal with the Irish, whether Southern or Northern, if one can do anything at all, it is sure to be either by way of creating an anomaly or of recognizing one."[22] Since postwar Britain's separate spheres of nationality stemmed not just from formal laws and informal practices but also from implied assumptions and perceptions, the patronizing tone of this defense and the public acknowledgment of national difference were as important in building a distinct Irish community of Britishness as the initial legal tricks of the 1948 act.

Absent from the negotiations, however, and representing the third element in the (Irish and British) politics of emigration, was any discussion of what these "unique" provisions represented: the conception of labor as a form of movable wealth open to manipulation by governing elites. London was ever eager to increase the volume of Irish migration, confident that such additions would work to the benefit of the UK economy; Dublin acquiesced in economic dependency and the loss of labor power in return for the emigrant remittances and disposal of its surplus population. During the war the UK Ministry of Labour had directed Irish workers to the economic advantage of Britain while the Irish government worried that after the war "up to as many as a hundred thousand or more unemployed men (who will, no doubt, have imbibed a good deal of leftism in Britain) [will be] dumped back here within the course of a few weeks."[23] Thus after the war both governments found it in their mutual interest to cooperate in finding a means by which migration might continue in its current form and at its current volume. In their mutual willingness to trade politics for migrants, both London and Dublin manifested a vision of labor as a commodity to be sold and distributed according to the needs of the state. As a result, the 1948 Nationality Act recognized Irish citizens as a distinct category with all the rights of subjecthood including the most significant right to enter the country freely. While this special category immediately benefited those Irish citizens who chose to take advantage of it, it also exemplifies the vulnerability of labor to state control. By acquiescing in England's use of Irish labor, by itself relying on the employment of Irish labor in foreign markets and thereby freeing itself of the obligation to provide employment at home, Fianna Fail helped define Irish migrants as workers first and citizens second. For its part, though granting the privileges of subjecthood, the United Kingdom acquired a labor source more vulnerable to direction and more likely to take up work in manual and casual trades—necessary work for any economy but not particularly attractive to indigenous labor. Thus, although by the 1948 act all Irish migrants became free agents within the British labor market, statistics reveal that the vast majority of workers took up employment in construction, agriculture, catering, domestic service, and nursing.[24] And while many continued to send remittances "home" to Ireland, they were increasingly categorized as part of the Irish diaspora rather than as Irish citizens temporarily working abroad. In this process, a symbiotic relationship stemming from both political and economic needs enabled policy makers on both sides to formulate a flexible interpretation of citizenship: the Irish government acquiesced in Britain's reliance on Irish citizens and treatment of such citizens as though they belonged to Britain rather than to Ireland, while the UK government acquiesced in the muddling of British nationality law and Ireland's public denunciations of British subjecthood. The result was an Irish community of Britishness based on pragmatic economic and political considerations, making this group British in practice but not in law.

III

In 1948 the Attlee government could justify the special treatment of Irish citizens, through Commonwealth ties between Eire and Britain under the External Relations Act (ERA). In September 1948, even before the 1948 British Nationality Act was due to come into effect (1 January 1949), the Irish Coalition government, led now by Taoiseach John Costello, announced its intention of repealing this last remaining link and proclaiming a republic. Thus, the whole question of Anglo-Irish relations once again opened up for debate. In light of the recent struggle to achieve a new understanding of the position of the Irish in Britain, Costello's announcement might at first glance appear ungracious or rash.[25] It seems likely, however, that the announcement had less to do with leaving the British Commonwealth and more to do with achieving the republic for which Irish men and women had been fighting and dying since 1916.[26] Notwithstanding the achievement of an Irish Free State to which the name Eire was subsequently given, an autonomous Irish republic, as proclaimed during the 1916 Easter Rising and over which a civil war had been fought (1922–23), remained elusive.[27] Costello and his Foreign Minister Sean MacBride believed the repeal of the ERA and the subsequent declaration of a republic would remove "an irritant" from relations with Britain and from politics within Eire. According to the Irish government, the repeal was not a hostile act but an attempt to move beyond the civil war and old grievances with Britain.[28] Thus, while the manner of Costello's announcement, during a press conference in Canada, may have appeared incongruous, still he was articulating a real aspiration of Irish nationalism, an aspiration couched still within the politics of emigration as the continuing importance of economic ties made clear.[29] Whatever the original motive, however, the effect of the announcement was to necessitate further discussion of Ireland's relationship to the Commonwealth and, by association, the position of Irish citizens in Britain.

Eire's projected repeal of the ERA forced the Attlee government in late 1948 to rethink the structures of Commonwealth membership. Coincidentally, a few months prior to Costello's announcement in anticipation of challenges from India, Attlee had already appointed a Cabinet committee to examine the nature of Commonwealth relationships. After much debate, this committee arrived at two major conclusions. First, recognition of the Crown for external purposes was the minimum commitment required for Commonwealth membership. Nations that could not accept even this "limited allegiance" to the Crown could not be recognized as Commonwealth members. Second, the Commonwealth was to remain a single body with only one level of membership; there would be no tiers of membership, no associate members. In both cases, the committee emphasized that only insistence on these principles could assure the future of the Commonwealth.[30] And yet even as the committee met, India and Pakistan declared their intention to assume republican status, and Ireland announced the impending repeal of the only remaining link between Eire and the Crown. In response, both ministers and officials worked hard to find a solution that would minimize disruptions to existing relationships and maximize Commonwealth strength. The intensity of these efforts manifests the degree of continuing UK commitment to the Commonwealth and the conviction that only through its preservation could individual members play a major role in international affairs. Premier Peter Fraser of New Zealand, for example, asked the Eire government to reconsider its decision to repeal the ERA, reminding its ministers of the need to stand together against the threat of world communism and emphasizing that Ireland's departure from the Commonwealth would be a "major disaster," which "would be seized on by our enemies and shake the confidence of our friends in the stability of the group."[31] In search of a mechanism that would secure Commonwealth stability while recognizing Eire's assertion of independence, the Labour government, just as it had done in 1945 in response to Canada's challenge, once again sought and found a solution within the politics of citizenship.

By chance Costello's announcement came just before a Commonwealth prime ministers' meeting and was thus from the beginning debated by both UK and dominion leaders. The Labour government first tried to persuade the Irish government that repealing the ERA would result in so many difficulties that it should not be done, or if it had to be done, then it should be replaced by some other link that would enable Ireland to remain within or reenter the Commonwealth.[32] A month later, in November 1948, in the manner of a "friendly warning," London prepared a note for the Irish government informing it of the consequences of repeal. As originally drafted, the note was uncompromising in tone, and it recognized no alternative in the event of repeal but to treat Ireland and Irish citizens as foreign. Once Ireland became foreign, it explained, international law and most-favored-nation treaties would compel the United Kingdom to control Irish migration to Britain, to treat Irish citizens in Britain as aliens, and to revoke Irish trade preferences.[33] Before it was sent, however, ministers weighed the potential benefits of publicizing the disadvantages of repeal in the hope that popular anger in Eire might force the government to rethink its case, against the need to secure full support for any course of action from other Commonwealth members. Stressing the administrative and political difficulties that would arise upon Eire's becoming foreign and the danger that Eire might raise the issue of partition at the United Nations, majority Cabinet opinion proposed that emphasis be placed on the spirit of Eire's desire to continue a special relationship with the Commonwealth rather than on the repeal of the ERA. Thus the Cabinet agreed to consult dominion leaders and to send a modified, milder note on possible consequences to the Eire government.[34]

Even as Cabinet ministers prepared to warn the Eire government against repealing the ERA, their officials were considering how to mitigate the effects of the likely repeal. As a result, Commonwealth Relations Secretary Philip Noel-Baker presented a Cabinet memorandum detailing just how inconvenient it would be for Britain should Ireland become foreign, in essence repeating the arguments of the previous year: the potential loss and certain disruption of a valuable source of labor with resultant damage to the export trade, the imposition on the civil service of much extra work for little gain, and the possible breakdown of the current aliens system. Indeed, the potential problems posed by the sheer number of Irish people currently living in Britain meant that it might be impossible to treat them in practice in the same way as other aliens. These difficulties were not thought to be insuperable, however. Eire citizens could, for example, without loss of their Irish citizenship, be offered a less stringent naturalization procedure, and legislation could be drafted to enable Eire citizens to continue to enlist in the UK armed forces. In general Noel-Baker concluded that whatever Eire might do, "in the interests of simplicity of administration and good relations with Eire . . . [British] legislation should in the first instance be drafted to furnish the maximum possible degree of mitigation."[35] Thus, Noel-Baker and officials from a variety of departments were prepared to implement a pragmatic interpretation of the obligations of alienage and the rights of citizenship in order to minimize inconvenience to Britain. They were prepared to construct an Irish community of Britishness, which, unlike that built in 1948, would be formally alien, but which, like that in 1948, would be relieved of the most troublesome burdens of alienage. This was a flexible enough conception of the politics of citizenship but the dictates of imperial policy demanded yet more flexibility.

Taking advantage of the proximity of Commonwealth heads of state, while London was preparing warning notes and mitigatory memos, Attlee invited Eire ministers to Chequers, his weekend residence, for talks; these were repeated a month later when UK, dominion, and Irish ministers and officials met again in Paris. The record of these talks reveals that UK and dominion policy makers saw this latest incarnation of the "Irish question" from very different perspectives. UK ministers Attlee, Jowitt, and Noel-Baker repeatedly stressed the inevitable difficulties that would follow upon Ireland's becoming foreign. The dominion ministers agreed, but after initial representations to Ireland not to repeal the act had failed, Australian Foreign Minister Herbert Evatt, New Zealand Premier Peter Fraser, and Canadian Premier-designate Louis St. Laurent all urged that some means be found by which Ireland, though repealing the ERA and thus no longer associated by allegiance to the Crown, could continue to be treated as a member of the Commonwealth. Though apparently surprised by the hastiness of the decision to repeal, Fraser was "earnestly anxious," St. Laurent "earnestly hoped," and Evatt believed "no effort should be spared" to avoid the "embarrassment" of Ireland becoming a foreign country. Furthermore, Evatt believed that Eire's action was motivated more by the desire "to take the gunman out of Irish politics" than by antiCommonwealth feeling. In summary, no dominion government wanted to be associated with "the severing of the last link" between Ireland and the Commonwealth. These comments built on Evatt's earlier suggestion to Attlee that it was incumbent on Commonwealth members to try to render "the constitutional arrangements of the Commonwealth acceptable to all, including Ireland."[36]

It is clear from the focus of dominion politicians' remarks that their position stemmed at least in part from fear of the political consequences in their own countries where the Irish lobbies were thought unlikely to welcome Ireland's alienage. Thus by a curious twist of fate "the classic Irish 'solution' to unemployment" now worked to the advantage of Irish nationalism as Irish communities abroad gave dominion politicians reason at least to accommodate if not to favor Irish initiatives. Thus, ironically, what London hoped to achieve by sending its citizens overseas was realized by Dublin. It was presumably with these communities in mind that dominion leaders stressed that if Ireland did become foreign "it should be made abundantly clear that this was by her own decision and that the Governments of the United Kingdom and other Commonwealth countries had done their utmost to make the consequences clear to her before any irrevocable step had been taken."[37] By contrast, Attlee believed it would prove difficult to "define the kind of intermediate position" Eire wished to occupy, and Lord Chancellor Jowitt questioned whether such a position, even if defined, would be recognized by international law.[38]

Most likely to be challenged, the UK delegation believed, were aspects of any new relationship which conflicted with Britain's most-favored-nation treaties. UK policy makers feared, first, that foreign nations would demand trade preferences akin to those enjoyed by Eire and, second, that foreign nations would conclude such arrangements with each other as a means of discriminating against nations with which most-favored-nation obligations existed, specifically, the United Kingdom. Fearing that successful challenges would undermine the whole system of imperial preferences, Attlee and his colleagues maintained that following repeal, international law would oblige the Commonwealth to regard Eire as foreign. Eire believed that most-favored-nation challenges could be resisted on the grounds that Eire had continued to enjoy special privileges since 1937 despite, according to Eire law, being outside the Commonwealth.[39] Irish Foreign Minister Sean MacBride repeatedly emphasized that Eire looked for continued friendly relations with the Commonwealth and that the repeal of the ERA did not prevent a "special kind of association." Specifically, the Eire government declared that the "special ties of blood and kinship," together with the long-standing social and economic ties already existing between Eire and the Commonwealth, could serve as the basis for a special association. Clearly, MacBride wanted to maintain the existing relationship with Britain with its economic privileges, including access to the British labor market, without having to pay the price of formal membership. That is, in the context of the politics of emigration, Eire wanted greater political independence despite continuing economic dependence.[40]

After much additional debate and only after the specter of a weakened Commonwealth had been emphasized, the UK representatives conceded that a way could be found to keep Eire from becoming a foreign country even though it left the Commonwealth. This solution depended on the further manipulation of the politics of citizenship. Specifically, Commonwealth representatives agreed that the reciprocal exchange of trade and citizenship rights was to constitute the basis of future association.[41] Furthermore, in order to protect the rights of Eire citizens currently in Britain and to avoid the necessity of drafting additional legislation, the Eire government agreed to postpone its repeal of the ERA until after the 1948 British Nationality Act came into effect. As further proof of Eire's nonforeign status, Irish affairs were to continue to be dealt with by the Commonwealth Relations Office rather than the officially more appropriate Foreign Office.

UK officials made it clear that Commonwealth unity was the overriding concern in accepting this compromise. According to the Lord Chancellor, the UK delegation acquiesced with reluctance and only because "it became clear to us that, if we persisted in the view that Eire must be regarded as a foreign country once the External Relations Act was repealed, we should find ourselves alone in maintaining that view. It was plain that Canada, Australia, New Zealand, like Eire, wished to follow the contrary view; and they all felt so strongly on this point that it seemed likely they might press it to the point of public disagreement with the United Kingdom Government."[42] The UK Cabinet approved the decision but "with reluctance, as they felt that Eire would thereby succeed in retaining many of the practical advantages of Commonwealth membership while renouncing its obligations. They recognized, however, that if they insisted on treating Eire as a foreign state after the repeal of the External Relations Act, the practical difficulties would be greater for the United Kingdom than for Eire; and furthermore that they would thereby forfeit the sympathy and support of Canada, Australia and New Zealand."[43]

This, then, was really the style and substance of negotiations. Perhaps because the government realized that some of the worst effects of Ireland's departure from the Commonwealth could be mitigated, it was initially the least willing to offer accommodation to the new republic. Or perhaps because they had gone to so much trouble to develop a third category of nationality just a few months earlier, the officials were simply angry about having to reopen the whole question at Ireland's bidding. Whatever the source of London's opposition, however, the larger imperatives of Commonwealth imperialism left it little chance to make itself felt. According to one civil servant summarizing Anglo-Irish relations in January 1949, "The records show that we were largely pushed into this compromise by the Prime Minister of New Zealand and the Foreign Ministers of Canada and Australia who when brought into the hasty consultations in Paris all took the line that whatever happened we must not let Eire become 'a foreign state.'"[44] Thus as the need for labor had produced a curious circumvention of alienage and citizenship during the writing of the 1948 Nationality Act, so the perceived need for Commonwealth unity and strength now provided that Ireland could formally secede and yet continue an association with Commonwealth members, creating an international no-man's-land. The arrangements were formalized in the Ireland Act passed into law in May 1949, which, while recognizing the Republic of Ireland's departure from the Commonwealth, pronounced Ireland and its citizens to be non-foreign to the United Kingdom.

Labour's willingness to construct a unique set of nationality provisions to accommodate the Irish government's assertion of its own national identity is only partly explained by the economic value of Irish migration and the political cost of Ireland's departure from the Commonwealth. At the outset, UK officials had tackled the issue of Irish nationality reluctantly, only when compelled to do so, and they seemed determined to find a solution that would minimize the disruption to the status quo. A few months later, during the negotiations surrounding the repeal of the ERA, UK representatives' language and judgments suggest an element of frustration at the Irish government's behavior, almost in the manner of a parent toward an errant child. Goaded by Irish politicians' determination to pursue repeal even at the cost of alienage, Labour appeared ready to accept the (mitigated) negative consequences but was prevented, as we have seen, by the concerted efforts of other Commonwealth members. The manner of negotiations in both cases suggests that eventual accommodation of the Irish was based on economic and political factors, but an additional factor also influenced the decision—an unspoken context of demographic acceptability. Thus the public defense of Ireland's unusual position rested on the "specially close relationship" arising from "ties of kinship," and the "ties of blood, history and intermingling of peoples which bound Eire to the older countries of the Commonwealth."[45] Likewise, an internal justification outlined the "historical, racial and geographical links" that bound the two countries together.[46]

Using elements of the same rhetoric of blood, migration, and intermarriage as was employed for the emigrating children of the empire, the governing elite articulated its conviction that Irish and British nationals shared a common heritage and indeed were members of a common, if extended, family. Useful as a means of *including* the Irish, this reliance upon blood and race as criteria of family membership served also to *exclude* "Asiatic" nationals. Fearful that India or Pakistan might also seek a reciprocal exchange of citizenship rights as an alternative to Commonwealth membership, UK and dominion ministers received assurance that this could not happen. Citizenship rights as negotiated in the case of Ireland were not an alternative to membership in the Commonwealth, nor were they the basis of membership, rather they provided the means by which Ireland avoided alienage to Commonwealth members and were based on "ties of blood, history and intermingling of peoples" which did not exist for "an Asiatic country."[47] Therefore, one may suggest that Labour constructed an Irish community of Britishness because Irish labor was economically useful, because Irish alienage was politically dangerous, and because

Irish aliens, though legally outside the boundaries of the state, fit into policy makers' constructed national identity. Though very much an abstract factor in the negotiations of the late 1940s, this supposition of Irish acceptability based on a racialized understanding of the imperial population assumed increasingly concrete form during the 1950s as Irish migrants were repeatedly compared to "coloured colonials."

IV

Throughout the 1950s, Irish aliens occupied an ambiguous position within British society. Privileged by the rights of subjecthood, they nevertheless suffered discrimination and rejection and remained concentrated within vulnerable manual and casual trades. Certainly official records suggest that though informally part of British society, they were regarded by politicians and officials as members of a distinct Irish sphere of Britishness. In 1951, for example, acting on what it said were "reliable reports" of squalor and overcrowding, the Irish Embassy requested that the living conditions of Irish migrants in Britain be investigated.[48] In their subsequent reports, UK officials revealed their prejudices and their conception of the Irish in Britain as a distinct community. A Ministry of Labour memorandum suggested that the Irish government publicly opposed Irish migration to Britain because it "cast a no doubt merited slur upon the conditions and prospects provided . . . in Southern Ireland." The memo further observed that Irish migrants to Britain were presumably "not used to good living conditions" since the majority had to be "disinfested" before entering the United Kingdom. Disparaging any justification for the Irish government's complaint, the British Embassy in Dublin framed its response within the unspoken politics of emigration, maintaining that while the Irish authorities acquiesced in emigration as an economic necessity, it would be "political suicide" for any government to be thought to be encouraging the exodus.[49] Four years later, an interdepartmental committee of officials remarked that the Irish, "accustomed to living in their own country in conditions which English people would not normally tolerate," tended to live in overcrowded and condemned buildings in the United Kingdom.[50] Suggestive of continuing assumptions of superiority over Irish migrants and the country from whence they came, these comments reveal that for some policy makers, Irish migrants occupied a position within the imperial hierarchy inferior to that of resident UK subjects, that they formed a community within a community. Barring any additional charges from Dublin, it is probable that this position would have remained largely unchanged throughout the ensuing decade. As it was, however, continuing Irish migration coincided with the onset of migration first from the West Indies and later from India and Pakistan.

A complete evaluation of both the Labour and Conservative governments' response to this new migration appears in the next two chapters, but for the purposes of comparison I note here that over the course of the next fourteen years Cabinets of both political hues instituted between fifteen and twenty investigations of the means by which further "coloured immigration" to the United Kingdom could be stopped. On each occasion, the unusual position of the Irish with regard to immigration and citizenship rights came up for discussion. On each occasion, successive working parties and Cabinet committees, while advocating informal or formal control of "coloured immigration," recommended against controlling immigration from the Irish Republic. This was the case even though a number of officials observed that the problems allegedly caused by immigration—overcrowding, strain on social services, and dangers to public health—were the same for both groups.

By contending that Irish migrants should not be controlled, UK officials did more than argue for the retention of Irish citizens' rights of subjecthood. The larger debate revolved around a demographic hierarchy and the division of British subjecthood into groups with the right to enter the United Kingdom and groups without it. Contained within this debate was the question of how a nonsubject group, the Irish, could be allowed access to Britain. The answer was a continuation of the existing "unique" relationship. Though not legally British subjects, the Irish were to be included in the higher category of those guaranteed entry to the United Kingdom. Thus, though perceived as a distinct community of Britishness, inferior to the domestic, Irish migrants apparently ranked higher on the imperial scale than British subjects of color. There was a variety of reasons for this high ranking, some of which, by the late 1950s, were well rehearsed. Making aliens of the Irish would have necessitated the imposition of border controls that would impede the flow of regular passenger traffic, require the employment of additional immigration officers at considerable expense, and in order to be effective, demand the creation of a border between Northern Ireland and the mainland. Furthermore, policy makers agreed that a steady flow of Irish labor was too important to UK industry to be disturbed in any way. And lastly, officials from a number of departments believed that revoking Irish citizens' practice of the UK franchise, as guaranteed by the 1948 Nationality Act, would prove both administratively and politically difficult.[51]

These practical considerations were undoubtedly real and were much the same as had been raised in earlier discussions of the Irish in Britain. At the heart of the comparisons made between subjects of color and Irish aliens, however, was the conviction that while many of the alleged social problems were the same, the one "outstanding difference" was that the Irish "whether they liked it or not were not a different race from the ordinary inhabitants of Great Britain." Nor did the presence of large numbers of Irish citizens give rise to "the same kind of problems or forebodings as the presence . . . of similar numbers of coloured people." In fact, "the population of the whole of the British Isles [was] for historical and geographical reasons essentially one." Thus, although the Commonwealth Relations Office believed that with regard to prospective immigrant workers it would often "be difficult to find any difference between a Jamaican and a New Zealander and an Irishman except for the colour of their skins," the color of their skins, or rather the significance attached to that color, played a major part in keeping one of the three out of the United Kingdom while allowing the other two free access.[52] Thus, despite British prejudice against the Irish, an "unpredictable and inconsequent people" according to a 1949 prime ministerial brief, they were nevertheless regarded as worthy of continued access to Britain thanks to "arguments of commonsense" and by virtue of the "outstanding" fact of their race.[53] In short, for both Labour and Conservative administrations, for all their wrangling about nationality, subjecthood, and legal challenges, the critical point when reviewing applications for membership in the familial domestic (as opposed to the political) community of Britishness was neither economics nor politics but genetics and the cultural patterns that were presumed to flow from biological structures. There was no underlying *single* reason for assumptions of Irish distinctiveness, but elite racism was a consistent contributing factor.

In 1962, as we shall see in more detail later, formally at least, if not in practice, the New Zealander was to join the Jamaican as an excluded subject. The Irish migrant, however, remained free to come and go at will. As throughout the preceding decade, this privilege was granted only after much internal debate. From the outset, as soon as controlling legislation for British subjects resident outside the UK began to be debated as a serious possibility in 1960, ministers insisted that it would be "impracticable" to try and control the Irish.[54] Over the course of the next few months, as the impetus for the control of "coloured immigration" grew ever stronger, so did the conviction that the Irish must in practice be excluded from control. The governing Conservative administration, led on this issue by Home Secretary Rab Butler, recognized the political difficulty, however, in privileging Irish aliens over British subjects and hoped to combat potential critics by formally including the Irish within the scope of control but excluding them in practice by subsequent order.[55] In general the favorable status to be enjoyed by the Irish was accepted as a practical inevitability, and only Commonwealth Relations Secretary Duncan Sandys expressed his unhappiness that Irish citizens should enjoy privileges denied Commonwealth citizens.[56] The rest of the Cabinet believed that the unusual position of the Irish might be justified by reference to the "special historical and geographical" relationship between Ireland and Britain and the existing special status with regard to nationality. Thus, one unusual step was to provide the justification for another.[57]

Seeking to defend the government's position against press and parliamentary criticism, Rab Butler suggested that he give a clear statement to the House establishing that while the Irish would be formally included within the scope of control, they would in practice not be controlled. Despite earlier ministerial references to the "facts of history and geography," the unusual position of the Irish was publicly justified not through blood and kinship but by reference to the practical difficulties of controlling either a land border between Northern Ireland and the Republic, or a sea border between the Republic and Britain, as well as the additional problems caused by the huge seasonal migrations of agricultural workers.[58]

In the event, in the political climate surrounding the introduction of the Commonwealth Immigrants Bill, and after Butler's initial efforts, the Macmillan government proved unwilling to expand further on why the Irish should continue to enter Britain freely, since any explanation offered appeared only to intensify the case against the government that the bill was racist. Opponents of the bill, and thus opponents of the principle of control, said that continued free entry for Irish migrants proved that the Commonwealth Immigrants Bill, though allegedly about numbers and the pressure of unchecked immigration on limited national resources, was in reality inspired by notions of race and designed to prevent the entry of people of color to Britain. Although the government resisted these criticisms, the willingness to admit fifty thousand new Irish migrants annually and the readiness to accept the arguments of practicality against border control where it suited certainly implied a preference for Irish aliens over British subjects of color. Also implying that preference were the "informal negotiations" with Dublin which had resulted in the agreement by the Irish government to police their ports to prevent parties of West Indians from entering the United Kingdom in return for the guarantee that the controlling legislation would not apply to Irish citizens.[59] Although explicit references to race and the Irish were few, that Irish migrants continued to make up the single largest national group entering Britain suggests that their demographic acceptability was taken for granted. Ministers did not have to make explicit reference to Irish citizens' white skin, though they sometimes did, because there was an unspoken assumption that Irish people were white. As a result, they were acceptable to the policy-making elite's construction of the national identity. As we shall see, Australians and New Zealanders were also white and also acceptable to policy-makers' constructed national identity, but since they were not an *essential* component of the labor force, the political difficulties of openly discriminating in their favor were to override the economic disadvantages of controlling their admission.[60]

Instead of explaining the ambiguous position of the Irish, the Cabinet concentrated on how best to meet criticisms of prejudice and preference without disturbing too much the arrangements already agreed upon with the Irish government which ministers believed represented the most practical settlement of the issue. Officials offered a number of alternatives by which the government might be seen to control Irish migration without actually doing so. One proposal involved the creation of a new citizenship of the British Isles which would include UKC citizens living in the United Kingdom and Irish citizens living in Ireland. After only a brief consideration the idea was rejected, principally because it would disturb the careful arrangements fixed by the 1948 and 1949 legislation.[61] Instead, ministers opted for a much simpler plan. Formally placed within the scope of the bill, Irish migrants were excluded from practical control, but the power to control them in the future was held in reserve should it prove to be necessary. To further mollify potential critics, the government promised to examine UK government records to acquire as much information as possible on the scope and nature of Irish migration to Britain.[62]

In 1948 UK officials went to a great deal of trouble to find a means by which the Irish could continue to migrate to Britain and thus continue to contribute to the UK economy. In 1949, with the Ireland Act, the same officials went to equal trouble to ensure that the Commonwealth remained a united and strong political force. The enabling context in both cases was the perception of UK officials that the Irish, notwithstanding a degree of cultural inferiority, were members of the same "family" as residents of the United Kingdom. Thus, the Irish community of Britishness was judged sufficiently British to allow the Irish to remain the largest single national group to enter Britain throughout the 1950s. By contrast, West Indians, Indians, and Pakistanis, though members of the political community of Britishness and though arriving in far smaller numbers, were not seen as family members. As a result their entry was contested, beginning with the very first arrivals in 1948.

CHAPTER 5

Keeping Britain White

News of Britain's labor shortage and subsequent recruitment of foreign labor extended beyond the refugee camps of Europe and the Irish labor exchanges. It spread also to the jobless and underemployed of the West Indies. The arrival of the *Empire Windrush* at Tilbury Docks, near London, on 21 June 1948 has traditionally been regarded as the opening of a new chapter in immigration to Britain. The 492 Jamaicans on board are typically represented as the first wave of a mass migration to the United Kingdom after World War II. Historiographical debate persists as to whether the Attlee government and its officials recognized the significance of the *Windrush* at the time, or whether its importance as a starting point came to be recognized only later, when many other colonial migrants followed these "pioneers." It seems likely that the truth lies somewhere in between. The UK policy-making elite did not have the foresight to recognize the *Empire Windrush* as a precursor of the 1950s migrant flow. Indeed, unless they were privy to US intentions to restrict West Indian immigration through the McCarran-Walter Act of 1952, it is difficult to see how they could have guessed how important the ship and its 492 passengers would be. Nevertheless, in formulating a response to the *Empire Windrush*, the Labour government set in play policy that would hold steady for the next seventeen years.[2]

Neither Clement Attlee nor the civil servants under his charge welcomed the ship, and both government and administration did all in their power to prevent further arrivals. Yet their actions were hamstrung by the dictates of formal nationality policy, which provided all British subjects with free entry to the United Kingdom. As a result, politicians and officials had to content themselves with making the best of a bad situation by working to minimize the dangers they believed the free migration of blacks posed to UK society. Throughout this process, they created and refined concepts of Britishness and national identity built on an existing racialized understanding of the imperial population but expanded to incorporate the presence of black Britons living in the United Kingdom. The Labour Cabinet proved capable of acknowledging colonial migrants' right as British subjects to move to the United Kingdom, even as they also assumed "coloured colonials" to be inferior stock likely to harm the interests of "British society." Through this process of acknowledgment and rejection policy makers participated in and, indeed, helped create the separate spheres of nationality prevalent in postwar Britain. These separate spheres both reflected and helped develop different communities of Britishness, each competing for the right to identify themselves as British. The significance of the *Empire Windrush,* then, lies not in the motivation of the migrants but in the response of the British state, which panicked when presented with what it assumed was to be a permanent "coloured" addition to the population. This chapter analyzes the process by which this panic matured into a clear-cut and fixed response to the idea of colonial migration. It suggests that this response set the pattern for subsequent administrations and eventuated in the 1962 Commonwealth Immigrants Act.

I

Jamaica, Trinidad, and Barbados were only some of the most significant of the Caribbean islands claiming membership of the British Empire. Since the seventeenth century British planters had relied on first indigenous and later imported slave labor to produce sugarcane. With the abolition of slavery and the end of the sugar boom, the West Indies was left with a poorly developed economy and a population too large for its natural resources. Throughout the nineteenth and twentieth centuries, the more densely populated islands relied on seasonal and permanent migration to make good their economies and to provide individual sustenance. Although as British subjects, all West Indians possessed the right to migrate to the imperial "motherland," migration channeled itself for the most part toward the United States—wealthier, geographically closer, and already host to a large settled West Indian community. Furthermore, the United States was a more practical destination for the majority of migrants, who intended a temporary sojourn, planning to earn only enough money to maintain lifestyles at home.[3]

Despite the popularity of the United States, some West Indians did make the trip to Britain and thus contributed to the black population that, whether as slaves, servants, or independent subjects, had played a role in UK society for over four hundred years.[4] In 1914 and 1939, war offered migration opportunities of a different kind to West Indians and increased the visibility of black people in Britain. Responding to the needs of total war, both the British government and the Merchant Navy recruited and accepted as volunteers several thousand colonial subjects for military labor battalions, munitions factories, or naval service. In all cases, colonial subjects, though theoretically equal to white subjects, in practice experienced de facto segregation and were treated as inferior. The majority lived and worked under the close observation of the Colonial Office, and at war's end, they were expected to return to their territory of origin.[5] These conditions of wartime service suggest that black British subjects were free to come to Britain only so long as they accepted the relocation to be temporary and the controls to be as unequal as they were strict.

Not all black Britons chose to follow Colonial Office directives. During the interwar years, several communities of color developed in port cities such as Cardiff and Liverpool. As British subjects, residents of these communities competed on equal terms for seafaring jobs with white Britons. Neither the ship-owning community of employers nor the central government looked favorably on this assertion of rights by black Britons, and they responded to it by trying to limit the rights of subjecthood wherever possible. Thus in 1925 the government enacted the Coloured Alien Seamen Order, ostensibly intended to prevent alien seamen from falsely claiming British nationality and thus rights of residence in the United Kingdom. In practice it was used, as the government had intended that it should be, to harass all "coloured seamen," "aliens and British subjects mixed," and to prevent as many as possible from settling in the United Kingdom.[6] By this order, "coloured" seamen without satisfactory documentation of British nationality had to register as aliens. The law was intentionally burdensome since, as the Home Office knew full well, the vast majority of black British seamen had no "proper" documentation and thus, by presumption became aliens, lost all privileges of citizenship, and became subject to deportation. The application of the 1925 Special Restriction (Coloured Alien Seamen) Order (CASO) to black British subjects has traditionally been attributed to both "popular racism" and overzealousness on the part of "provincial police and officials." In fact, it appears to have been "the first instance of state-sanctioned racial subordination inside Britain," representing an attempt by the state, in collaboration with employers, to segregate the labor market, to prevent further black migration, and to deny black Britons' claim to Britishness.[7] This attempt to restrict Britishness was not an isolated incident. Instead, the CASO stands as a clear example of an ongoing practice, which continued and matured into the post–World War II period.

By 1945 Britain boasted a community of color variously estimated at between 10,000 and 30,000 strong.[8] This community received its first significant postwar addition in the form of 108 passengers traveling on board the

Ormonde in late 1947. These were soon followed by the 492 Jamaicans on the *Empire Windrush*. It was perhaps fitting that the first postwar contingent of West Indians should hail from Jamaica, since with a birthrate estimated variously at between 2 percent and 4 percent and an unemployment rate of between 20 percent and 35 percent, the island was one of the poorest of Britain's colonial possessions.[9] For these individuals, migration to Britain offered not just a chance of a well-paid job—the majority of the *Windrush*'s passengers were skilled or semiskilled workers—but a chance to renew or realize connections with the imperial "motherland." Throughout their tenure as British subjects, the populations of the West Indian isles had been encouraged to think of Britain as home, as the cultural and political center of "their" empire. Accordingly, by 1948, after several centuries of colonial occupation, the vast majority of Jamaicans and their island compatriots regarded themselves as British in both name and substance. Not only their legal nationality but also much of their identity depended on their Britishness. Thus, though it was farther away than the United States, traveling to Britain constituted something of a homeward journey. This was not the perception of those awaiting them at "home," however, who believed generally in several definitions of Britishness and specifically in a West Indian Britishness located within an exterior, political community and best maintained at the periphery of the empire, not the core.

II

The impending arrival of the *Empire Windrush* received an immediate response from government officials, who recognized that its passengers were unlike any who had come to Britain before.[10] These colonial subjects had not been recruited by the British government and were not seamen. Rather, they were traveling as independent British subjects and were thus beyond the public control of the Colonial Office. These perceptions shaped the bureaucratic response to the *Windrush* and thereby conditioned the migrants' experiences in Britain. The Cabinet Economic Policy Committee, meeting in mid-June 1948, before the *Empire Windrush* had even docked, acknowledged somewhat wistfully that as "private persons traveling at their own expense" the Jamaicans could not be stopped, but the committee suggested that they might be sent on to East Africa to work on the groundnuts scheme. In any case, the committee requested a report from the Colonial Secretary, Arthur Creech Jones, both on "this incident" and on proposals for preventing its repetition.[11] The subsequent report had a distinct air of the battle station about it, supporting the characterization of one later observer that the government saw

The *Empire Windrush* approaches Tilbury in June 1948. Many of the 492 British subjects on board had served in the British army during the war and were traveling in response to news of Britain's labor shortages. (The Hulton Deutsch Collection.)

the *Empire Windrush* as "a sort of slave transportation engineered by evil agencies somewhere in the Carribean."[12]

The Colonial Office report made clear to Cabinet members that the individuals on board the *Windrush* were British subjects and therefore entitled to come and work in Britain. The migration was "a spontaneous movement" that neither the colonial government of Jamaica nor the imperial government of the United Kingdom had the "legal power" to prevent. Regardless of their rights, however, Creech Jones emphasized that the Jamaicans' imminent arrival was a "problem" that had to be "tackled as one outside ordinary provisions . . . and as a combined operation without too much insistence on normal departmental responsibilities."[13] If it were not, "public scandal" would surely result. The choice of language and indeed the report's very title reveal that from the outset these colonial subjects were classified as a "problem." Unlike the refugees from Europe or aliens from Ireland, these would-be laborers were not called volunteer workers or even British subjects but "Jamaican Unemployed." By identifying the migrants as Jamaican, the Colonial Office placed the colonials outside the United Kingdom and built a barrier between Jamaicans and UK residents. The effect was to lessen or weaken the migrants' claim to Britishness. Equally damning, by describing the migrants as "unemployed," policy makers categorized them as an economic burden, as people in search of financial support. These twin negative images, alien and needy, ensured that the colonials faced greater hurdles than other migrants. And though inaccurate—the migrants were British subjects whose employment would benefit the UK economy—this image of foreign parasites remained the stereotypical prism through which both Labour and Conservative administrations viewed colonial migrants for the next seventeen years.

Tackling this "problem" outside normal departmental guidelines meant that the *Windrush*'s passengers were treated as cattle or as so many units of labor. The Colonial Office telegraphed the ship ahead of time requesting that migrants be presorted for ease of classification upon landing. Ministry of Labour representatives boarded the ship in order to arrange employment for as many as possible, as soon as possible.[14] Those colonials without prior arrangements were to be temporarily housed, with a warden, in the air raid shelter at South Clapham tube station. These arrangements enabled Creech Jones to assure the Cabinet that "the whole matter is being vigorously dealt with." Responding to a request from Attlee for identification of the organizers of the "incursion," the Colonial Office admitted that it did not know the identity of the "ringleaders" of the "enterprise," but it had taken steps to ensure that further "influxes" were discouraged.[15] Again, the actual language is important: it identified the migrants as alien invaders who were somehow trying to circumvent imperial rules by independently migrating to Britain. Clearly, for all the talk of universal Britishness and even as the 1948 British Nationality Act was in the midst

One *Empire Windrush* passenger prepares to settle down for the night in Clapham Tube Underground Shelter, June 1948. His carefully packed luggage and attention to detail would appear to decry the notion of an ill-considered "incursion." (The Hulton Deutsch Collection.)

of its parliamentary readings, these migrants from Jamaica occupied a separate sphere of Britishness. And yet it is important to stress that both ministers and officials recognized the Britishness of the migrants. Indeed, the tone of the Cabinet debate and the absence of any attempt to deny the colonials' nationality suggests that ministers perceived the migrants to be unfairly taking advantage of the rights accorded them by their status as British subjects. Labour accepted migrants' Britishness but believed that it was different from their own.

The reception facilities provided by the Colonial Office for the *Windrush*'s passengers could perhaps be interpreted as the continuation of the wartime close concern for colonials' welfare or as offering the same facilities for subjects which had so recently been made available to alien refugees.[16] Had the Colonial Office not met the *Empire Windrush*, and had the Ministry of Labour not worked quickly to find jobs, the government could perhaps have been accused of showing a preference for aliens over citizens. Superficially, being met and cared for seems preferable to being left to sink or swim at the docks. As the language of the Colonial Office report reveals, however, the Cabinet regarded the two groups quite differently. European Volunteer Workers were channeled through selections, medicals, hostels, and train journeys as part of a long-term scheme for the recruitment of foreign workers and future citizens. The colonials were met and housed to avoid "disorder" and with the determination that this was to be a once-only affair. The government demonstrated its long-term commitment to EVWs by negotiating deals with trade unions, arranging for the transport of dependents, and investing time and money in helping the Europeans adapt to the "British way of life." By contrast, apart from the initial reception at Tilbury, colonial subjects who migrated to Britain in the postwar years received no accommodations, no arts and crafts fairs, and no organized sports. Instead, they encountered only public disapproval.

Speaking in Parliament, Minister of Labour George Isaacs expressed the hope that "no encouragement will be given to others to follow their example." Similarly, Arthur Creech Jones reassured the House that while the government could not "interfere with the movement of British subjects," the episode was unlikely to be repeated. The most telling public explanation of the colonials' treatment, however, came from Parliamentary Under Secretary for Labour Ness Edwards, who announced that while the government would offer short-term assistance, it could "do no more for these men than we do for our own men."[17] With this comment Edwards joined the Colonial Office in categorizing the colonial subjects, despite war service as British troops and despite passports proclaiming their British nationality, as something other than "our own men." They were outsiders looking to come in. Their admittance depended on the goodwill of those inside, and while this batch was to be tolerated, government speeches left onlookers in no doubt that further "incursions" should not be encouraged. The government's response to colonial migration hardened with each arriving ship. From 1948 through 1953, around two thousand West Indians migrated to Britain each year. Yet as early as the arrival of the third ship of the year, the *Reina del Pacifico,* in December 1948, officials decided that no further assistance on the lines of that provided to the *Windrush* and its successor the *Orbita,* would be given in future. Officials feared that by meeting the ships, and distributing free travel warrants (in an effort to disperse the "coloured population" throughout the country), they were in fact encouraging other colonials to migrate.[18] Thus, from 1948 onward, while recruited Italian and Irish workers received tea and buns and luggage labels en route to their new jobs, colonials entering Britain as British subjects were left to fend for themselves.

From the very beginning colonial migrants posed a conflict of interest for (some) UK policy makers and (some) UK employers. As we have seen, government officials disliked the notion of migrating colonials and tried to prevent further arrivals. Yet, at a time when "you couldn't get an armless, legless man, never mind an able-bodied one," the colonial workers proved a necessary stopgap.[19] So necessary in fact, that some employers, most famously the British Hotels and Restaurants Association and London Transport, actively recruited colonials for specific jobs in Britain. Other industries proved willing to absorb the migrant flow passively. As the UK economy boomed in the 1950s, indigenous workers vacated menial labor and repetitive assembly-line work for the plusher offerings of the white-collar sector or high-paying factory employment. As a result, West Indians and later Indians and Pakistanis found jobs in the labor-hungry textile industry in the North, metal manufacturing in the Southeast and Midlands, and transport and catering all over and thus entered some of the same industries for which the government had recruited alien labor after the war. Indeed, even as the *Empire Windrush* was docking, the Foreign Labour Committee was rejoicing over its discovery of a thousand Sudeten women suitable for importation into the United Kingdom. As the decade progressed, however, the supply of European refugees ran dry while employers continued to need workers, whatever their skin color. This conflict of interest persisted throughout the next decade and it was only with the onset of a slight recession in the late 1950s that the Conservative Macmillan government was able to justify exclusion on economic grounds.

In response to questions concerning colonial migration, the Attlee government gave ambiguous public statements that upheld the legal right of West Indians to migrate while hinting that they would be better not to do so.[20] The nature of these statements helped foster a hostile climate within Britain and to shape the circumstances under which the passengers on board the *Windrush* and those who would follow them were able to sell their labor power. This conditioning worked to limit colonials' economic and social opportunities.

The majority of West Indians, though skilled or semiskilled workers in the West Indies, had little option but to take up low-paying unskilled work in Britain. As newcomers, colonial migrants might have expected to *begin* their UK careers with the lowest-paying jobs. What they could not have expected was that for the most part, these jobs would remain their economic ghetto for the next forty years. Many accounts of migrants' experiences in Britain document the de-skilling and discrimination endured by black Britons, including those born of migrant parents in Britain. Contemporary investigations into hiring practices found that West Indians, Indians, and Pakistanis were almost invariably rejected as potential employees for all but the most menial work. To the majority of employers, a black or brown skin signified a less capable, poorly educated individual.[21]

Colonial migrants also faced a hostile reception from many landladies and landlords, who refused to let rooms to "coloureds." Colonials found accommodation easiest to get if they restricted themselves to certain neighborhoods or even streets. As a way around this discrimination, migrants often pooled their resources and bought accommodation capable of housing several families (and future additions) at once. Whereas such enterprise might have earned praise in a different group or setting, in postwar Britain it merited only further anger as migrants were accused of "taking over" streets and neighborhoods and ousting the white residents. In general, facing the effects of racial discrimination in a society that denied that it was happening, migrants were constantly reminded of the unfriendliness and unfamiliarity of the environment in which they were living. Personal accounts of West Indian migration to the United Kingdom emphasize colonials' shock at discovering that they were seen as outsiders both by officials and by fellow subjects, regardless of the culture that had taught them to regard England as the "motherland" and themselves as members of the British Empire.[22] Years spent learning British history and imbibing British imperialism had not prepared the colonials to be treated as members of a separate sphere of Britishness. Nor need they have been. The Attlee administration could have welcomed the colonial workers as relief for the British economy; could have initiated a propaganda exercise similar to that undertaken on the Europeans' behalf; could at least have refrained from hoping that "no encouragement will be given to others."

For deep-seated reasons related to their sense of community and identity, officials adopted none of these courses. The Attlee government and the permanent officials of the Ministry of Labour and the Home and Colonial Offices clearly feared the Jamaicans' independence and worried particularly that other islanders would copy it. Internal reports document alarm at the prospects of a strain on the welfare state and the potential dangers of long-term colonial unemployment. These fears alone, however, do not explain the virulence with which postwar officials approached the question of free colonial migration.

The intensity of feeling displayed by civil servants and politicians toward the *Empire Windrush* stemmed rather from something less tangible. By moving from the periphery to the center, these 492 Jamaicans were challenging the imperial system. As we have seen, this system of formal equality in fact rested on a hierarchy defined by race, gender, and social class. The system could be maintained only if all British subjects hewed to their positions within the hierarchy. By asserting their rights as British subjects to travel to the United Kingdom in search of work, the colonials appeared to be trying to merge separate communities of Britishness. Instead of separate black and white communities with informally unequal rights, there would now be only one community of white and black mixed. The prospect of merging the domestic community of Britishness with the political imperial community frightened the Labour government and many of the officials under its direction.

III

Official resistance to colonial migration went beyond hostility toward the *Empire Windrush*. In March 1948 the Colonial Office had proposed a scheme for the recruitment of colonials along the same lines as EVWs. Superficially, it may seem odd that a department could, on the one hand, urge the recruitment of colonials for work in Britain and then, three months later, be startled when it seemed that the colonials had thought of the same idea. What seems to have alarmed officials, however, is the autonomy of the colonials' behavior. When the Colonial Office recommended the import of colonials, it envisaged a *scheme,* an organized arrangement that would select the best of the colonials and employ them in much the same way as had been done during the past two world wars. The scheme would be strictly limited and under the direct control of the Colonial Office. That nearly five hundred people could simply board a ship and come presented officials with a premonition of a limitless, uncontrollable invasion. It seems likely that the Colonial Office intended its recruitment proposal to serve more as a public relations exercise on behalf of the imperial Parliament than as a full-scale effort to reduce unemployment in the colonies or supply needed labor in the United Kingdom. Indeed, the manner of senior official Sir Thomas Lloyd's proposal itself was hesitant and apologetic, relying for its weight more on the good that could be done for Colonial Office policy than on the advantages to Britain of organized recruitment.[23]

The Ministry of Labour opposed the suggestion from the outset. Sir Godfrey Ince, the Permanent Secretary, acknowledged the apparent contradictions in employing aliens rather than citizens but explained away alien recruitment as a contribution toward the resolution of the European refugee problem.[24]

Downplaying the economic imperative behind continental recruitment allowed Ince to dismiss the potential utility of colonial labor. In reality, the ministry's continuing recruitment of Italian and Irish labor suggests that hostility toward colonial recruitment went deeper than Ince's economic focus suggested. Senior civil servant M. A. Bevan, for example, commented that with "regards to the possible importation of West Indian labour . . . we must dismiss any idea of this from the start." A month later a colleague reiterated that the ministry should "rule out any question of a concerted plan to bring West Indian colonial workers here." By the fall, the ministry's attitude remained "entirely negative" and officials were referring to an "alleged" manpower shortage in Britain and expressing frustration that the Colonial Office was trying to use the recruitment proposal to "get rid of some of their troubles and give us some help in ours." The same official believed that the colonials "would be far more trouble than they are worth."[25]

Despite this intense hostility on the part of the Ministry of Labour, an interdepartmental working party consisting of representatives from the Colonial and Foreign Offices, the Ministries of Labour, Agriculture, Fuel and Power, Health, the Treasury, and National Assistance was established in the fall of 1948 to "enquire into the possibility of employing in the United Kingdom surplus manpower of certain Colonial territories in order to assist the manpower situation in this country and to relieve unemployment in those Colonial territories."[26] The Ministry of Labour sustained its initial opposition by setting out to convince the working party that the previously advertised shortages no longer existed. In labor sectors where shortages could not be denied, the ministry concentrated on demonstrating that colonial citizens would make unsuitable workers.[27] *Empire Windrush* passengers, for example, had proven "useless and unwilling" for agriculture, and the forty-three thousand textile vacancies were an unlikely home for West Indian women, who would be unable "to stand up to the Lancashire climate for any length of time" and were illiterate besides; the isolation of domestic service likewise rendered its fourteen thousand openings unsuitable as a colonial occupation. Colonials could take up none of the eighteen thousand vacancies in the woolen industry because the only accommodation available entailed sharing with Poles and EVWs. Shared housing was again the limiting factor in the silk, rayon, hosiery, pottery, tinplate, and sheet steel industries.[28] This proclamation of an absence of vacancies and a lack of accommodation contradicts the statement prepared a few months earlier for the International Labour Office, in which ministry officials had estimated a total foreign labor requirement of 60,000 for the twelve-month period beginning in June 1948 and divided equally between men and women. Although preference would be given to skilled workers, the ministry was prepared to train unskilled workers and guaranteed accommodation for all. Although Ministry officials later downgraded this estimate for the year ending September 1949 to only 22,500, the total required still massively outweighed any potential Caribbean recruitment.[29]

The ministry anticipated criticism for its position, admitting that the Colonial Office might wonder at the recruitment of "ex-enemies" while "English-speaking British subjects remain unprovided for." To deflect this criticism, ministry officials decided to place responsibility "where it properly belongs . . . on the shoulders of the industries concerned."[30] Thus, in addition to the practical issue of shared accommodation, the ministry emphasized that trade unions would probably be generally hostile to the introduction of "other races."[31] This argument was employed even when the trade unions had not been consulted. In one instance ministry officials agreed that since "there is certainly not a dog's chance of the Unions agreeing at this juncture to the introduction of coloured labour," the working party should be left with the erroneous impression that the union had been consulted and its response to the proposal had been negative. Justifying the failure to consult the union in the first place, ministry officials emphasized their reluctance to disturb the unions.[32] This reluctance contrasts sharply with the government's earlier determination to brook no resistance to its plans for European alien immigration.

Acknowledging the difficulty of rejecting young English-speaking female British subjects for textile jobs that clearly existed, ministry officials questioned whether they should justify exclusion on wider grounds. This broadening of its case was based on the general conviction that Britain's "small coloured population" should not be increased and on the specific proposition that "the moral standards of the young women in the Isles are quite different from those that prevail in this country."[33] The ministry's arguments had their effect. A perceived lack of suitable vacancies, a shortage of accommodation, and a general fear of the social implications of introducing "coloured persons" led the working party in the summer of 1949 to advise against the large-scale recruitment of colonial labor. The Colonial Office accepted the decision with equanimity, being grateful for the authorization it received to recruit a small number of selected female colonials to work as hospital domestics. In truth, this was probably all they had ever expected or wanted to achieve since Lloyd's original proposal had accepted "the complications . . . of settling in employment peoples of other races" and his reply gratefully accepted that "even small schemes if carried out with imagination can have a favourable and not unimportant effect on public opinion" in the colonies.[34]

Had the Colonial Office challenged the Ministry of Labour's presentation of "the facts" it might have discovered that they were open to question. This much was revealed by the Ministry of Labour's negative response to a suggestion that a group of ex-RAF colonial citizens should be recruited for work in the textile industry. Despite a Colonial Office reassurance that the men were "probably a cut above the ordinary run of the plantation," the ministry rejected the idea on the grounds that there were no further male vacancies. In internal correspondence, however, ministry officials commented that it was "fortunate" that the RAF people referred to were presumably all men "for had the enquiry related to women as well as men we should have been on much weaker ground—having regard to the fact that we have recently created employment opportunities in this country for both German and Italian women."[35] Significant here is that the ministry would not have employed the women but merely have found the rejection much more difficult to explain. The episode demonstrates that the ministry's reluctance to recruit colonials stemmed not from lack of employment opportunities but from a determination to block the employment of colonial workers and a preference for the recruitment of foreigners where jobs existed.

This resolve reflected the governing elite's racialization of the imperial population. As we have seen, the term "racialization" refers to "a representational process whereby social significance is attached to certain biological (usually phenotypical) human features, on the basis of which those people possessing those characteristics are designated as a distinct collectivity."[36] These collectivities are subsequently assigned certain behavioral and mental traits which come to be regarded as genetic and therefore fixed and immutable. Thus ministers and officials assigned colonial migrants all the stereotypical characteristics they associated with blackness. They presumed them to be quarrelsome, suspicious, violent, unlikely to settle down, and in need of discipline. The migrants could not be housed in government hostels for fear of the trouble that would "invariably" follow but could not be allowed to house themselves since they would only exacerbate the "squalid" and "sordid" conditions in the existing "coloured ghettoes." Officials believed that the acceptance of colonial migrants would impose a high cost on the UK government while raising a great many "social implications."[37]

Thus skin pigmentation no longer merely denoted racial group (even if one were to accept the legitimacy of racial groups) but rather denoted fixed mental and physical capacities. Within the British Empire, as we have seen, racialization first divided the imperial population into white and colored, and then within these groups privileged some national or ethnic groups above others. "Coloured" British subjects were deemed inferior in every way to white Britons. Racialization was at the heart of the separate spheres of Britishness enabling members of the UK elite to accept the otherwise contradictory situation of practical inequality within a theoretically equal empire. That is, for imperialists the separation of whites and blacks was not a conscious decision of elites but rather an "inevitable" function of skin color.

The significance attached to skin color in the postwar period and in the specific incidents under review here cannot be overstated. The working party assumed from the outset "that a large majority of any workers brought here would be coloured" and bore "this fact and its repercussions" in mind throughout their discussions.[38] The Home Office was brought into the discussions early on since it was thought likely "to have very definite views in the light of actual experience about increasing the male coloured population of this country." M. A. Bevan proposed that before consulting trade unions, officials first establish the extent to which they were prepared to use "coloured labour" in light of the likely problems of accommodation, transport, and long-term maintenance.[39] Thus from the outset, potential colonial migrants were primarily identified by their skin color, not by their nationality. This linguistic tool created additional barriers between the migrants, identified as "coloured," and UK residents, implicitly identified as white. By simple logic, if the British population was white and the colonials were black, then the colonials could not be British.

The associations attached to the colonials' skin color were sufficiently strong to override the presumptive rights of their legal nationality. Indeed, the policy-making elite perceived the functional differences of skin color to justify the separation of Britishness into separate spheres. Thus Sir Harold Wiles, Deputy Permanent Under Secretary at the Ministry of Labour, had no difficulty in announcing that "whatever may be the policy about British citizenship," he did not think that "any scheme for the importation of coloured colonials for permanent settlement here should be embarked upon without full understanding that this means that a coloured element will be brought in for permanent absorption into our own population." Furthermore, by dint of their skin color, colonials could not fairly be compared to EVWs, who "are coming definitely for permanent settlement here with a view to their intermarrying and complete absorption into our own working population." Following Wiles's logic, because they were black, colonials could not be so absorbed and were thus unfit for permanent settlement. Therefore Wiles, a senior policy-making official, was able to dismiss the rights attaching to the formal imperial British nationality policy in favor of the logic of the "commonsense" identity. He could do so because his (and others') understanding of Britishness allowed for separate spheres of nationality and the differentiation between "a coloured element" and "our own population." The different communities of Britishness which lay at the heart of this separation also lay at the heart of the working party's conclusions that the "early training and way of life" of "coloured workers born abroad" "must make it more difficult for them to settle down with British born workers." In the same vein, the Ministry of Labour proposed that "immigrant coloured workers are unfamiliar with our way of life and in various ways behave differently from workers who were brought up in this country." And perhaps most glaring in its implicit emphasis on skin color over alienage, one civil servant found it "difficult to believe that the CO really contemplate taking a lot of coloured girls from their native environment in the West Indies and dumping them in what must be the very alien community of a Lancashire town and hope that it will be a success all round."[40] That neither this official nor those in the working party questioned that the Ministry of Labour could do precisely the same with over 300,000 continental aliens whose connection to Britain might be presumed to be somewhat weaker again suggests that Britishness was something that could be acquired by the right people and something that could be denied others.

And yet the working party was not insensitive to the colonials' status as British subjects. Indeed, this was the major secondary strike against them. In his letter to M.A. Bevan immediately after the Colonial Office proposal, Sir Harold Wiles advised against the recruitment of "coloured British subjects" who, unlike former prisoners of war or other aliens, could not be deported "when they had served their purpose."[41] Sir Godfrey Ince believed it unlikely that the colonials could be held to the terms of any recruitment contract "against their will" as was the case with EVWs, who, if they broke their contracts, theoretically risked a return to the Continent as a displaced person.[42] Civil servants worried particularly about the implicit assumption of responsibility in organized recruitment schemes, suggesting that colonials would expect considerable assistance and would blame the government for misfortune.[43] In its presentation to the working party, the Ministry of Labour noted that one of the major difficulties in the proposal to recruit colonial workers would be that once in Britain "colonial workers, being British citizens, would not be liable to a[n] effective . . . degree of control. They would in fact be entitled, as British workers are, to a considerable measure of freedom in selecting the kind of job they would most like to do." Furthermore, the ministry assumed that even unemployed colonials would prefer to remain in Britain to "abuse" national assistance rather than face poverty at "home."[44] Incorporating the ministry's arguments, the final conclusions of the working party presented colonials' freedom within the labor market and their freedom from deportation as suitable reasons not to undertake large-scale recruitment.[45] Thus, while color prevented colonial participation in the search for long-term demographic increase, citizenship disqualified colonials from short-term recruitment projects. This is a curious view of citizenship and its prerogatives—as an unfortunate happenstance rather than an inalienable birthright and badge of equality. It derived from policy makers' ability to recognize colonials' status as British subjects even as they dismissed the rights attaching to that status. Thus once again, as they had done for the Irish, the Labour government and its officials separated the status of British nationality from the rights of British nationality. This time, however, the effect was to deny rights rather than expand them.

The working party's conclusions and the assumptions on which they were based were not isolated cases of bureaucratic racism. Rather, they formed part of a general climate of hostility toward the prospect of colonial migration. Shortly after the arrival of the *Empire Windrush,* a group of Labour MPs stated in a letter to the Prime Minister their fear that uncontrolled immigration without any selection on grounds of health, education, character, or customs constituted a threat to the "profound unity" of the "British people." Specifically, the MPs feared that "an influx of coloured people domiciled here is likely to impair the harmony, strength and cohesion of our public and social life and to bring discord and unhappiness among all concerned."[46] These Labour MPs assumed a "uniformity" in the British "way of life" and assumed also that their color placed colonials outside this circle. At the same time as the MPs drew this circle and made it appear strong, however, their expressed fear that it could be impaired suggests its fragility. That the constructed national identity could not accommodate people of color and was vulnerable to their presence suggests that the competing communities of Britishness were bounded by impermeable, yet vulnerable barriers.

IV

These same barriers were evident in the report of the Royal Commission on Population, which after deliberating for five years published its report in 1949. As we have seen, the Coalition government had instituted the commission in response to popular and academic fears that the UK population was in decline. We have also seen its recommendation that Britain continue to foster imperial emigration as a means of securing continuing British world influence. Sanctioning the dispersal of an already scarce resource led the commission to consider alternative means of restoring the depletion. With both mortality and marriage rates found to be operating at peak efficiency, the commission was left with family size and immigration as the only possible methods of population increase. Of the two, the commission unequivocally favored an increase in the UK birthrate and listed several methods by which this might be brought about. The scope of the commission's suggestions is quite startling. They included a determined fight against maternal and infant mortality, an increase in the family allowance, tax benefits to favor larger family size, the provision of child-care facilities at hospitals and doctors' offices, holiday and rest homes for mothers, financial aid for family holidays, the development of children's playgrounds, the building and modernization of larger houses, and greater use of pain relievers during childbirth. The variety and extent of these suggestions testifies to the importance the commission accorded population increase.[47] Propelling the commission toward a pro-natalist position was the fear that an aging British population would be a declining population, suffering a lack of energy, initiative, and enterprise. In the consequent absence of progress the British population would "become dangerously unproductive, falling behind other communities not only in technical efficiency and economic welfare but in intellectual and artistic achievement as well."[48] Anxious to avoid this possibility, the commission called upon the government to implement its pro-natalist suggestions and to demonstrate to the population at large a national commitment to an increase in the birthrate.

The commission's conclusions and the scope of its enquiry make clear that its members differentiated between the imperial British population and a white British population. For example, although charged with the investigation of the United Kingdom's population, the commission, apparently as a matter of course, examined the population of the whole empire. Within this discussion, however, the commissioners expressed concern that "the white population of the Empire" would soon be overtaken by the "Asiatic," which enjoyed a much higher birthrate. This racialization of the imperial population shaped the commissioners' understanding of the demographic possibilities facing the UK government. They had no doubt that postwar Britain required more population. The report even estimated the annual number of young adult immigrants—170,000—which would be necessary to assuage fears of population decline and to allow the continuation of imperial emigration. And yet despite this conviction, the commission sanctioned only the very limited immigration policy outlined in Chapter 2, namely the limited import of European aliens to Britain in order to facilitate the export of "British stock" to the dominions. Large-scale migration into Britain was rejected on the grounds that newcomers could only be welcomed "without reserve" if they were of "good human stock and were not prevented by their religion or race from intermarrying with the host population and becoming merged in it."[49] Implicit within this statement was the assumption that the host population was white. Thus, although not identified by name, the black population of the empire implicitly stood outside the inner circle of whiteness and was unacceptable as a demographic replacement for the departing "British stock." With this conclusion, the members of the commission helped to draw the boundaries between the different communities of Britishness present in the politics of citizenship in postwar Britain.

The Cabinet's reaction to the *Empire Windrush*, the collusion of official departments in the rejection of colonial labor-recruitment schemes, parliamentary representation, and the commission's report all illustrate certain central assumptions current in postwar conceptions of British nationality. First, despite the famed extent of the British Empire, "the British people" were not "coloured," and conversely, "coloured" people were not British. Second, "the British people" and the "British way of life" were threatened by uncontrolled "immigration" of the wrong sort. Third, black people were the "wrong sort" since skin color was assumed to be an unmodifiable racial characteristic. Fourth, skin color formed the basis of the separate spheres of nationality inhabited by black and white British subjects. Fifth, these different communities of Britishness could not be merged. In short, the colonial workers on the *Empire Windrush* and the colonial citizens who followed them may have had British passports, may have served in the Allied Forces during the war, may have been citizens of the United Kingdom and Colonies, but because they were black, they were not and never could be British to the first degree.

V

Though concentrating its efforts on black Britons, the Attlee government also gave its attention to others who appeared likely to disturb the separate communities of Britishness and the rigid hierarchy that made up the British Empire. In fact, it was not a racial but a political issue that prompted the first suggestions that the "open door" to all British subjects be closed, or at least be made subject to opening with a key. In July 1949 the Attlee Cabinet discussed the recent London dock strike and the "subversive activities" of British subjects, in this case Canadian seamen, in "fomenting" the strike. Ministers debated whether the law should be changed to prevent "Communist agitators who were British subjects from other parts of the Commonwealth" from entering Britain. Though aware of the "time-honoured principle" of British nationality law, which permitted freedom of entry to all British subjects, the Cabinet agreed that the deportation of British subjects engaged in "subversive activities" might not be inconsistent with the "general principles" of British nationality law. Although ministers refrained from actually instituting a change of policy in this case, they did, a year later, agree that future alien applications for British nationality would be vetted politically, so that neither communists nor those who "appeared to have an enduring loyalty to communism" would be eligible for naturalization.[50] By regulating admission to nationality in this way and by threatening to strip the rights of nationality from existing subjects, the Labour government hoped to preserve what it believed to be the essential conservatism of the constructed national identity and the domestic community of Britishness. In so doing the Cabinet demonstrated a readiness, which would be copied by future Cabinets of a different political persuasion, to abide by the presumed spirit of the law while disregarding the letter.

Even as they were discussing communists, ministers extended their review of nationality and immigration policy to include the "recent movement from the West Indies." Ministers weighed the damage controlling legislation might inflict on Britain's position "as the mother country, or at least the hub, of the

Commonwealth" against the potential danger that West Indian migrants might continue to be attracted by Britain's higher standard of living.[51] In their very first discussion of the possibility of new legislation, Labour ministers had touched on what would prove to be the kernel of the debate: how to prevent unwanted colonial migration without endangering the strength and unity of the Commonwealth.

The Attlee government attempted to limit and, if possible, prevent colonial migration to the United Kingdom even as it passed a nationality act that confirmed the right of the colonials to migrate. This conflict between a formal nationality policy that confirmed the right of all members of the British Empire to enter Britain and an informal constructed national identity that reserved that right for people who really belonged reflected separate spheres of nationality that produced different communities of Britishness. What is interesting is that in 1949, despite the arrival of the *Empire Windrush* and its successors, the Colonial Office (and other departments) believed that migration to Britain was still something they could control. The working party had authorized the recruitment of a small number of suitable females with the implicit assumption that this would be the extent of West Indian migration. This assumption corresponds to Creech Jones's earlier statement to the Cabinet that the absence of suitable transport made future arrivals on the lines of the *Empire Windrush* unlikely. Instead, he anticipated only "a steady trickle, which . . . can be dealt with without undue difficulty."[52] Over the course of the next fourteen years first Labour and then Conservative administrations attempted to deal with a trickle that became a river. In trying to dam this flood, ministers were trying always to reconcile real but competing communities of Britishness with the mythical ideal of a single universal British nationality. Considerations of Commonwealth and empire prevented them from abandoning the myth; commitment to a white community of "Britishness" prevented them from accepting the merger of separate communities. In place of such radical change, policy makers relied on the implementation of administrative controls on colonials' practice of their subjecthood and citizenship. This tinkering at the edges of nationality and Britishness constitutes the substance of Chapter 6.

CHAPTER 6

Tinkering at the Edges of Nationality

The decade between the passing of the 1948 British Nationality Act and the 1962 Commonwealth Immigrants Act constitutes a critical period in the politics of citizenship in postwar Britain. These two events could not have taken place under more different levels of secrecy. As we have seen, elected politicians together with officials from a variety of departments began the era by passing a nationality act that, by confirming Britain's position as the migratory center of the Commonwealth, tried quietly to uphold the nation's position as an important international power. Much of this work was completed out of public view in departmental conference chambers and through internal correspondence. Fourteen years later, some of those same politicians and officials, along with new colleagues, faced a loud and distinctly public clamor for the passing of legislation that would effectively nullify the substance of the 1948 act by policing Britain's borders. How the politics of citizenship shifted from the private to the public sphere and how the border was (partially) closed constitute the subject of this chapter.

In November 1958 the *Economist* reported that officials in Whitehall believed that "the liberal line—uncontrolled immigration—can be held for a few more years, but not indefinitely. Far from thinking that the British people will get used to colour . . . this school of opinion in Whitehall and beyond feels that when the tide of colour rises to a certain, as yet unspecified, point, the mass of British voters will demand that some check be imposed."[1] A superficial reading of the headlines and editorials of the popular press of a month or two earlier, in response to the Notting Hill and Nottingham "race riots" appears to confirm the civil servants' thinking: "The public demands swift and effective action from the Government." "The Government must not dither for fear of being considered unsympathetic to the coloured immigrants."[2] "Can Britain avoid controlling immigration?" The number of immigrants must be kept down so that they can be assimilated into the population."[3] In addition to these contemporary affirmations, many historiographical interpretations of race relations and "immigration" in Britain subsequently confirmed Whitehall's version of events: namely, that a liberal UK government was forced by a frightened and hostile public to impose immigration controls on subjects and citizens of color.[4]

As persuasive as this version of history is, an alternative reading of events suggests that the UK government, whether Labour or Conservative, was never "liberal" with regard to "race and immigration" and indeed tried very hard to prevent the migration of people of color to the UK.[5] As we have seen, this official hostility to black British subjects had manifested itself in 1948 upon the arrival of the *Empire Windrush* and upon the suggestion of the Colonial Office that "surplus colonial labour" be recruited for work in England. During the subsequent decade this hostility matured as first Labour and then Conservative politicians and their appointed officials concentrated their energies on finding a means to stem the continuing migration of colonial subjects and citizens of color to Britain. The catch to this investigation, however, was that the prevention/limitation had to be achieved without endangering either Britain's international position as the center of a multinational and multiracial Commonwealth or the domestic political fortunes of the governing administration. It was not an easy circle to square.

Over the course of the decade, colonial migration to Britain increased incrementally. From 1948 through 1952, between 1,000 and 2,000 people entered each year, climbing to 3,000 in 1953; 10,000 colonial migrants entered in 1954, 42,000 in 1955, 46,000 in 1956, and 42,000 in 1957. Numbers dropped significantly in 1958 and 1959 to only 30,000 and 22,000 respectively. In 1960, however, the net intake of colonial migrants increased substantially to 58,000 and more than doubled again in 1961 to 136,000.[6] There appears to have been a clear turning point in 1954. By the end of this year, the annual rate of colonial migration had climbed to 10,000 and Gwylim Lloyd George had replaced David Maxwell-Fyfe as Home Secretary. Also during this year, and partly in response to these two events, some Conservative ministers, along with some officials, became convinced that the solution to their problem lay in publicizing the dangers of uncontrolled "coloured immigration" to a general public perceived to be as yet too liberal to initiate change on their own behalf. The language and content of various committees, reports, parliamentary speeches, and Cabinet debates suggest that ministers and officials envisioned an educational campaign designed to produce a majority public opinion opposed to continuing colonial migration, and in favor of controlling legislation. Fostering a public climate of hostility in this way enabled ministers to escape responsibility for legislation curtailing colonial migration and to attach the blame instead to an apparently illiberal public clamoring for control. It is my contention that this campaign is the key to understanding the shift from private to public sphere and from open to closed borders. Thus, according to this interpretation, the infamous "race riots" resulted not from a desperate *popular* hostility toward people of color but from the policy-making *elite*'s racialized understanding of the world's population and their propagation of this belief to the rest of society.

I

Even before this formal effort to shape public opinion got under way in 1954, both Labour and Conservative politicians manifested hostility toward British subjects of color through the appointment of five internal investigative studies into colonial migration.[7] Policy makers' conceptions of colonial migrants substantially matured with each new report. The first study, for example, consisted of a simple interdepartmental meeting called by the Home Office to discuss reaction to the "continuing influx." Focusing on stowaway migrants, the meeting resulted in a decision to revert to the prewar policy that allowed only specific documents as proof of British nationality and subsequent right of entry. Individuals failing to produce such documents were immediately returned to their port of origin.[8] In a second study, in March 1950, Labour Cabinet ministers discussed the "difficulties of finding suitable employment for the coloured people who had come to this country in recent years" and invited Attlee to review what further means might be adopted to check the migration into the United Kingdom of "coloured people from British colonial territories."[9] Thus, in little over a year, policy makers had moved from returning stowaways to reviewing how fare-paying citizens could be encouraged not to migrate.

The third study, presented to the Attlee Cabinet in February 1951, concluded that there was no justification for new legislation, but all practicable administrative measures should continue to be enforced.[10] In October 1951 a Conservative administration led by Winston Churchill replaced Attlee's government. The attitude of policy makers toward colonial citizens remained the same, however. In November 1952 Churchill, believing that five or six hundred "coloured workers" was a number sufficient to warrant further investigation, instituted a general study into Post Office employment practices. In his subsequent report, Postmaster General Earl de la Warr stated that it was not for the Post Office alone to discriminate and that if it was felt that "coloured workers" should not be allowed to obtain employment in the United Kingdom, then the proper course would be to deny entry to the country in the first place. The Conservative Cabinet took the Postmaster General at his word, and moving ever farther along a path of active hostility toward black Britons, commissioned additional investigation into the means by which "coloured people" could be prevented from seeking employment in the UK.[11]

This fifth investigation into the status of "coloured people" in Britain was the most substantial thus far, drawing on the resources of several departments and meeting regularly for almost a year. The hostility of the working party to the prospect of continuing colonial migration manifested itself in both the substance and the style of its final report, presented in December 1953. The substance of the report noted a current "coloured population" of forty thousand and observed that further migrants could not be stopped "however large in number and however unsuitable for settlement here they might be." "Coloured workers" allegedly found employment difficult to obtain because of their "low output . . . high rate of turnover . . . irresponsibility, quarrelsomeness and lack of discipline." "Coloured" women were described as "slow mentally," and "coloured" men as "more volatile in temperament than white workers . . . more easily provoked to violence . . . lacking in stamina," and generally "not up to the standards required by British employers." Further proof of colonials' unsuitability for settlement manifested itself in the "primitive, squalid and deplorable" living conditions of the "coloured community" already in Britain.[12]

The linguistic style of the working party expanded on that adopted by officials responding to the *Empire Windrush* and established a pattern that would endure even to the present day. The significance of the use of this language to describe migrating colonials cannot be overstated. In a world recovering from a fight against supremacist fascism and in a country supposedly striving for a new relationship with its imperial possessions, officials could not publicly focus on the migrants' skin color as the source of the problem. Thus, what was perceived as a race problem had to be disguised as an "immigration" problem—a much more politically and socially acceptable issue. In turn the subsequent public discourse of control was framed within the ostensibly objective basis of numbers—too many people coming in who, though individually acceptable, collectively threatened to overwhelm the nation's resources. Deftly manipulating language in internal reports, parliamentary and press statements, and official documents, both elected politicians and appointed officials undertook a tiered process of reconstruction, transforming migrants of color from British subjects into Commonwealth immigrants while racializing the term "Commonwealth immigrant" to refer only to migrants of color. When complete, the process placed two implicit, apparently impervious barriers between colonial migrants and the indigenous UK population: they were foreigners and they were black. These barriers were important for two reasons. First, as others have shown, the term "immigrant" indicates a population with exterior origins, whose access requires scrutiny, and may be denied."[13] Furthermore, in many societies, including the United Kingdom, the term may also bear the negative associations of overcrowding, poverty, and social disorder. Thus the prism of parasitical alien established in 1948 in response to the *Windrush*, remained in play throughout the 1950s. Second, by highlighting skin color as a distinguishing feature rather than nationality as a binding fact, the policy-making elite's terms of reference implicitly identified the UK indigenous population and the colonial migrant population as opposites. If the migrants could be separated out as "coloured," then the indigenous society must surely be noncoloured or, more simply, white. By isolating the colonials as "blacks," this oppositional status inhibited the opportunities for integration and cooperation and strengthened the public perception that the primary identity of colonials was black.[14] Thus, although the migrants themselves changed not at all, by changing their names, policy-makers first changed the rights they were presumed to hold and, second, building on these presumptions, changed migrants' actual rights.

Having thus divided the UK population into their "proper" spheres of Britishness—white and British, colored and immigrant—postwar governments went on to construct immigration itself as a problem.[15] This process involved both notable inactivity and proactive initiatives in migration policy. First, both Labour and Tory cabinets chose not to preempt the negative attitudes a white population bred on imperialist mythology might have been expected to produce in response to the introduction of a black population. Second, neither party invested sufficient infrastructural capital to enable migrants to settle without apparently stretching existing resources. In fact, the social services budget was sometimes cut in order to finance other policy areas. Third, government spokespeople referred to colonial migration in terms suggestive of disapproval and likely to excite popular concern. Fourth, at least some officials and politicians were willing to undertake a public relations exercise designed to convince the general public of the benefits and necessity of legislative control of migration. The combined result of this activity and inactivity was the construction of "race and immigration" as a problem in need of solution. To hold policy makers responsible for the construction of "race and immigration" as a problem is not to accuse them of instigating a conspiracy or of running hate campaigns. Rather, it is to suggest that by subjecting colonial migrants to political attention, by drawing society's notice to their presence, and by accepting and confirming links between colonial migrants and health risks, unemployment scares, and national assistance abuse (etc.), the policy-making elite helped shape the popular understanding of colonial migration as a problem.

Convinced of the dangers of continuing unrestricted migration, the 1953 working party quickly focused on finding a means to curtail it. Officials rejected an aliens-type work-permit system both because controlling colonials' right to work might merely result in greater reliance on National Assistance and because officials feared that during current conditions of full employment it would be difficult "to avoid making it plain that the measure was aimed at coloured colonial subjects." Instead, believing that deporting criminals or the habitually unemployed would both eliminate the worst of the "coloured population" and demonstrate to potential migrants the futility of coming to Britain in hopes of living off National Assistance, the working party recommended that the government assume powers of deportation against specific classes of migrant. Cognizant of the violation of British subjects' traditional freedom of movement and right to live in Britain, the working party nevertheless pursued deportation as a means of ridding the United Kingdom "of thoroughly undesirable people who cannot be said to belong to it in any real sense."[16]

Once again, the working party's constructions of nationality are plain to see. Like Sir Harold Wiles before them, this collection of officials from a variety of departments was able to dismiss the formal nationality policy in favor of a commonsense national identity. The report's inclusion of the word "real" is surely significant in this regard, manifesting not only officials' recognition of colonials' legal status but also their confidence that legal status was not sufficient to override a commonsense understanding of Britishness. Despite the strength of the working party's recommendation to deport and the convictions that lay behind it, the Cabinet opted to acquire further information before acting. In part this postponement stemmed from Churchill's belief that "the problem had not yet assumed sufficient proportions to enable the Government to take adequate counter-measures."[17] Evident here is that at this stage, in the early years of the decade, policy makers were still tinkering at the edges of nationality, trying to limit migration with internal or domestic tools, trying to eliminate the "riff raff." They were not yet proposing the total abrogation of subjects' rights.

Within a few months, however, a steady increase in migration numbers convinced some ministers that migration of a certain kind was fast assuming proportions that would soon be "unmanageable" if the government relied on deportation alone.[18] Lord President of the Council, Lord Salisbury, elaborated on the Cabinet's fears by warning that assuming powers of deportation "would only be tinkering with what is really becoming a fundamental problem" and suggested that it was "not merely a question whether criminal negroes should be allowed in or not; it is a question whether great quantities of negroes, criminal or not, should be allowed to come."[19] Similarly, Colonial Secretary Oliver Lyttelton believed that some form of legislation was necessary "if there is to be any means of controlling the increased flow of coloured people who come here largely to enjoy the benefits of the Welfare State."[20] Likewise, Churchill framed his migration views in terms of avoiding "a mag-

British subjects of color reading the small ads in a London newsagent's window, 1950. Such notices would advertise jobs, rooms to let, and items for sale. (The Museum of London, Henry Grant Collection.)

pie society."[21] The belief that deportation would not solve the "fundamental problem" and the exclusive focus on "coloured people" illustrate that notwithstanding disclaimers to the contrary, discussions about "immigration control" were really discussions about "color control." Racialization ensured that these officials, like many of their colleagues and constituents, regarded blacks as dangerous simply because they were black rather than exclusively on account of any behavioral problems they were alleged to carry with them. For had it been merely a question of the criminal few, then a deportation bill would have satisfied the restrictionists' demands. As it was, the real desire to keep Britain white resulted in a preoccupation with finding the type of legislative border control which would prohibit all blacks' entry without endangering the Commonwealth ideal.

It is at this point, in March 1954, that the first signs appeared of a deliberate campaign to sway public opinion in favor of control. Cabinet Secretary Sir Norman Brook wanted a formal review of colonial migration on the grounds that "although the essential facts are already well-known to the Government, enquiry by a responsible committee would help to educate public opinion on the subject."[22] In light of the content of the December 1953 working party report with its "documentation" of violence, irresponsibility, and mental slowness, it is reasonable to assume that Brook believed that such publication would serve as evidence of the case against continuing colonial migration and perhaps lay the ground for future legislation.

Further support for this position came in October of the same year with the replacement of Maxwell-Fyfe by Gwylim Lloyd George. Throughout his tenure as Home Secretary, Maxwell-Fyfe had consistently opposed the imposition of any formal control on colonial citizenship. Within a month of taking office, Lloyd George was advocating immigration control as urgently needed to curtail a "flow of immigrants into the United Kingdom of a kind which does not readily assimilate itself to the native population of this country."[23] Lloyd George also favored the appointment of a committee of inquiry because it "would serve to focus public opinion on this question and would help to gain public support for legislation to deal with it."[24] The new Colonial Secretary, Alan Lennox-Boyd, agreed, suggesting that "although there are many signs that responsible public opinion is moving in the direction of favouring immigration control, there is still to my mind a good deal to be done before it is solidly in favour of it." The appointment of a departmental committee, said Lennox-Boyd, would have two advantages. It would enable the government to have its legislation ready for immediate application and thereby avoid an "immigrant" rush to "beat-the-ban," and at the same time it would allow "public opinion to develop further and be crystallised."[25]

Ministers' readiness to encourage the crystallization of public opinion was perhaps bolstered by a parliamentary debate in which a small number of MPs had spoken in favor of controlling legislation. Initiated by John Hynd, Labour MP for Attercliffe, the discussion focused on alleged abuse of the welfare state by "immigrants" and the supposed threat to law and order posed by "virile young men." For its part, the government defended the colonials' right to enter the UK but acknowledged "the importance of the problem . . . its urgency and . . . the deep concern which it causes in many parts of the country" and promised "to press on with [their] work to see that a satisfactory solution is evolved."[26] This defense almost exactly mirrored that given a few months earlier when the government assured the House of its awareness of the "public concern that this matter is causing."[27] Through these presentations, the Colonial Office identified colonial migration as a problem in need of urgent solution. And yet the content of the speech ran directly counter to the Colonial Office's own information, which reported that same month that the "great majority" of colonial migrants were gainfully employed, and that the UK economy could usefully absorb a great many future migrants.[28] By making public speeches suggesting social danger while ignoring the reality of economic utility, the government surely fostered an unfavorable public atmosphere for colonial migrants. At the same time, its ostensible upholding of colonials' citizenship enabled the government to maintain a liberal guise.

II

Outside the House, Hynd's procontrol views received some support from the popular press which occasionally ran sensationalist stories describing the growing "coloured community" as a "critical problem" and calling for something to be done.[29] A different kind of support could perhaps be drawn from the black-white clashes that took place in Camden Town, London in August 1954. This two-day violence had its predecessor in rioting in Liverpool and Birmingham in 1948 and Deptford in 1949. These outbreaks of violence can be interpreted either as the start of postwar popular hostility toward "New Commonwealth" immigrants or as continuing a tradition of "communal riots" involving territorial warfare over contested areas and rights. Since the causes of the disturbances closely mirrored those of earlier "riots," it seems appropriate to place them within this tradition of communal contestation.[30]

Apart from these outbreaks of physical violence, it is difficult to gauge the reaction of the indigenous UK population to the presence of blacks in Britain and next to impossible to discern popular response to the arrival of additional colonial migrants. The first major opinion polls were taken only after the news-making Notting Hill "riots" and, perhaps equally significant, only after ten years of government discouragement of colonial migration. It would be presumptuous to apply the negativity found toward "Commonwealth immigrants" back in time to the early years of the decade. What are available, however, are accounts from contemporary sociologists and other early practitioners of the new field of "race relations." Anthony Richmond, one of these practitioners, estimated in 1955 that one-third of the UK population could be said to be tolerant, one-third mildly prejudiced, and one-third extremely prejudiced. While Richmond expected little of the last group, he believed that a "judicious educational campaign" on the part of the government could do much to give the lead against popular "bias and discrimination." Michael Banton, another contemporary academic, recorded that only 4 percent of three hundred whites believed blacks to be "uncivilized," and less than 10 percent believed that mixing between people of different skin colors should be avoided. In general, although they noted and acquiesced in a certain degree of popular caution from whites toward blacks, Richmond, Banton, and others believed that greater educational initiatives to acquaint the UK population with colonial aspirations and backgrounds could achieve much.[31]

Some observers suggest that this potential base for education in tolerance persisted as late as the 1960s. Maintaining that only a dedicated minority of 15 percent was determined to arrest all inward migration of people of color and suggesting that committed antiracists made up another 10 percent of the population, Michael and Ann Dummett claim that the remaining 75 percent of the population was "hesitant, ambiguous and confused" in their attitudes toward the new visible minorities in their midst.[32] One small review of available primary sources appears to confirm this theory. Of eighteen letters concerning colonial migrants sent by branch officers to the Trades Union Congress headquarters between 1954 and 1957, eight supported colonial rights, six called for control, and four asked for more information.[33] The distribution of opinion is similar to that in letters sent to headquarters about the recruitment of aliens. Both Bournemouth Trades Council and the Midland Region of the TUC Advisory Committee expressed written alarm at the continued influx of foreign labor but emphasized that they were not referring to the people of the Commonwealth countries. Similarly, Andover and District Trades Council supported incoming labor from within the empire but called for stricter control over alien recruitment, and both Shingfield and Bedford District Trades Councils condemned UK employers and Italian workers for operating a color bar against Jamaicans.[34] In general, the letters portray a work force worried by visible difference, surrounded by an imperial tradition of racial hierarchies, yet aware that discrimination and injustice were wrong. In short it was a work force unsure how to receive additional labor, whether colonial or alien, but expecting guidance from national leaders.

Further support for colonial migrants appeared in some sections of the news media. The *Daily Sketch* condemned the informal color bar sometimes operating in Britain, particularly when 300,000 jobs were "going begging," and called on the country "to receive these men and women on equal terms."[35] The *Economist* declared that to refuse to fill some of the jobs vacant in Britain with West Indians "would be an admission of both economic ineptitude and moral defeat" and called on the government "to live up to this country's professions of political aims." The *Economist* described West Indians as an economic asset and derided the argument that they were taking jobs and houses away from natives of Britain as "a polite hypocrisy . . . a cover for some genuine social problems." According to the *Economist,* the real issue surrounding colonial entry to the United Kingdom, despite the public rhetoric, was not jobs but skin color. As an alternative solution to the "problem" of colonial migration, and in contrast to policy makers, the *Economist* called not for migration control but for social and economic initiatives that would reflect "both Labour's attitude to a multi-racial Commonwealth, and the evolution of a new Tory Commonwealth."[36] Both publications feared that a color bar in Britain would damage Commonwealth relations and held prejudice to be the fault not of the policy of free entry but of the subsequent practice of social and economic discrimination. Thus, there was a great deal of room in the early 1950s for the government to promote popular acceptance and understanding of colonial migration. Such a campaign might have been similar, perhaps, to that which had been launched to facilitate the integration of alien continental immigrants in the immediate postwar period. While one must set these signs of support or ambiguity against the actual experiences of West Indians looking for accommodation and jobs, who found only "No Coloured, No Irish" signs, the point is not whether the indigenous UK population accepted West Indians with open arms but to what extent a popular reluctance to accept difference was fostered by a policy-making elite determined to prevent a permanent "coloured addition" to the UK population.[37]

III

In December 1954, despite their hopes that it would educate the public, ministers decided against the appointment of an investigative committee on the grounds that its conclusions could not be guaranteed to favor control. Though unable to agree on this step, however, the Cabinet was sufficiently confident to instruct the Home and Colonial Secretaries—the principal advocates of control—to prepare an immigration control bill.[38] The Cabinet's decision was partly influenced by the tide of colonial migration, which, according to Gwylim Lloyd George, had risen from two thousand in 1953 to ten thousand for 1954. In response to this significant increase, and convinced that "these large parties do not just happen" UK officials searched for those responsible. They need not have looked far. Throughout the nineteenth and early twentieth centuries, the vast majority of West Indian migrants had remained within the Caribbean or traveled to the United States, where entry was fairly easy for those who could pass basic literacy and medical tests since the Caribbean was included within the generous British visa quota. In 1952, however, responding to domestic pressures to reduce black immigration, the US government through the McCarran-Walter Act separated the West Indies from the United Kingdom and gave all the islands a much reduced single visa quota of eight hundred. This dramatic curtailment of opportunity forced potential emigrants to find an alternative destination. Holding British passports and hearing only of jobs and good fortune from those who had gone before them, many turned to the United Kingdom. Their primarily economic motivation did not make them less British. The majority still carried the cultural baggage of colonialism and might reasonably have expected a welcome from the "motherland."

They met instead a Conservative government intent on preventing their migration. Twice in 1955 ministers reviewed the bill drawn up at their request in December 1954. On both occasions, however, they encountered the same two factors that had inhibited decisive action thus far: fear of public opinion and disagreement on what form immigration control should take. In view of their dislike for "coloured immigration" and their perception of colonial residents as black and United Kingdom residents as white, policy makers' most obvious route would have been to introduce a bill controlling the immigration of citizens of the United Kingdom and Colonies resident outside the United Kingdom. Since residents of the "old dominions" were British subjects, not UKC citizens, this maneuver would have enabled the government to "welcome the comparatively few good young Canadians or New Zealanders who wish to work here, while restricting an excessive number of West Indians or West Africans."[39] Ministers believed that such a specific bill, however, would reveal "the obvious fact that the object is to keep out coloured people."[40] Significantly, policy makers rejected this specific bill not because they disliked the prospect of legislating a color bar but because it would be "politically impossible."[41] Churchill's private secretary, Sir David Hunt, retrospectively identified "the difficulty": "The minute we said we've got to keep these black chaps out, the whole Commonwealth lark would have blown up."[42] In short, by revealing the narrowness of Britain's constructed imperial national identity, the hollowness of the "time-honoured principle" of a single universal British nationality, a color-specific bill would have exposed the government to public and perhaps international condemnation.

Prevented from pursuing their preferred course, ministers considered the alternative of introducing a universal bill that would apply to all British subjects equally, regardless of skin color or territory of origin. The potential consequences of a universal bill were equally dangerous, however, since it would catch in its net migrants "of good type from the 'old' Dominions . . . who come here, with no clear plans, in order to try their luck."[43] Officials feared that restricting the rights of these people to return to "the land which they still regard as home" threatened to undermine Britain's position as a metropolitan motherland around which the empire rotated, and from the empire, we recall, Britain drew strength to sustain its status as a substantial international power.[44] The Commonwealth Relations Office, in particular, argued against a universal bill, contending that British subjects' right to enter and reside in the United Kingdom played an ever-increasingly important role in binding the empire together and countering "centrifugal tendencies within the Commonwealth."[45] Commonwealth Relations Secretary Alec Douglas-Home, the future Prime Minister, supported the general need for controlling legislation but feared that to include India and Pakistan could provoke retaliatory measures against the British business community in Asia.[46] And yet the third alternative—to do nothing—appeared most dangerous of all. Ministers feared that unchecked colonial migration would produce "a significant change in the racial character of the English people."[47] Such a prospect was alarming both on its own account and because officials of all departments believed that the existence of "a large coloured community as a noticeable feature of [the nation's] social life" was "certainly no part of the concept of England or Britain to which people of British stock throughout the Commonwealth are attached" and might well "weaken the sentimental attachment of the older self-governing countries to the United Kingdom."[48]

Given these circumstances, the architects of the draft bill, presented to the Cabinet in January 1955, attempted to devise a fourth alternative, a bill universal in theory but specific in practice. Under the terms of this bill, permission to land would be granted only to those British subjects able to convince the landing officer that they would not become reliant on public funds. The advantage of the bill was that it avoided the imposition of full immigration control on every incoming passenger and targeted only "the immigration of coloured people."[49] An interdepartmental committee of officials believed that whereas all British subjects would have the formal right to prove financial independence, "the type of person whom it is desired to exclude would seldom be able to do so."[50] Furthermore, landing officers would be given license to operate the law with the "minimum of inconvenience" to British subjects from the "old dominions" and could "without giving rise to trouble or publicity, exercise such a measure of discrimination as we think desirable."[51] Despite these layers of operation, the Cabinet in January 1955 refrained from introducing the bill for fear that they would be unable to ensure its success.[52]

A second version, presented in November, formalized a split within the previously universal imperial British nationality. Its terms identified as not subject to control any person who "belonged" to the United Kingdom. In this instance to belong was to have had one's passport issued in the United Kingdom, Channel Islands, or Isle of Man. Since the ostensible ground for control was to avoid unemployment and overcrowding, the bill controlled entry by requiring British subjects not belonging to the United Kingdom to provide evidence of employment and accommodation in Britain. Those unable to produce such documentation would be denied admission. Again, officials believed that the bill could in practice be made to effect only the desired discrimination and to leave migrants from the "old dominions" free to enter. Even with this reassurance, however, the Cabinet, particularly Lennox-Boyd, doubted the efficiency of employment and housing permits as tools to limit colonial entry and feared that granting only a specific class of subject the absolute right to enter would nullify the substance of the imperial British nationality. Furthermore, ministers believed that employment qualifications would prove difficult to justify at a time when immigration of all kinds "was a welcome means of augmenting our labour resources." Indeed, colonials were sufficiently valuable laborers that the Cabinet briefly discussed instituting a contract labor system whereby colonials would be admitted only for specific periods of time. Such a measure appeared to be an attractive means of continuing a useful labor supply while avoiding long-term damage to the demographic makeup of society. Yet even this fifth alternative failed to square the Cabinet's circle. Though it would limit the migration of people of color, ministers feared that it would also highlight the Cabinet's preferences and the racialized hierarchy of the imperial community of Britishness. Thus, the Cabinet again refrained from decisive action and passed the whole matter back to Prime Minister Anthony Eden for his further consideration.[53]

The second inhibiting factor throughout 1955, as before, was the perception that "public opinion" would oppose a controlling bill of any nature. Specifically, despite the debate of November 1954, ministers noted the "lack of public anxiety" surrounding the question and believed it unlikely that they would be able to carry a control bill through the House since the Labour Party, the TUC, and even some of their own members would not publicly support an immigration control bill.[54] The government was at a seeming impasse. Sure in their own mind of the dangers of unrestricted colonial migration, ministers yet faced a public unwilling or unable to perceive the depth of the problem. Thus, policy makers returned to the idea of educating the public to the "problem" of colonial migration.

In February 1955 ministers reviewed a draft White Paper detailing immigration restrictions already operating in other parts of the Commonwealth. In calling for the document, ministers had hoped that "public opinion might be influenced in favor" of controlling legislation "if more publicity were given" to existing controls. The draft proved unsatisfactory for its intended purpose, however, as ministers realized the potential danger to Commonwealth unity of publicizing the administrative means by which dominion governments excluded British subjects of color.[55] More promising as a potential educative tool was Cyril Osborne's proposal to introduce a private member's immigration control bill—an opportunity to assess the prospects of gaining parliamentary approval for legislation. Osborne's subsequent withdrawal of his bill and the lack of support for it garnered a mixed reaction from the Cabinet. It avoided the embarrassment of debating controlling legislation during Princess Margaret's visit to Jamaica, but it also prevented "the expression of public and Parliamentary opinion."[56] Preparing for the May 1955 general election, and despite declining public interest, Lloyd George recommended a firm and open commitment to controlling legislation since "public opinion is still uninformed." Reluctant again to publicize their readiness to infringe the rights of British nationality, ministers agreed instead that candidates should only confirm the troublesomeness of the issue and promise a future enquiry.[57] The drive to educate the public rarely involved policy makers in open statements against migration. Rather it consisted of subtle warnings of "the possible social consequences of unrestricted entry into this country" and fears of what the future might hold. At all times these warnings were accompanied by a stated recognition of the need to maintain ties between the United Kingdom and other members of the Commonwealth. Privately, however, policy makers were much more blunt in their assessment of what it would take to bring the UK public around to a procontrol position.

A month after the election, at Eden's instigation, Lloyd George again brought colonial migration before the Cabinet and again pressed the case for an independent committee of inquiry. According to Cabinet Secretary Brook, and following his earlier summary, the purpose of this committee "would not be to find a solution (for it is evident what form control must take) but to enlist a sufficient body of public support for the legislation that would be needed."[58] The Cabinet agreed, concluding that "the first purpose of an enquiry should be to ensure that the public throughout the country were made aware of the nature and extent of the problem; until this was more widely appreciated the need for restrictive legislation would not be recognised." In light of this need "to focus the problem and educate public opinion," the Cabinet doubted whether the public committee envisaged by Lloyd George "would be such as to rally public opinion in support of restrictive legislation" or even whether it would "have the effect of guiding public opinion in any definite direction." Instead, "an authoritative statement of the increasing volume of immigration, and of the social and economic problems to which it was likely to give rise, might prove a better basis for action." Accordingly, an interdepartmental working party was set up to explore the "problem" of "coloured workers."[59]

IV

This interdepartmental working party, chaired by the Home Office and modeled on its 1953 predecessor, remained in existence right through the passing of the 1962 Commonwealth Immigrants Act. It reported at least semiannually, first to the Cabinet and later to a Cabinet committee of ministers. Its reports were extremely thorough, identifying current problems, predicting future difficulties, and suggesting possible solutions. Although it was implemented with high hopes, the working party's first report, presented to Anthony Eden's Cabinet in September 1955, did not provide the "basis for action" the government sought but rather produced "an objective statement which, if published, would not lead to a demand for legislation."[60] The objectivity to which the Cabinet referred included the information that the majority of West Indians were employed, law-abiding, and generally making a "useful contribution to our manpower resources." The working party found no evidence either of undue demands on National Assistance or of racial tension.[61] Yet even such an "objective" report concluded by recommending in favor of immigration control on the grounds that if allowed to continue, colonial migration would create both a critical housing shortage and a "race relations" problem. This conviction led the working party to assert "the right which any country must claim, and which most other Commonwealth countries exercise, to control immigration from outside in the interests of its own citizens." This was a reasonable assertion, perhaps intended to "rally public opinion" to the cause, but it ignored the reality that those who would be excluded were not aliens but citizens. The working party's readiness to distinguish between the United Kingdom's "own citizens" and West Indians makes clear that these officials, like all their predecessors, shared the conception of West Indians as foreigners, as members of some other nationality and certainly not members of the domestic community of Britishness.

Faced with a report that identified an inner-city housing shortage as the only *current* problem for which colonial migration could be held responsible, the Eden Cabinet decided against publication. The working party had essentially failed in its appointed task. It had been established in the belief that its report would provide the justification policy makers perceived they required for the introduction of controlling legislation. Without this social and economic base, ministers feared that immigration control would be recognized as a racially inspired measure and the government identified as illiberal. Thus, legislation had again to be postponed.

In November 1955, unable to proceed either with the publication of the report or with legislation, the Cabinet passed the issue back to Eden, who in turn appointed a Cabinet-level committee of ministers to which the interdepartmental working party would report directly.[62] Thus, in the years immediately preceding the outbreak of the 1958 "riots," the Conservative government received a minimum of three reports each year detailing the condition of the "coloured population" and suggesting on what grounds the total number of "immigrants" might be reduced. Each report followed much the same format: detailing the increasing number of "coloured people" among the UK population, identifying this growth as "a problem," advocating the urgency of action when "public opinion" should allow it, and debating the various methods by which control might be achieved.

In its first meetings and reports in 1956, for example, the ministerial committee, consisting of the Lord Chancellor Kilmuir (Maxwell-Fyfe), Lord President Salisbury, Home Secretary Lloyd George, Commonwealth Secretary Home, Colonial Secretary Lennox-Boyd, Minister of Labour Iain Macleod, and Attorney General Reginald Manningham-Buller, noted that the "coloured" population of Britain had risen to 100,000. The majority were law-abiding, employed, and aroused "little, if any, public expression of race feeling." Indeed, the "ordinary people of this country," were believed to be "by no means intolerant of coloured people in their midst." In light of this tolerance, legislation to control entry "would come as a shock for which public opinion is still not prepared" and would likely provoke "most people—certainly the more vocal elements"—to express concern about the "illiberal" nature of the government's proposals. Before taking action on such a controversial matter, the government needed to count "on a satisfactory volume of public support," which was unlikely to be "forthcoming at present."[63]

Even as it sought public affirmation of its general position, the Eden administration was still confined by the inability to choose among a variety of possible methods of control, unable to decide which would most effectively limit the entry of blacks without being seen to discriminate. A deposit system was rejected on the grounds that too small a sum was unlikely to deter any migrants who could afford the fare, and too large a sum would expose the government to criticism that it favored the wealthy.[64] A quota system was rejected on the grounds that establishing quotas for the entry of British subjects would amount to an advertisement in favor of migration. Furthermore, and more significant, to avoid charges of open discrimination, publicly known quotas would have to be applied to each territory, and thus the objective of keeping out "coloured people" probably could not be achieved.[65] In preference to quotas, the working party of civil servants recommended the housing-permit system which had been first outlined in the 1955 draft bill. Intending migrants would first have to obtain a certificate of available accommodation from the local authority in which he/she intended to live. Officials believed that the distribution of permits could be manipulated so as to limit "coloured immigration" without appearing openly discriminatory. This option was preferred over proof of a job waiting since officials feared that labor-hungry employers and potential migrants would quickly be brought into contact with each other by agencies. This fear demonstrates both civil servants' acceptance of the economic value of migrants and the multifaceted nature of the postwar state—in this case the conflicting interests of governing and business elites. For its part, the ministerial committee believed that the "old dominions" would be likely to sympathize with the predicament of the United Kingdom and to recognize that the principle of the open door had grown up "at a time when the coloured races of the Commonwealth were at a more primitive stage of development" and there had been no fear of a "coloured invasion." Thus, by 1956 policy makers' thinking had matured to the point where they actively sought not only the exclusion of legitimate Britons but also the connivance of other "white" countries to help bring this about. Notwithstanding the absence of domestic public pressure, officials and ministers emphasized their conviction that the flow of "immigrants" would continue to grow and that legislation would have to be enacted when the problems of absorbing a "different racial strain" overcame all other considerations.[66]

Of particular concern in 1956 and 1957 was the changing demographic makeup of the migrant flow. As residents in a Commonwealth country, Indians and Pakistanis, though not citizens of the United Kingdom and Colonies, were British subjects, and under the terms of the 1948 act still enjoyed the right of free entry to Britain. They first began to migrate to Britain in significant numbers in 1956 when they accounted for a quarter of the year's 40,000 increase in the "coloured population." In 1957 the interdepartmental working party expressed alarm at this sudden spurt of migration from Asia, describing the migrants themselves as illiterate, "of very low social standing and suitable only for menial work."[67] In 1958 the working party wrote at length on Indian and Pakistani migrants, comparing them unfavorably with West Indians, who were presumed to be not only English-speaking but much more accustomed to "English ways" and for the most part drawn from the enterprising and skilled elements of their communities. Despite the succession of reports advocating legislation or the imposition of some sort of check on West Indian migration, the 1957 working party believed that West Indians had presented "few problems" and did not constitute grounds for legislation.

This sudden show of support for West Indian migrants was remarkable in two respects: it counteracted all the previous warnings against colonial migration, and it was issued just as the character of West Indian migration was changing. Between 1948 and 1955, the typical West Indian migrant was skilled or semiskilled, originated from an urban setting, and migrated to Britain primarily for economic motives but also out of a desire to enhance middle-class status by journeying to the motherland. After 1955 typical migrants tended to be semiskilled and unskilled, from poorer and sometimes rural backgrounds, and more heavily influenced by the desire for economic improvement.[68] Perhaps officials' observations on the relative value of West Indian migration reflected the professional backgrounds of early migrants and their efforts to "fit" into British society. Thus, by 1956 officials were able to comment on their apparent "English ways," against which Indians and Pakistanis of "a poor type and quite unassimilable" compared unfavorably.[69]

The working party's conclusions were echoed by the Colonial Office, which contrasted "the skilled character and proved industry of the West Indians with the unskilled and largely lazy Asians."[70] Indians and Pakistanis were described variously as illiterate, of poor stature and health, dirty, poorly skilled, and in general as "feckless individuals who . . . make a bee-line for National Assistance." The Colonial Office, at least, believed that Britain had no obligation "to act as a dumping ground for the rag-tag and bob-tail of Asia."[71] Officials deemed the rising rate of total "coloured immigration" to be sufficiently serious to merit the warning that although there were currently no economic grounds for "immigration" control, "the real danger lay in the prospect of a multi-racial society." Thus, they advised ministers to act "now rather than when it might be too late to undo the damage."[72]

Despite these warnings and the hope of the "white" Commonwealth's understanding, the Eden Cabinet and later the Macmillan repeatedly shied away from introducing legislation. Following an earlier pattern, each suggestion was noted by the Cabinet and set aside to await the maturing of public opinion and the discovery of some means by which "coloured immigration" might be controlled without exposing the government's racialized preferences and without damaging Commonwealth unity. Thus, in 1957 legislation was postponed on the grounds that the rate of migration had recently declined, and "public opinion was not yet ready for a statutory regulation of immigration from other parts of the Commonwealth . . . and its introduction at present might bring about serious political repercussions."[73] Reviewing their options, ministers again considered whether the appointment "of some inter-departmental enquiry into the social and economic problems arising from coloured immigration might offer a suitable means of stimulating public opinion on this subject." This time around, the proposal was rejected on the grounds that "as the problem became more serious the public would inevitably be made aware of it by other means, e.g. the Press, and there would then be demands for Government action."[74] Public opinion appears to have been taking a long time to express its concerns, however. A few months later, in March 1958, the ministerial committee noted that while colonial migration was again assuming proportions that gave cause for concern—new totals suggested a total "coloured population" of 180,000—"there seemed to be little evidence of any marked anxiety among the general public in the country as a whole." Ministers were not simply awaiting the expression of public concern but apparently wanted to control its expression. Thus they rejected the idea of ascertaining "the public mind on the subject by stimulating discussion in the Press" for fear that the result might be an "explosion of opinion" in favor of "immediate action," which they could not undertake, having not yet decided what form control should take.[75] In June 1958 ministers seem to have given up the idea of legislation since "public opinion generally does not appear yet to be seriously concerned by the problem" and was not yet "unanimously ready to welcome legislation." As a result, the Cabinet committee recommended that the government should avoid such "contentious" routes and rely instead on administrative means to control "coloured immigration."[76] In addition to fearing domestic public opinion, the Cabinet accepted Home Secretary Rab Butler's strongly worded argument that the introduction of legislation would undermine the unity of the Commonwealth and thus damage Britain's international interests.

Thus, almost a decade after the first consideration of the nature of possible controlling legislation, ministers still could not bring themselves to initiate legislation that might threaten Britain's role as the center of a Commonwealth and empire. Indeed, whereas the disaster of Suez might have been thought likely to have already undermined Britain's position as an international power of weight, UK policy makers apparently still considered the Commonwealth the most likely means of securing what little international substance Britain had left. For example, in early 1958, after a recent Commonwealth tour, Prime Minister Macmillan spoke of the Commonwealth's important role "in the world struggle between the forces of tyranny and of freedom" and drew strength from Australia, Canada, and New Zealand's continuing desire for UK migrants and capital.[77] In light of the significance accorded the Commonwealth ideal, ministers were still reluctant in 1958 to pass legislation that might weaken Commonwealth ties. As a result, ten years into the debate, the competing communities of Britishness which first faced Labour continued to be unreconciled under the Conservatives.

These competing communities assumed ever more concrete form in the 1957 British Nationality Act. The 1948 act had provided that individuals born and living outside the United Kingdom of "pure European descent" whose father was also born outside the UK and who thus would not automatically become UKC citizens had one year to register their presumed UKC status. The problem in 1956 was that for a variety of reasons many such individuals, living mostly in India and Pakistan, had failed to register within the time allotted. Angered by "exile" from their "birthright," those concerned petitioned both directly and through the media for the reinstatement of their right to register as UKC citizens. The tone of internal correspondence between officials and politicians makes clear that this group was regarded as fully British, part of the familial community of domestic Britishness. Somewhat legalistically, Lloyd George referred to them as "British subjects of UK ancestry"; according to the Home Office, they were "as much white men as any of us" and "of British stock."[78] For Malcolm MacDonald, High Commissioner to India, the "fundamental problem" to be resolved by the 1957 bill "was the position of these persons of British origins and connections who are regarded as members of the UK community but who are not UK domestic citizens."[79] MacDonald's inclusive language, along with that of his colleagues, embraced these "Britons abroad" and made clear that although they had little intention of living in the United Kingdom, they had the perceived right to call it home. As a result, the 1957 British Nationality Act, along with some other adjustments, provided an additional five years for those eligible to register as UKC citizens. Thus by taking care of "European families who had served Britain well," London demonstrated its continuing perception of itself as an imperial heartland assuming a parental role.[80]

Left out of the 1957 act, however, was any provision for the three million or so Indians and Pakistanis who had also been left without UKC citizenship and who might also have described their efforts at imperial living as having "served Britain well." Under the terms of the 1948 British Nationality Act, any dominion resident failing to become a citizen of that dominion upon its passing of nationality legislation automatically became a citizen of the UKC, provided that Westminister passed its own enabling legislation. This ruling was yet another aspect of Britain's self-appointed and jealously guarded role as metropolitan center, but despite India and Pakistan's passing of separate nationality legislation, London did not act to pick up stateless citizens. The Home Office explained this lapse by reference to the three million Hindu and Muslim refugees with "not the remotest connection with this country" who would have qualified for UKC citizenship had Britain so acted. While drawing up the terms of the 1957 Act to extend UKC citizenship to individuals of "pure European descent," officials debated whether this deficiency should now be rectified. Having argued for several years against the idea, the Home Office in late November 1956 argued in favor of rectification on the grounds of moral responsibility. Determined opposition from both the Commonwealth Relations Office and the Foreign Office, however, resulted in a nationality act that, while inviting "lost" British stock to join their fellow Britons, left the Indians and Pakistanis explicitly without formal UKC citizenship and implicitly outside the community of domestic Britishness.[81] Thus, though a comparatively minor piece of legislation, the 1957 act is significant both for the light it shone on the competing communities of Britishness within Britain and for its role in sharpening the divide between separate spheres of nationality.

V

This divide was maintained through a comprehensive system of administrative controls. Effectively, the UK government hoped to establish a sufficiently rigorous system in the place of origin to discourage potential migrants from leaving their countries and thereby do away with the necessity for any system of control in the United Kingdom. Both the Indian and Pakistani governments proved extremely cooperative in this pursuit. They actively discouraged the emigration of unskilled and illiterate persons to the United Kingdom and attempted to stop the traffic in forged passports. In the case of India at least, this cooperation was forthcoming primarily because the government believed that the arrival of "low-caste and illiterate Indians" would damage the reputation of other Indians in Britain, namely, students and the "well-to-do."[82] The Pakistani government increased passport application fees, demanded deposits to cover possible repatriation costs, submitted all unskilled laborers' applications to the Protector of Emigrants for special permission (rarely given), and denied passports to any applicants without "firm prospects of establishing themselves." In addition, applicants were expected to be literate and possess a working knowledge of English. The Indian government required proof of sound financial status and literacy and subjected all claims of prospective UK employment to rigorous scrutiny, while requiring all emigrants departing by sea to obtain special leave to depart in addition to their passports. Furthermore, applications from "low-class" Indians were forwarded to the UK Home Office for more intensive vetting of employment and accommodation claims. Applicants seeking a passport for travel to a country within easy reach of the United Kingdom received equally intensive scrutiny by Indian authorities. And in both India and Pakistan, the UK High Commissioner publicized in vernacular newspapers UK-originating material detailing the allegedly difficult conditions likely to greet new arrivals.[83] For their part, the West Indian colonial governments, though not as elaborate in their practices, went some way to limit migrant traffic. Jamaica no longer granted passports to criminals, children without jobs or guardians, people aged over fifty, and pregnant women. In addition, and presumably to assist in tracking migration statistics, all travel agencies in Jamaica, the primary source of migrants, had to be registered with the government.[84] From the perspective of UK civil servants, what mainly hampered the efficiency of all these measures was that any British subject who succeeded in reaching UK shores and could prove his or her nationality had an absolute right to admittance.[85]

In addition to these efforts by colonial governments to discourage migration, London implemented some steps of its own. As we have seen, since September 1949 the Home Office had targeted British subject stowaways by reverting to the prewar practice of accepting only specific documents as proof of British nationality and right of entry.[86] In an effort to better track the flow as a whole, immigration officers, on the instructions of the Home Office, had secretly been keeping count of the entry and departure of "coloured" British subjects since October 1954. Likewise, the Colonial Office had developed its own counting mechanism by requesting colonial governors to send notice of each emigrant ship bound for Britain. The Colonial Office attempted to enlist yet further help from West Indian governments in slowing down the migration rate by sending telegrams that emphasized the likelihood of unemployment upon arrival in Britain and warned of the difficulties for those already in Britain should additional migrants continue to travel. The Colonial Office ensured that material reaching the UK High Commissions emphasized migrants' problems and ignored successes and achievements.[87] In addition, ministers discussed the possibility of employing the BBC to interview migrants who had returned to their "native countries" dissatisfied with their experience in Britain. Kilmuir's Cabinet committee hoped that "publicity of this kind might be effective in discouraging other immigrants from setting out." Aware of the potential political dangers of this step, ministers urged that it be pursued with "due discretion, avoiding any appearance of government intervention."[88] Such discretion manifested itself in the Colonial Office's presentation to colonial governments of the pressure to legislate as emanating "from individuals, often belonging to the lunatic fringe."[89] In reality, as we have seen, successive Cabinets and many ministers not only voiced their own desire to limit "coloured immigration" but bemoaned the apparent absence of a parallel desire among the general public.

The range of administrative methods used by territories of origin and the United Kingdom to prevent colonial migration was so extensive that one might suggest that those migrants who did succeed in obtaining a passport, completing an English-language interview, bearing up to scrutiny, and accepting propaganda at its true value were indeed hardy souls. Certainly, many appear to have proactively taken control of their situation and circumvented the host of regulations either by making use of corrupt or incompetent officials in order to get the necessary documentation for travel to England or by dealing studiously with each obstacle presented. Complementing this image of the 1950s migrant as a motivated individual were reports from colonial governments stating that it was "the more robust and energetic people" who emigrated. This evidence contradicts UK officials' depiction of West Indians as unskilled, lazy, and prone to violence. Rather, in losing people to Britain, the Jamaican authorities believed themselves to be "losing their best stock."[90]

This view from the colonies mattered little to UK officials, who credited the extensive range of administrative steps with decreasing the rate of migration to Britain. So pleased were they, in fact, that they wanted more impediments.[91] Believing the measures in place in India and Pakistan to be more effective than those operating in the West Indies, Colonial Office officials urged the governments of the West Indies to adopt tougher tactics. Colonial Office officials were particularly aggrieved that the administrative checks in place in the West Indies were not sufficient to prevent the migration of any

Recent arrivals at Victoria Railway Station. The formal attire of the principal figure is hardly in keeping with the stereotype of the idle and irresponsible migrant beginning to take shape by 1956. (The Hulton Deutsch Collection.)

honest able-bodied person in search of employment.[92] To prevent just such migration, the Colonial Office was on the verge in the late summer of 1958 of suggesting that West Indian governments stop issuing passports for a period of perhaps six months.[93] Had this measure been approved, the Colonial Office would have gone some way toward squaring the government's circle by curtailing unwanted migration from the colonies while allowing demographically acceptable migration from the dominions to pass unhindered, and all without any public admission of the UK government's role in bringing this about. To gain its objective, the Colonial Office employed almost threatening language to the West Indian, Indian, and Pakistani authorities, implying that if nothing more were done by the sending territories to halt migration at the point of departure at least temporarily, then London would have to act and control migration at the point of entry, perhaps permanently.[94]

The Macmillan government justified its request for administrative controls by reference to the downturn in the British economy. Correspondence with West Indian, Indian, and Pakistani governments emphasized the unemployment rate in Britain and the likelihood that it would continue to rise for "coloured immigrants." The Colonial Office promised to do all it could to assist incoming migrants but believed that these efforts would be hampered if additional migrants continued to arrive. In this case, the factor ostensibly responsible for the limitation on colonial migration was not the British state, or even the British public, but the recession—a supposedly unbiased player. In reality, since the Ministry of Labour admitted that much of the West Indian unemployment, though four times the national average, could be accounted for by recent arrivals in the process of finding a first job, the recession provided the occasion not the reason for control.[95] Unfortunately for the Colonial Office, however, just as it had found allegedly objective proof of the case against colonial migration, the government's other strategy of encouraging public opinion bore fruit.

VI

On Saturday, 23 August 1958, in the St. Ann's area of Nottingham, what began as a pub brawl over a black man and white woman talking together "turned suddenly into a major race riot." By the time the "riot" was over, ninety minutes after it started, more than a thousand whites had participated in attacks on West Indians and eight people had been hospitalized. A week later, in Notting Hill, London, after much press publicity and after two MPs had called for "immigration" control in response to the Nottingham "riot," crowds of whites numbering up to four hundred and using an assortment of homemade weapons launched a series of attacks over two successive nights on black people, their houses, and their businesses. On the third night of rioting, blacks began to arm themselves and fight back. On the fourth night, the police finally stepped in and asserted their control over the area.[96]

Traditional accounts tend to regard these incidents as the first eruption of public concern over colonial migration. Or more succinctly, the "riots" are said to represent the United Kingdom's realization that it had acquired a black component to its population. This interpretation depicts the "riots" as a starting point for future action. As I have suggested, however, there is another reading of these events. The very origin of the fights—whether black men should associate with white women—reveals a great deal of ignorance and barely thought-out prejudice which had been allowed to fester. One may see in the whites' reported chants that the blacks should "go home" the success of policy makers' reconstruction of subjects into aliens and proof that the language of the Cabinet room and parliamentary chamber had finally moved to the public highway. For the white youths in Nottingham and Notting Hill, the blacks whom they attacked were clearly interlopers, aliens who had gained admission to the United Kingdom somehow immorally if not illegally. The anger of the whites over jobs lost, amenities shared, and housing stock stretched represents the logical fruition of successive governments' failure to match infrastructural development with population growth. In this case, not doing something—not educating, not investing—imposes just as much culpability as doing something. And in a variety of areas policy makers opted not to act or to act in the direction opposite to that which might have produced a welcoming atmosphere for colonials.

Notably absent from interdepartmental reports throughout the decade, for example, was any suggestion of possible ways to improve or solve the "problems" allegedly caused by migrants. Neither working party nor Cabinet committee reports recommended educational measures to familiarize the public with migrants or suggested promoting a general atmosphere of tolerance. Rather, policy makers looked rather dourly and pessimistically into the future and feared for what "racial" tension might one day develop should migration continue on its current pattern. Indeed, much as had been the case when the *Empire Windrush* first docked in June 1948, the working parties of the 1950s pointed toward a negative outcome; they were charged with investigating "the social and economic problems arising from the growing influx into the United Kingdom of coloured workers from other Commonwealth countries." This directive established, first, that the migrants were classified according to skin color—clearly there was no need to research the migration of white Australians—and, second, that the migrants were presumed to produce problems even before the working party's first meeting. Thus, Brook's observation of 1954 rings true. There was no real need for a committee to explore possible solutions, since everyone knew what the solution must ultimately be, but a committee would publicize the problems.

This lack of concern with potential solutions was echoed at Cabinet level. On each occasion on which colonial migrants were discussed, ministers asked only how to prevent further migration, never once investigating how the problems they believed were caused by migration could be ameliorated without recourse to nationality law. This focus suggests the kernel of the issue: both Labour and Conservative administrations consistently regarded the inward migration of colonial subjects and citizens of color as an "immigration" problem. The only question was how the border could be better policed without sacrificing the domestic and international political advantages given by the Commonwealth. Never did they contemplate the kind of measures adopted on behalf of the European Volunteer Workers, concern for whom had extended to the institution of a publicity campaign, English-language teaching, and even the provision of games facilities. Instead, colonial migrants were left alone, having no more done for them "than for our own men," and social pressures and conflicts, especially between working-class whites and migrants were allowed to fester and to be perceived as problematic. For example, even as Macmillan's Cabinet discussed the social and economic problems caused by "immigration," they authorized a cut of between £25 and £30 million in the budget for "social investment" to which housing, education, and hospitals were expected to make major contributions.[97] By increasing pressure on available housing and further stretching the resources of the welfare state, these cuts would seriously aggravate the very problems with which the Cabinet claimed to be so concerned when they were presumed to have been caused by migrants. One might easily understand that those experiencing the increased competition for these services might blame the migrants. Indeed, as at least one observer has noted, in times of economic distress, "it is less convenient for people to trace the source of problems to structural changes in the economy; more convenient to place the burden of responsibility on a strikingly different and identifiable group."[98] Thus, the likely result of decreased public spending on social services and education would be a further development of hostility toward colonial migrants on the part of indigenous whites. To condemn the government for cutting its budget is not to accuse it of deliberately intensifying grass-roots hostility. Rather, by inattention to the likely consequences of these cuts, policy makers facilitated the transformation of popular anger stemming from social and economic causes into racial hostility. By so doing, policy makers manifested their own conviction that the "coloured immigrants" were a "problem" simply because they were in the country in the first place.

Official reaction to the 1958 "riots" was extremely hostile. Public expressions of hostility emphasized the breakdown of law and order and the unwarranted assault on the liberty of British subjects. Prime Minister Macmillan, for example, denounced the violence and upheld the right of British subjects of whatever skin color to walk the streets unmolested. Privately, however, officials condemned the "riots" not because they were antimigrant but, first, because they were outside the control of the state and thus a threat to the order of society and, second, because they disrupted plans for the imposition of additional administrative controls on migration. As we have seen, prior to the "riots" officials had hoped that a brief spurt in unemployment would provide sufficient justification for a passport moratorium. In the wake of the "riots" officials believed it politically impossible to press for any kind of border control since it would suggest that the government was pandering to a racist populace. Within the Colonial Office, for example, one civil servant who had been pressing for the imposition of formal control since 1954 now believed that it would be "shameful" and impossible to achieve before Britain had "clear[ed] its good name."[99] Others, less willing to be railroaded into inactivity, yet admitted the difficulty of pressing ahead with demands for control in light of the recent violence.[100] Similar sentiments came from colonial governors who accepted the economic legitimacy of control but believed that the "emotions stirred up by the riots" would make it difficult for local colonial governments to agree to any increased restrictions.[101] Action was likewise curtailed by the immediate reaction of the press, which largely condemned the rioters and branded the white attackers as hooligans likely to bring the reputation of Britain as a tolerant society into disrepute. The *Observer* called legislation "the easy way out" and said it would "be a shameful admission that the problem is too difficult for us to solve and that a multi-racial society is impossible." The *Daily Sketch* regarded the "riots" as "a . . . blot on our national good name for tolerance" and suggested that the imposition of formal migration control would only make matters worse. The *Manchester Guardian* consistently stood by the open-door principle; the *Times* remained noncommittal.[102]

The Bank Holiday "riots" temporarily threw the government's objectives off course. In early September, having flown to Britain in direct response to the violence, the Prime Minister of Jamaica, Norman Manley, rejected the passport moratorium proposal on the grounds that the true rationale was not jobs and houses but race.[103] Despite this setback, the government's long-term objective remained the curtailment of colonial migration by any means. And if officials now found it difficult to conceal the color bar behind every suggestion, politicians were able to use the disturbances as evidence that "something had to be done." In his speech immediately after the riot, in which he condemned the breach of public order, Macmillan at the same time declared that the government would examine the problem of "Commonwealth immigration." The emphasis of his speech was on the color blindness of English law rather than sympathy for the victims of violence. Neither focus would likely increase popular awareness of migrants' status as British subjects and citizens with the confirmed right to enter the country freely. Immediately after the "riots," officials' correspondence suggests that the Home and Colonial Offices sought to separate the outbreak of violence from the perceived need to introduce control, still claiming that control was an economic necessity. When this strategy failed, policy makers reversed it and soon followed Macmillan's example of linking the violence to a growing imperative to introduce control so as to maintain public order. As a result, black Britons were held responsible for the outbreak of disorder when whites attacked them.

While the "riots" themselves were not responsible for the introduction of legislation, they did play an important role in shifting the debate from the private to the public sphere and in transforming "immigrants" into "coloureds." Laying the groundwork for this movement in April 1958 John Hynd, Labour MP for Attercliffe, initiated a parliamentary debate on the dangers of continuing unrestricted colonial migration as evidenced by the strains placed by "immigrants" on the housing stock and the threat posed to law and order. Conservative MP Martin Lindsay (Solihull) supported Hynd by calling on the government to face its duty and introduce control regardless of the accusations of color prejudice which might follow. Responding for the Home Office, Patricia Hornsby-Smith denied that "immigrants" constituted a drain on Britain but admitted that "coloured unemployment" had more than doubled in the past six months, owing largely to the illiteracy, poor language skills, and "poor physique" of migrants from India and Pakistan. In her defense of colonial migration, Hornsby-Smith further reassured the House that although certain "coloured immigrants" appeared disproportionately prone to violence, it was most often directed "against their own fellow countrymen." Thus Hornsby-Smith, like so many of her predecessors, both problematized colonial migration and drew a barrier between colonial migrants and UK residents, placing them, as residents of different countries, in separate spheres of nationality.

Presumably sparked by the events of Notting Hill, "coloured immigration" was on the parliamentary agenda twice in just two months at the end of 1958. On both occasions a small group of perhaps four or five MPs linked West Indians with unemployment, crime, drugs, prostitution, disease, and abuse of the welfare state. Martin Lindsay went one step further by creating the specter of a "multiracial" society, which by its very existence imperiled the "national character." Responding for the Home Office, David Renton followed the pattern of Hornsby-Smith and those before her. He emphasized the significance of freedom of movement to the harmony of the empire and rejected legislative action, yet conveyed the impression that "coloured immigration" should be curtailed. Significantly, his public rejection of legislation was based less on principle and more on the proven effectiveness of the administrative checks already in place. This manner of rejection further identified the government with a desire to see migration decrease and thereby further fostered a hostile climate for blacks in Britain.[104]

Throughout 1959 the Macmillan Cabinet continued to explore the best means to exclude British subjects and citizens of color from Britain. Caution still prevailed, and the show of parliamentary support for the idea of control proved insufficient to persuade ministers to act. Even the middle measure of deportation was rejected in 1959 because, although it would demonstrate recognition of the seriousness of the "problem" and commitment to finding a solution, it would also likely discredit the government. Instead, impressed that administrative controls introduced by the Jamaican government had halved the number of passports issued during the past two months, the Cabinet hoped for continued success from this source. At the same time, however, and revealing their own preferences, ministers instructed officials to continue exploring potential legislation.

In an effort to limit migration, the Colonial Office requested that more publicity of this kind be made available to potential migrants, 1959. (Public Record Office, Kew Document Reference: CO1031/2538.)

This preparation was undertaken despite the fact that throughout this period, internal reports still found only housing a matter of immediate concern. Migrants continued to be law-abiding and apparently healthy, and there was "still no evidence of any significant increase of racial tension outside London."[105] Despite its inability to document any actual social and economic problems, the working party in late 1959 nonetheless reported that "coloured immigration" was dangerous and ought to be stopped. This recommendation came in spite of heightened efforts by colonial and Commonwealth governments to enforce administrative controls more rigorously. The Indian government, for example, though it would not compel intending migrants to undergo tuberculosis testing, agreed to encourage them.[106] The West Indian government, ever since the "riots," had undertaken "vigourous action" to dissuade potential emigrants from setting out without prior arrangement of accommodation and employment.[107] Ministers noted happily that although the UK "coloured population" had grown in 1959, the rate had been much slower than in recent years. Thus, once again the Cabinet held back from legislative action in the hope that it would prove unnecessary. Notably, ministers had not become any more accustomed to a "coloured" presence in Britain. Rather, they were inhibited by the same concerns that had always prevented action—fear of the consequences.[108]

VII

The following year, 1960, saw a sudden spurt in migration numbers and a consequent increase in government concern. Home Secretary Rab Butler brought the rising figures to the Cabinet's attention in July 1960, suggesting that if current rates continued, legislation would once again have to be considered. For the moment, however, he did not recommend any public action.[109] In November when the matter again came up for review, Butler proposed that the defunct Cabinet ministerial committee be reconstituted to keep the "disquieting" situation under review. The "disquieting" situation was the migration of 43,500 West Indians in the first ten months of 1960 compared with 16,400 in 1959 and 29,800 in the previous peak year of 1956. As always there was "no immediate problem of unemployment," but the Ministry of Labour believed that it would become increasingly difficult to place unskilled "coloured" labor over the coming years.[110]

It seems likely that Butler's sudden anxiety stemmed less from the warnings of the Ministry of Labour, which had been consistent since 1948, and more from the recognition that the migrants were never going to stop of their own accord. According to Butler, the "immigrants" were attracted by full employment and high wages and would continue to migrate as long as conditions remained favorable in Britain. The administrative efforts of the West Indian, Indian, and Pakistani authorities to publicize the risks of emigration were consistently counteracted by encouraging letters, often enclosing passage money, from friends and relatives already in Britain. This realization, coupled with the rise in numbers, appears to have prompted Butler for the first time to offer his personal support for controlling legislation. His fears had little to do with unemployment per se but resulted from the realization that if current rates continued, the "coloured population" might reach 2.7 percent of the total UK population.[111] Moreover, colonial governments appeared increasingly likely to relax their controls because of domestic complaints that the majority of emigrants, despite official warnings to the contrary, *were* finding employment in Britain. Thus, only London possessed the power to control entry.

A few months later, in February 1961, the Cabinet Commonwealth Migrants Committee adopted a similar line. This committee consisted of Lord Chancellor Kilmuir as chair, Home Secretary Rab Butler, Colonial Secretary Iain Macleod, Commonwealth Relations Secretary Duncan Sandys, Minister of Labour John Hare, Minister of Health Enoch Powell, and Minister of Housing Henry Brooke. Notwithstanding ministers' perception that migrants already in Britain had largely been accepted, the committee based its recommendation for control on the "startling" numbers of incoming migrants. In 1960 alone, the net intake of "coloured people" from all parts of the Empire, though predominantly from the West Indies, reached a new high of 58,000, almost three times the previous year's figure. Even more alarming was the projection based on the past six years' figures that the black population in the United Kingdom (then estimated at 300,000) could be expected to reach 1.5 million by 1980.[112] This focus on a growing "coloured" element contrasts with the lack of expressed alarm at either general population growth or the percentage increase in the Baltic, Irish, or Polish communities. Further emphasizing this focus on skin color as the defining feature of Britishness, the Ministry of Labour acknowledged that it had kept a separate count of "coloured unemployment" since 1953. The ministry was now able to report that of the "West Indian labour force," 5 percent was unemployed, compared to a national average of 1.6 percent. At the same time, the ministry admitted that the vast majority of West Indians were employed and that all of their fears about unemployment were based on future projections, not current facts. These projections, however, continually provided sufficient grounds for the ministry to recommend immediate control.

Throughout 1961, policy makers focused on perceived problems and repeatedly separated colonials from white UK residents, placing them in separate spheres of nationality. For example, ministers remarked on migrants' propensity to live in "grossly over-crowded and ever-growing colonies," under the tenancy of a "coloured landlord" determined to overfill a house with "his own people." Likewise, although the Cabinet committee had few facts in the area of health, it yet reported that "immigrants living in difficult social circumstances" contributed greatly to increases in venereal disease and tuberculosis. Against this problematic ministerial focus, local police described the general attitude of white people toward "coloureds" as "sympathetic tolerance" and reported that while the majority of blacks both lived and married within their "colonies," those who had moved out or married white Britons were generally accepted by white neighbors.

In early 1961, despite its desire for legislation, the ministerial committee recommended against its introduction until the House had more fully expressed its opinion in a forthcoming parliamentary debate. In the meantime, government spokespeople were to be authorized to recognize the problematic nature of colonial migration, reiterate the difficulties of restricting the entry of British subjects, and welcome a full expression of parliamentary opinion. They were not to admit that legislation was already being prepared or contemplated, and they were to confirm the government's refusal to countenance any discrimination based on race. Thus once again, the government chose to withhold its own hand until public, in this case parliamentary, opinion had revealed itself. There was no doubt of the Cabinet's own beliefs, however, as it once again invited the Cabinet Commonwealth Migrants Committee to consider the likely form legislation would take.[113]

It was in the midst of these discussions in London that Prime Minister Macmillan visited both the West Indies and the United States. Prompted by the soon-to-be (albeit briefly) Prime Minister of the West Indian Federation Sir Grantley Adams, but supported by officials at home, Macmillan raised the issue of West Indian migration in a memo to President John Kennedy. Adams had hoped that upon independence the West Indies might be included within the generous British immigration quota for entry to the United States. London liked this idea but feared that to push it too strongly "would create the impression that we [are] trying to push off our domestic problems on to United States' shoulders."[114] With this caution in mind, Macmillan was briefed only to raise the issue of immigration, to hope that the existing West Indian quota would not be reduced following independence, and to suggest that West Indians might be allowed in without visas to work temporarily as domestics. That the topic was raised at all testifies to the seriousness with which it was regarded in London, as though any potential window of relief of the "pressure" felt in Britain was significant enough to explore.

Back in London, the "startling increase in the number of coloured immigrants" prompted a second Cabinet discussion just a few months later, in May, and a third in July 1961. With a prospective total of 200,000 "coloured immigrants" for 1961 alone, and a projected population of color of 2 million by 1975, the Cabinet committee recommended that ministers prepare themselves for the introduction of control in the very near future unless they wished to face a US-style "colour problem."[115] Ministers believed the increase was due both to a breakdown in the administrative controls by which the flow had so far been regulated and to colonials' fear that the UK government was about to introduce legislation. The Cabinet committee rejected health, housing, and quota controls as impracticable. It is perhaps fitting, given its early and intense resistance to the idea of colonial labor, that it was the Ministry of Labour that eventually found the "solution" to the government's policy dilemma of controlling blacks without appearing to be instituting a color bar. The ministry proposed a work-permit system. Recognizing that most employers would take on "coloured labour when it offered itself," the ministry believed that employers would be far less likely to employ workers whom they had not seen and who were applying for a permit from overseas. Thus, once again, government and business interests conflicted. The ministry was not entirely insensitive to economic dictates, however, recommending that any scheme of control should be flexible enough to keep pace with the changing requirements of the economy.[116] The system worked by dividing potential migrants into three groups—the skilled, those with jobs to come to, and the unskilled. All would have to apply for a Ministry of Labour permit or voucher in order to enter Britain for the purpose of taking up employment, but only the third group would be subject to numerical caps. With this scheme, ministers believed that they had finally found a way to square their circle, since it was assumed that most migrants from the "old dominion" countries would be either skilled or en route to a specific job, and thus they would be exempt from controls under the proposed plan. The third category would presumably cover only the "coloured" territories, but in formal terms the legislation would be nondiscriminatory.

As ideal as the scheme appeared, however, there were four major difficulties to be arranged. First, it would be difficult to justify an employment permit scheme publicly when the majority of migrants were doing work "of real importance to the country."[117] Furthermore, the Treasury, joining the working party at a very late stage, stated its outright objection to any controls, maintaining that young migrants provided flexibility and expansion opportunities to the UK economy, and should therefore not be discouraged. Incorporating the Treasury's views, the working party summarized the conflict thus: Commonwealth sentiment and economic interests against "the long-term social consequences of the presence in this country of large and growing coloured communities that are difficult of assimilation."[118] Officials and later ministers found against the Treasury and in favor of control, with Home Secretary Butler admitting that since they "could not legislate openly on grounds of color" an employment scheme provided the "best public stand."[119] Second, the scheme evaded rather than solved the Irish question. As we have seen,

throughout the decade in which thousands of colonial citizens had been subjected to scrutiny, a cross traffic between Ireland and Britain of over one million was allowed and even encouraged. Unwilling to disturb this traffic but
conscious of the importance of appearances, the Cabinet agreed that Irish
citizens would formally be subject to control while informally allowed free
entry. Third, Ministers still could not agree on which British subjects should
automatically be free from control. Minister of Health Enoch Powell argued
for a formal split within the existing UKC citizenship, so that residents of the
United Kingdom and residents of the colonies would each enjoy a separate
citizenship.[120] This strategy would have had the advantage of matching policy
makers' own conceptions of Britishness, but it would have necessitated significant legislation to redraw the 1948 act, would have formally differentiated
within the imperial nationality by creating an apparently inferior colonial nationality, and as in 1948, would have required consultation with other Commonwealth members. Instead, ministers chose compromise. Subject to control would be all British subjects born outside the United Kingdom, Channel
Islands, and Isle of Man. Such a territorial and limited prescription had the
advantages of being formally color blind and existing only for the purposes of
migration. For all other purposes, including international law, the existing
citizenship of the United Kingdom and Colonies remained intact.[121] And finally, initiating any legislation threatened the prospects for the success of the
current negotiations to unite all the British Caribbean under a single independent flag as the West Indies Federation. To avoid jeopardizing these talks, the
Cabinet agreed that no announcement of impending legislation should be
made before October 1961 at the earliest. In addition to helping the West
Indies Federation this delay "would have the advantage of enabling public
opinion to express itself about the recent striking increase in immigration."[122]
Thus, as late as the summer of 1961, even with the format of the legislation
beginning to take shape, officials still looked for a more forceful expression of
public opinion in the hope that it would be seen to have led the way. Thus,
thirteen years after they had first wished that the passengers on board the
Empire Windrush could be prevented from landing, Cabinet ministers were
finally edging toward a resolution of their problems. And thirteen years on,
these problems were still perceived largely in terms of skin color. Indeed, the
final official report given to ministers before they decided to legislate for control concluded that "by and large, the immigrants are as healthy and respect-
able as other people, and have no difficulty in finding jobs; and the ugly racial
incidents of 1958 have not been repeated."[123] Nevertheless, despite this social
and economic assimilation, policy makers were convinced that Britain was not
really the migrants' home and that it was therefore legitimate to find some
means of curtailing their freedom of entry.

The Cabinet took the formal decision to introduce controlling legislation on 10 October 1961 although public announcement was to await the Conservative Party conference and the warning of Commonwealth governments. The decision was based on Butler's estimate that the "immigration" total for 1961 was likely to reach over 100,000 and his conviction that "it was evident that the country could not assimilate coloured immigrants on the current scale."[124] In Butler's presentation at the time, and his memoirs subsequently, the language is that of exhaustion, of concession, of inevitability, and fatality. "Under pressure," Butler presented the bill in "defensive and apologetic terms," emphasizing the necessity for control in the light of recent numbers.[125] He referred to the administrative help the colonial and Commonwealth governments had given over the past few years but gave the impression that even these informal controls were no longer sufficient to stem the migratory flood into the United Kingdom. Butler made no reference to the color of the majority of those UKC citizens who would now be made subject to control. Referring to legislation as "a sad necessity" and speaking of "a general feeling in the country," the language suggested that border control had been forced on the ministers.[126] Whether this forcing had been done by a racist public or greedy colonials mattered not. The point was that the ministers themselves were only responding to events. In reality, as we have seen, for the past thirteen years a succession of officials and politicians had taken an extremely proactive role in developing enough momentum to make control acceptable.

VIII

The 1962 act codified what successive Labour and Tory Cabinets had been thinking and saying in private since the early postwar years. The act divided would-be British subject migrants into three groups, each eligible for A, B, and C vouchers respectively: those with jobs to go to, those with skills or experience deemed advantageous to the United Kingdom, and unskilled laborers in search of work. Only the last category was to be subject to numerical control. The number of vouchers available was not fixed, and this feature was to work against potential migrants, as voucher allocation varied according to political and economic considerations. The voucher system significantly reduced primary migration to Britain. From a high in the first six months of the act's implementation, for example, when over 51,000 voucher holders were admitted, the number fell to just under 13,000 by 1965.[127] Although the act was ostensibly color blind, Butler believed that its "great merit" was that it could be presented as nondiscriminatory even though in practice "its restrictive effect is intended to, and would in fact, operate on coloured people almost exclusively."[128] Furthermore, the act empowered the Home Secretary to deport British subjects of less than five years' residence in the United Kingdom upon conviction of a criminal offense carrying liability to imprisonment, and thus it dealt with the "criminal element" that had caused so much concern in the early 1950s. The act also reserved a great deal of discretion to immigration officers to prevent the landing of individuals unable to convince officers of their right to enter the country or their ability to support themselves without having to work. It thereby enabled the Home Office to discriminate in favor of subjects whose entry it had no wish to control. To make the act more effective, British subjects denied entry were to have no access to appeals and were to be returned at the carrier's expense. Finally, the act created a class of British subjects who were defined as "belonging" to the United Kingdom and were not subject to immigration control. This group, as in the 1955 bill, was defined as those who had been born in the United Kingdom or whose passport had been issued on behalf of the United Kingdom. Thus, the term excluded UKC citizens resident in the colonies whose passports were issued by and on behalf of the colonial government, but it included those living overseas whose passports were issued by UK high commissioners. Subject to control but to be admitted without entry permits at the immigration officer's discretion were students, visitors, economically self-sufficient British subjects, and dependents of voucher holders. Once admitted, all British subjects would remain free from further control—no police registration, no employment controls, no curtailment on length of stay. The absence of internal controls was an important tool in demonstrating that British subjects were still a category above alien immigrants and represented the government's attempt to paper over the cracks it had opened in the imperial nationality.

Some commentators have speculated that policy makers enacted the 1962 legislation without reference to the act of 1948—that the UKC citizenship created by that act was "featherweight" compared to the "the enormous weight of legal tradition and political history concerning the British subject."[129] As we have seen, however, the Macmillan government and its predecessors were fully cognizant of the value of the UKC citizenship and consciously chose to leave it undisturbed by any separation of colonial from UK citizenship. Rather, by enacting legislation that exempted a specific class of persons from control—those belonging to the United Kingdom—policy makers were still trying to get the best of both worlds: minimum disruption of colonial relations with limited entry of migrants of color. In the event, neither goal was achieved. To lessen the apparent inhumanity of the act and to placate the anticontrol lobby, dependents of British subjects who had already entered the country or were subsequently admitted were allowed free entry. Fearful that the provision would be removed at some point, many dependents migrated within a year or two of the act's passage. Hence, not only did migration figures keep pace with the numbers that had prompted the institution of control in the first place, but the act made permanent what had originally been intended as a temporary migration. In fact "New Commonwealth" migration into Britain between 1960 and 1962 was greater than the sum of all postwar colonial migration preceding it.[130]

To secure public and parliamentary support for the bill, Macmillan's government played down its significance. One way of doing so, as had been done throughout the political debate thus far, was through language. The act was titled Commonwealth Immigrants Act and consistently referred to "Commonwealth immigrants." Under the terms of the 1948 act it would have been equally appropriate to call it British Subjects Migration Act and to identify those to be controlled as British subjects. By 1962, however, the transformation from British subject to "coloured immigrant" was complete and the act carried the title that most clearly explained its purpose. Likewise, Butler directed its provisions against the "quarter of the globe's population" who were "legally entitled" to come to Britain, rather than the British subjects or UKC citizens who regarded Britain as an imperial home.[131] By this language, Butler helped define potential migrants as non-British individuals connected to the island only through some legal error rather than through three hundred years of colonialism. Notwithstanding this linguistic deftness, the 1962 bill was bitterly condemned by the Labour Party in general and Hugh Gaitskell, its leader, in particular as "a surrender to racialism." Labour also attacked the bill for its ambiguities, its inclusion of the Irish, its unilateralism, and its betrayal of imperial obligations. Labour front bencher George Brown astutely attacked the bill for its recourse to nationality as "inadequate" and "misleading" when the problems were, in fact, of a domestic nature and of the government's own making.[132] Here was impassioned opposition from the party that only a few years before was so keen on maintaining the integrity of the constructed British national identity that it had suggested shipping off certain sections of the population to East Africa to raise groundnuts. Some commentators have accounted for the shift by reference to Gaitskell's personal aversion to racism and belief in the empire; others believe the Labour Party foresaw benefits to be had from uniting around an issue of constitutional importance. Whatever the origins of the opposition, however, it succeeded only in amending the act, not in preventing it, and the law controlling the entry of British subjects became operative on 1 July 1962.

Within the space of just over a decade, the debate on colonial migration had moved from the private to the public sphere, and the United Kingdom had partially closed its borders. Superficially, it appeared as though Conservatives had found a means of squaring the prisonlike circle that Labour's earlier passage of the 1948 Nationality Act had created. Certainly, a succession of officials and administrations had toiled long enough in search of a breakthrough. And yet, as the next chapter makes clear, concepts of nationality were no clearer after the 1962 act than before. Ironically, it is possible that had policy makers acted when they first expressed alarm, they might well have made their future position easier. A bill to control entry applying to British subjects and aliens alike in 1948 or even 1950 might have been slightly easier to pass off as color blind. As it was, by waiting until 1962 and by transforming British subjects into immigrants and immigrants into "coloureds," policy makers ensured that an act to restrict immigration would be seen as an act to restrict people of color, predicated on a racialized understanding of the world's population.

This effective admission of a racial hierarchy within the allegedly universal imperial nationality fractured the Commonwealth ideal and opened the door to requests for additional controls. In the mid-1960s and beyond, the issue of "race and immigration" exploded into the public domain, and some politicians joined extremist groups in demanding that the formal nationality policy be further narrowed to better match the constructed national identity. Meanwhile, colonial migrants and their descendants continued to fight for the right to claim their identity as Britons living in Britain. The concluding chapter outlines the still confusing politics of citizenship down to the present day.

CHAPTER 7

Still the Same Old Story

Within a year of passing the 1962 Commonwealth Immigrants Act, the Macmillan government began to rework its administration hoping to reduce the number of "coloured immigrants" further. Within six years, in a frenzied attempt to block the entry of British subjects of Asian descent who had "escaped" control in 1962, Harold Wilson's Labour government introduced and passed a second Commonwealth Immigrants Act, which drew a line around a yet more exclusive community of domestic Britishness. Three years after that, in 1971, Edward Heath's Conservative administration passed an immigration act that gave concrete form to the separate spheres of nationality which had effectively governed British nationality and migration policy since at least 1945. In 1981 Margaret Thatcher's Conservative administration formally redrew Britain's nationality law by creating tiers of British citizenship and abandoning even the language of a United Kingdom and Colonies citizenship.

Each of these legislative acts reflected a continuing discourse of the contested terrain of citizenship in postwar Britain. Furthermore, between 1981 and 1996, several incidents made it clear that even the 1981 act failed to resolve all the contradictions within the politics of citizenship. In the spring of 1982 Margaret Thatcher dispatched a naval task force to the Falkland Islands in defense of "British kith and kin," some of whom only a year before had failed to meet the criteria for classification as British citizens. By contrast, over the course of the subsequent decade, residents of Hong Kong witnessed Thatcher's acquiescence in their imminent reconstruction from citizens of a British Dependent Territory to citizens of China. Meanwhile, residents of the European Community, though aliens in name, saw their right to enter Britain reaffirmed by international treaty. This concluding chapter explores each of these events, as well as the public debates surrounding post-1962 legislation and finds that the framework within which UK policy makers conceive British nationality and migration policy in the late 1990s remains haunted by much the same mixture of imperial, economic, and demographic imperatives as in the late 1940s.

I

Even before the 1962 Commonwealth Immigrants Act came into force, Macmillan's Commonwealth Immigration Committee, consisting of Kilmuir as chair, Duncan Sandys, Enoch Powell, Reginald Maudling, David Renton and Attorney General Reginald Manningham-Buller, debated the benefits of a flexible and liberal operation of the act against the desirability of limiting the "net coloured intake."[1] Essentially, discussion centered upon how many employment vouchers should be issued each year. Initially the issue was fixed at 750 per week, but within a few months, the Ministry of Labour requested an increase to 1,000, since many vouchers were not being used and the backlog of applications had already produced a waiting list for a C voucher of between six and twelve months. The committee responded by increasing the issue to 900.[2] As this generosity suggests, the early operation of the act appeared satisfactory to ministers who believed that it was working to control unwanted colonial migration.[3] By the summer of 1963, however, signs of disquiet began to appear as ministers noted that the number of applications for a C voucher had sufficiently exceeded supply that the delay had increased to fifteen months and was soon expected to reach three years.[4] Significantly, it was not the length of delay that concerned them but the overwhelming numbers seeking entry. By October 1963 John Hare as Minister of Labour forecast a "net coloured intake" of between 50,000 and 60,000—"more than could hope to be absorbed."[5] Eight months later Home Secretary Henry Brooke declared the 1962 Commonwealth Immigrants Act "inadequate" to control migration.[6] Ministers began actively considering additional means to "keep the rate of coloured immigration within acceptable bounds."[7]

The easiest means of achieving this objective was to reconstruct the administrative terms of the 1962 act. As we have seen, according to the act as originally passed, would-be migrants intending to settle permanently or intending to take up employment in the UK applied for one of three vouchers issued by the Ministry of Labour. Within a year, ministers had reduced the weekly issue of vouchers to 400 and placed additional qualifications on each of the three categories. Category A vouchers became subject to greater bureaucracy as UK employers nominating Indians and Pakistanis now had to produce photographs of, and more information about, their intended employees. Category B vouchers underwent the most complete reconstruction. Available to university graduates and professionals and intended originally to facilitate "the entry of persons from the white dominions," 83 percent of these vouchers had gone to residents of India and Pakistan during the first year. Noting that the majority of applicants were teachers, the Ministry of Labour in collaboration with the Ministry of Education imposed new standards of eligibility on university degrees. Officials believed that the changes would reduce the number of eligible applicants by two-thirds, and of equal importance, whereas all degrees issued in Australia and New Zealand would qualify, only first-class honors would do so in India and Pakistan.[8] The largest number of applicants were those applying for the unskilled C vouchers. In July 1963, in an effort to control distribution, the Cabinet committee ruled that no single country could receive more than 25 percent of the vouchers in this class. Although applicable to all countries, the practical effect of this rule was felt only by India and Pakistan, which together supplied an average of 3,200 applicants a week. The result was that within less than a year, the queue of applicants from these two countries alone had grown to 270,000. With this backlog and at the current rate of issue, policy makers anticipated that Indian and Pakistani individuals applying for a nonpriority C voucher in the spring of 1964 would not receive it until 2014.[9] Even though this delay should have deterred even the most determined applicants, the Commonwealth Immigration Committee tightened the rules governing C vouchers still further by deciding to issue a maximum of 50 per week, even if A and B vouchers failed to reach their limit of 350.[10] Furthermore, in June 1964 the government announced that because of the long waiting list and in order to avoid unnecessary expense both to applicants and the ministry, no further applications for nonpriority C vouchers would be accepted. Not announced was the decision to cease issuing C vouchers altogether in September 1964.[11]

In the first year of controlled admissions, from July 1962 through June 1963, the net intake of colonial migrants was 34,500. Over the course of the next year, this figure rose to 68,000.[12] This constant inflow of colonial migrants disappointed ministers, who evidently had hoped for dramatic decreases. They discovered that the right of dependents to join settled residents accounted for the steady migration figures, and the act prevented the imposition of any ceiling on movement. Ministers debated whether "men who sought employment in this country might reasonably be expected to maintain their families at home and to return to them in due course, instead of establishing themselves permanently in this country." Thus they were beginning to frame their consideration of British subjects in terms akin to those offered to guestworkers in continental Europe. In the event, the proposal was rejected after only a brief discussion because of the difficulties of justifying the separation of families and of dealing with the social problems that might result in the areas where single men settled.[13] Notably, the rejection was motivated less by principle than by pragmatism, since ministers did investigate the means by which the pool of eligible dependents could be reduced. Discovering that denying the right of entry to children over the age of sixteen, fiancées, and widowed or elderly parents would reduce the total admitted by only two or three thousand, however, ministers turned instead to reducing the number of primary vouchers issued as a means of reducing the number of eligible dependents. Looking for doctors, nurses, teachers, and transport workers, ministers discussed restricting vouchers to migrants with job offers in the public sector.[14] Home Secretary Henry Brooke, believing that the "rate of net immigration is too great . . . for things to be left as they are," suggested a reduction to seven or eight thousand vouchers a year, issued only to people coming to take up work of "national importance."[15]

As Brooke's proposal makes clear, and as had been the case prior to the 1962 act, controlling additional migration involved wider issues than simply closing the door. Most significant, too inflexible a policy threatened an economy currently benefiting from a migrant labor supply and further endangered relations with the "old dominions."[16] To ensure that any tightening of the 1962 provisions hit only their intended target, ministers implemented several devices designed to protect the privileges of Australians, New Zealanders, and Canadians. Shorthand typists, for example, though neither professionals nor university graduates remained within category B because the majority were women from the "old dominions."[17] Similarly, immigration officers turned "a blind eye" to "working holiday-makers" from the "old dominions" who, though admitted as visitors, took jobs.[18] Discrimination, however, was limited to that which could be explained or defended. In August 1964 officials from the Home Office and Ministry of Labour believed that "if it were permissible to discriminate openly between coloured and other people . . . the task of restricting the flow would be technically simpler."[19] As it was, though believing "coloured immigrants" to be the sole source of trouble, officials were forced to discover a less obvious means of discrimination. Operating the 1962 Commonwealth Immigrants Act at these dual levels reinforced the differentiation of communities of Britishness: the imperial, familial community consisting of white-skinned Britons was privileged and protected from the letter of immigration law, while the political community of Britishness consisting of black-skinned Britons was subjected to increasingly tight regulation.

For thirteen years this regulation had been the concern of a succession of Conservative governments. In October 1964 Harold Wilson's Labour Party assumed office, but policy toward migration and nationality remained much the same. As we have seen, the Labour Party in opposition had strongly condemned the 1962 act. Within a very brief period, however, this opposition was transformed into advocacy of yet greater controls. By the time of the election in 1964, the Labour Party's manifesto carried a promise to retain the act and a statement that "the number of immigrants entering the United Kingdom must be limited." Ameliorating this commitment, however, was a promise that subsequent control was to be effected in consultation with other Commonwealth countries. Within a month of taking office, and in light of the 330,000 voucher applications pending, Labour Home Secretary Frank Soskice and Commonwealth Relations Secretary Arthur Bottomly believed it "imperative" that the 1962 act (due to expire at the end of the year) should be renewed and that promised discussions with other members of the Commonwealth should be very informal and raise no hopes that the system would be changed.[20] Furthermore, Soskice, borrowing from the repertoire of his predecessor, labeled the 1962 act "inadequate" for limiting the flow of "immigrants" to a rate fixed by the government.[21] At the same time, some of the Home Secretary's colleagues emphasized that "net coloured immigration" should be contextualized within all immigration and that the "right course" would be to reduce racial tension by alleviating strains in housing, education, and health.[22] Despite this attempt at an alternative definition of the "problem of coloured immigration," the full Cabinet supported Soskice's subsequent memo, which declared that the "net intake of coloured Commonwealth immigrants" in 1964 was too high at 62,000, 9 percent higher than it had been in 1960 when there were no controls in place. Soskice suggested that too many people were evading control, either by entering as visitors or students but staying as workers or by posing as dependents where no relationship existed. In response, Soskice planned a parliamentary statement outlining the tougher measures to be employed by immigration officers to verify the "bona fides" of students, visitors, and dependents.[23] By February 1965 Wilson went one stage beyond Soskice, suggesting that in addition to "tightening up" existing controls, additional "tougher legislation" might be required.[24]

These words assumed concrete form in the August 1965 White Paper *Immigration from the Commonwealth*. Building on the Commonwealth mission promised in the manifesto and undertaken a few months earlier by Lord Louis Mountbatten, the government concluded that although migrants were making a "very valuable contribution" to the economy, there was "a limit to the number of immigrants that this small and over-crowded country can absorb."[25] As a result, the White Paper instituted significant changes in the operation of the 1962 act. Henceforth the annual distribution of vouchers was reduced from 20,000 to 8,500 (with 1,000 reserved for Malta and no more than 15 percent to go to any one country). Ministers expected that approximately 5,500 vouchers would go to doctors, dentists, nurses, qualified teachers, experienced science and technology graduates, and experienced non-university-graduate professionals. With the acquiescence of the Cabinet, the

Ministry of Labour hoped that the remaining 2,000, though distributed on a general first-come-first-served basis, could be directed to persons with offers of employment from hospitals or public transport.[26]

The second major change instituted by the 1965 White Paper concerned dependents. Home Secretary Soskice appeared as alarmed as his Conservative predecessors by the "half million dependents" who already had the statutory right to enter the United Kingdom. To prevent this number from growing, Soskice recommended that future migrants be admitted on the understanding that their dependents' entry could not be guaranteed.[27] In discussion, ministers opted for a softer exclusion, deciding that henceforth children over the age of sixteen were not to be admitted even to join parents already settled, nor were children under sixteen to be admitted to join relatives other than parents. Furthermore, all dependents would be subject to a more rigorous check, with immigration officers instructed to give preference to dependents carrying entry certificates and empowered to refuse entry to any whose authenticity they doubted.[28]

The third change instituted by the White Paper moved migrating British subjects one step closer to the position of aliens by allowing immigration officers to attach landing conditions to migrants of whose status they were in doubt. In addition, the Home Secretary was now empowered to deport without a court recommendation individuals deemed to have entered Britain by evading the 1962 act. Hoping to minimize Commonwealth dissent, the Cabinet rejected Soskice's original request for powers of deportation equal to those he possessed for aliens.

All the extra hurdles contained in the White Paper, though perhaps minor in themselves, made a British subject's passage to Britain ever more difficult and visibly more contested. More contested because, as had been the case throughout the postwar era, the linking of the cessation of further migration with the fate of "this small and over-crowded island" served to make all migration appear suspect. And although Wilson's language, like that of his predecessors, was formally color blind, the relationship between migration and people of color was by 1965 sufficiently tight that few were left in doubt of the true objective of the White Paper—to keep out further "coloured immigration." Indeed, during the parliamentary debate, both supporters and opponents of the White Paper called on the House to recognize that the issue revolved around "the question of color."[29] As a result, the status of British subjects of color already in the country became more vulnerable.

This vulnerability persisted despite the Wilson government's introduction of legislation to combat racial discrimination. Britain's first Race Relations Act, passed in 1965, prohibited incitement to racial hatred and attempted to combat acts of discrimination based on race, ethnicity, or nationality in places of public resort. The act did not extend to housing, on the ground that the government should not interfere with personal rights, or to employment because it would likely be ineffective.[30] The introduction of any legislation to combat acts of discrimination based on race was an advance of sorts for subjects of color in Britain and may be thought to mark the first official move away from the path set by Attlee's response to the"incursion" of the *Empire Windrush*. Unfortunately, its limited sphere of operation and the absence of any criminal sanction made it "declaratory rather than effective or efficient."[31] Furthermore its permanent association with migration control weakened its impact. Ministers themselves referred to the legislation as the counterpart to their efforts to limit further admissions. Moreover, it manifested the continuing existence of communities of Britishness.

These communities of Britishness shaped policy makers' public statements on race and immigration throughout the coming decades. Even when ministers spoke of "assimilation" and "integration," the shadow of their absolute conviction in separate spheres of nationality overlay their words. Thus, discussing the potential for further entry restrictions in late 1964, Alec Douglas-Home's Conservative Cabinet believed that a distinction must be made "in any public statement," between "immigrants" already in the country and "immigrants" seeking admission. The former were to be "treated without discrimination in accordance with our liberal traditions," and the latter were to be kept outside in order to avoid creating "insoluble social problems."[32] Likewise, Wilson's government promised to alleviate the "difficulties" caused by "the presence in this country of a number of immigrants with differing cultural and social backgrounds" by both promoting integration and limiting further admissions. Hence the value of the Voluntary Liaison Committees of 1965, the Race Relations Act and Commission of 1968, the Race Relations Board in 1975, and the Race Relations Act of 1976—all designed to promote integration—was seriously weakened by an enveloping context of control. Thus, despite the laudable objective of equality, by classifying would-be migrants as unwanted outsiders, the language used ensured that settled migrants were regarded in the same unfavorable light. The general public, hearing that "immigration" needed to be further controlled in order to reduce the associated social problems, would find it difficult to distinguish migrants of color already resident in the United Kingdom from migrants of color seeking admission. Rather than the number of years of residence, overt physical characteristics became the markers for opinions on whether or not a particular migrant was part of the problem. Despite kind official words to the contrary, both settled and would-be migrants would likely be regarded as troublesome non-British immigrants. What would stand out to the public, as it stood out to policy makers, was not the legal nationality that UK residents and all British subject migrants still held in common, but the "social problems" that official discourse associated with "coloured immigration." By 1965 this discourse, and the whole issue of "coloured immigration," was firmly located within the public sphere.

II

If, according to the traditional historiography, the "riots" of Notting Hill provided the contextual tinder for the 1962 Act, then the Smethwick election result seems concrete proof that popular anger at rising "immigration" shaped subsequent official migration and nationality policy. Labour won the 1964 election with a national swing of 3.2 percent, but in the Midlands constituency of Smethwick the Conservative candidate Peter Griffiths won with a swing of 7.5 percent. The campaign was the first to be fought on the issue of "race and immigration" with Griffiths refusing to condemn those of his supporters who used the slogan "If you want a nigger neighbour, vote Labour." Griffiths's success, and the earlier formation of residents' associations based around negative images of migrants of color, appeared to suggest the electoral value of adopting an antimmigrant position. Writing shortly after the election, Richard Crossman, Labour Minister of Housing and Local Government, referred to "immigration" as "the hottest potato in politics," and he believed it would be a vote loser for Labour if the party were thought to be "permitting a flood of immigrants to come in and blight the central area of our cities."[33]

Certainly, Crossman's words and the fact that the 1965 White Paper with its tightened restrictions followed Smethwick would appear to suggest the validity of the traditional interpretation: a hostile public pushed an otherwise liberal administration toward ever greater "immigration" control. This is the same picture presented by early histories of the 1945–1962 period, for it was the picture presented by policy makers themselves. As in the immediate postwar years, however, popular sentiment seems unlikely to offer a full explanation. Owing to the thirty-year rule, I had no access to state papers after 1965, but it seems doubtful that policy makers adopted a radically different operational code from that employed in the immediate postwar era. During that period, as we have seen, both Labour and Conservative politicians and the officials under their direction were intent on preventing the settlement of migrants of color and worked steadily to reclassify certain British subjects as immigrants and then as "coloureds." It is difficult to imagine that policy makers became passive in the 1960s. More likely, as the early deliberations on the effectiveness of the 1962 act suggest, they continued to pursue a zero-tolerance policy for additional migrants of color. From this perspective, the increasingly harsh restrictions on migration, together with the various immigration and nationality acts, were driven not by the explosion of "race and immigration" into the electoral arena but by imperatives internal to the governing elite. This is not to deny the reality of popular hostility—many polls and electoral victories suggest a great deal of fear and loathing on the part of white subjects towards subjects of color—but to suggest that its origins may lie equally in the policy-making elite's discourse of nationality and migration, which separated "coloured immigrants" from "white Britons," and in a continuing competition for resources most easily explained, in the absence of any better explanation, by the arrival of visibly different groups.[34] As a result, one may hold that the elite were at least partly responsible for both the initial explosion of "race and immigration" onto the public stage and the subsequent narrowing of the popular British national identity.

Thus, the formation and language of the extreme right-wing political party, the National Front, can be seen in part as a response to the official discourse of "race and immigration." Certainly, its call to protect "our British Native Stock" by terminating "coloured immigration" fits within the same framework as policy makers' concern for the effects of a "coloured element in . . . our own population" and reliance on "British stock" to populate the dominions.[35] In both cases, the language separates the "coloureds" from the British. Likewise, the position of Conservative MP Enoch Powell, usually identified as "extreme," which became synonymous in popular lore with opposition to "coloured immigration" in the 1960s and 1970s actually fell within the realm of established "official" conceptions of British nationality. It is true that his call for repatriation, his stories of old white ladies having excrement pushed through their letterboxes by black men, his dramatic references to the "River Tiber foaming with much blood," and his judgment that Britain "must be mad, literally mad, as a nation to be permitting the annual inflow of some 50,000 dependents" earned him dismissal from Edward Heath's Shadow Cabinet in 1968.[36] Nevertheless, Powell was himself a member of the Cabinet committee that formally decided in favor of legislation in 1961 and later debated the withdrawal of the right of family reunification. Similarly, Powell's most infamous statement—"The West Indian or Indian does not, by being born in England, become an Englishman. In law he becomes a United Kingdom citizen by birth; in fact he is a West Indian or an Asian still"—reflected the perceived communities of Britishness which had guided policy makers' understanding of British nationality since at least 1948.[37] Thus, Powell merely sought to do in 1968 what Attlee, Churchill, Eden, Macmillan, Home, Wilson and their Cabinet colleagues and officials had been trying to do since 1948: protect the domestic community of Britishness from the presumed social impurities carried by subjects of color. And Heath followed in the same tradition, accompanying his dismissal of Powell with the assurance that it was the policy of the Conservative Party that "immigration must be more stringently limited and that immigrants wishing to return to their own countries should be helped financially to do so."[38] Heath thereby placed himself within the discourse of the postwar politics of citizenship which regarded British subjects of color as "outsiders" belonging to "some other nation." Though he would not call for forced repatriation and still insisted on assimilation, Heath's speeches stemmed from the same perspective of separate spheres of nationality as Powell's, and both in turn originated within a framework established by postwar policy makers.

III

This framework received its most concrete addition in the 1960s through the passing of the 1968 Commonwealth Immigrants Act. Rapidly rushed through its parliamentary readings, the act further restricted the automatic right of entry to the UK to UKC citizens who were themselves or who had a parent or grandparent born, adopted, registered or naturalized in the United Kingdom. It was designed to prevent the entry of so-called Kenyan Asians, British subjects and UKC citizens whose ancestors had been encouraged to move from India to Africa in the late nineteenth century to help establish a colonial infrastructure designed to serve the "mother country." The Kenyan government's implementation of an Africanization campaign upon independence in 1963 prompted many to migrate to Britain rather than face continued discrimination. Since their passports were issued by the UK High Commission, rather than a colonial government, they were not subject to the 1962 act. What they faced instead, however, was complete hostility. Richard Crossman's diary records the horror of Cabinet colleagues at the prospect of these "Kenya Asians with British passports" gaining entry.[39] Suggesting that holding a British passport was somehow a technical aspect of far less importance in defining identity than the status of "Kenyan Asian," Crossman's language reinforced policy makers' belief in separate spheres of nationality and different communities of Britishness. Evidently the "Kenyan Asians" were British in law but not in form, unlike Kenyans of European descent, who had been protected by a special Nationality Act in 1964 which ensured their right to return to the United Kingdom.[40] The right of British settlers to return "home" had always been one of the principles of British nationality policy; it was the freedom of movement that held the Commonwealth together as well as an expression of the motherland's obligations to her colonizing children. And yet in 1968, it was applied only to the children who had departed the native territory, not to those who had been adopted into the family as part of imperial expansion.

The Wilson government's treatment of British subjects of color resident in Kenya was condemned by much of the quality press as "racialist" and as a "betrayal," and some contemporaries questioned the authority of one group of citizens to withdraw rights from another. One distinguished barrister of the day summarized the injustice: "In passing [the act], a group of citizens temporarily in office have deprived another group of citizens of a fundamental right of citizenship, the right to enter and live in the only country in which they were legally entitled to do so." A legal scholar remarked that the act "authorises the violation of the duty imposed on the United Kingdom by international law to admit its own citizens." Moreover, it was "a deliberate and not simply an unwitting abandonment of principle."[41] But vocal condemnation achieved little against an official view that depicted the "Kenyan Asians" as so many hordes seeking to take advantage of their passports and gain admission to Britain, where they would inevitably strain the nation's social and economic resources. This view of the "immigrants" prevailed despite the Labour government's earlier recognition that the migrants spoke English, were "familiar with Western ways," and possessed useful skills.[42] It also prevailed despite the political imperatives pertaining twenty years earlier. During the negotiations over Indian independence, the Colonial Office had urged that all "Indians settled within the Empire should be British subjects and therefore owe full allegiance to the Crown." To avoid an irredentist problem, the Colonial Office believed that Indians in Africa and elsewhere should "cease to be able to look to the government of India for protection" and should look only to Britain.[43] Thus, the United Kingdom had seen to it that when the independent Kenyan government instituted its Africanization campaign, the "Kenyan Asians" looked not to New Delhi but to London. As late as 1963, Conservative Home Secretary Henry Brooke had suggested that it would be "out of the question" to subject "UKC citizens of Asian origin" to immigration control. Such an action would not only "be seen to be a discrimination based on racial origin" but "would be tantamount to a denial . . . of one of the basic rights of a citizen, namely to enter the country of which he is a citizen."[44] Likewise, a year later, Wilson's Labour government had reviewed the growing trickle of "Asians" entering Britain from Kenya but, recognizing that "depriving them of their existing rights and status would be difficult to justify," had deferred action until the numbers rose. Four years later, with the introduction of legislation, it would appear (although records are not yet available) that the numbers had reached whatever magic figure was necessary to overcome the government's earlier fear of being seen to revoke citizenship based on "purely racial" motives.[45]

The separate spheres of nationality which had shaped policy-making debates since 1948 were given concrete form in the Heath government's 1971 Immigration Act. By controlling the migration of subjects of color while allowing white subjects to migrate at will, the act solved what had previously been a critical issue for policy makers. As we have seen, throughout the 1950s, legislative action had been inhibited by reluctance to impose border restrictions, which, for form's sake, would have had to be applied universally throughout the Commonwealth and thus would have affected migrants from the old and new Commonwealth alike. In 1962 this difficulty had been circumvented by the discriminatory practice of a nominally universal bill. Nine years later, ministers were sufficiently confident of public support to be able to pass a bill that formally divided British subjects into patrials and nonpatrials and placed nonpatrials on virtually the same footing as aliens. Under the terms of the act as operated, patrials consisted of British subjects and UKC citizens who had themselves or whose parent or grandparent had been born, adopted, naturalized, or registered in the United Kingdom, or UKC citizens who had lived for five years in the UK. British subjects and UKC citizens without this close familial connection or who had not lived in the UK legally for five years (and all aliens) were classified as nonpatrial. Although nonpatrial British subjects living in Britain at the time of the act's passage retained their right to live in the United Kingdom, nonpatrials living outside the United Kingdom could enter only with a work permit, which carried no right to permanent settlement.[46] Since those with ancestors born in the United Kingdom tended to be descendants of UK colonists, patrials were overwhelmingly white. Nonpatrial subjects tended to have ancestors in the colonized lands and tended to be people of color.

Through this reconstruction of subjecthood, the act legally differentiated between the familial community of Britishness composed of the truly British—those descended from white colonizers—and the political community of Britishness composed of individuals who had become British through conquest or domination. The latter community discovered that as a result of the 1971 act their British nationality amounted to little more than a name on a passport and that their access to Britain was restricted in much the same way as it was for aliens. That the communities were separated above all by skin color is evidenced by the fact that though ostensibly passed to control migration into Britain, the 1971 act, by removing controls from patrial British subjects living in the "old dominions" who when identified as "Commonwealth immigrants" had previously been subject to control, actually increased the number of British subjects free to migrate to the UK by several million. Furthermore, just as had been the case in 1948, 1949, and 1962, the Irish were placed within a distinct Irish community of Britishness. Under the terms of the 1971 act, Irish citizens continued to be free from immigration control provided that they entered the United Kingdom from the Common Travel Area, defined as Great Britain, Ireland, the Channel Islands, and the Isle of Man. By 1971 this Irish community of Britishness constituted 1.3 percent of the total population of Great Britain.[47]

This distinction between familial British and political British went undisturbed even by the admission of thirty thousand "Ugandan Asians" in 1972. Following the Ugandan government's Africanization campaign, these British subjects were caught in much the same position as had been their Kenyan compatriots. The major difference was the "Ugandan Asians" were admitted. Their entry was shackled with sufficient qualifiers, however, to make clear that theirs was a special case deserving of exceptional treatment. Prime Minister Heath revealed his assessment of their situation in his request that other Commonwealth countries "share the burden" by accepting some of the migrants for settlement. In short, the "Ugandan Asians" were admitted not because the government recognized them to have rights but because, despite their nonpatrial status, Heath saw little alternative to admitting them. Also admitted were white Rhodesians fleeing the country's transition to majority rule. Since the Rhodesians were patrials, however, their unrecorded and apparently unremarked entry did not result in an "immigration" scare.[48]

Ten years after the Heath government had openly recognized the different communities of Britishness comprised in postwar British nationality, Prime Minister Thatcher introduced a new nationality law prompted by the public's alleged fear "that this country might be rather swamped by people with a different culture."[49] Making explicit the assumptions present in policy-making discussions for over thirty years, Thatcher's words legitimated the notion that migrants of a different culture or color were a threat to British society and hence had no real right to admittance. Following the same line of argument, and further separating Britons into "insiders" and "outsiders," Home Secretary William Whitelaw defended the 1981 British Nationality Act as necessary because some "holders of the present citizenship may not unnaturally be encouraged to believe, despite the immigration laws to the contrary, that they have a right of entry to the United Kingdom."[50]

The 1981 act was intended to remove any such misconceptions. It did so by dividing British nationality into three tiers: British citizenship, British Dependent Territories citizenship, and British Overseas citizenship. British citizenship was largely acquired by former UKC citizens who themselves, or whose parents or grandparents, had been born, adopted, naturalized, or registered in the UK, and former UKC citizens who had been legally settled in the UK for five years. In general terms, legally settled non-UKC citizens who under the terms of the 1948 act had enjoyed the right to be registered as UKC citizens retained the right to register as British citizens for five years. Those choosing not to register retained their settlement rights. British Dependent Territories Citizenship was acquired by former UKC citizens who claimed this same relationship with a UK dependency. British Overseas Citizenship was held largely by nonpatrials and other British subjects who fell into neither of the other categories.[51] With the right of abode in the United Kingdom confined to the first tier, it appeared as though policy makers were reconstructing the British national identity to suit the geographical borders of the United Kingdom. It was not quite this simple, however, for the act gave former patrial British subjects resident in the "old dominions" who did not qualify for British citizenship the lifetime right to migrate to Britain and to register as British citizens. Similarly, the act provided that children born abroad within five years of the Act's commencement to British citizens by descent (a category generally unable to pass on citizenship) retained the right to be registered as British citizens if their grandparental connections would have ensured patrial status but for the passing of the 1981 act.[52] The act also created new criteria of eligibility for British citizenship, ruling that children born in the UK of parents not legally settled, became eligible for British citizenship only after ten years' continuous residence. Thus despite its territorial appearance, these rulings in fact placed greater significance on parentage than on geography and so position the 1981 act within the larger postwar discourse of blood, family, and kith and kin. Likewise, its stratification reflects the separate spheres of nationality present in postwar Britain.

The Conservative government's explanations of the act seem to suggest that Britain was finally giving up its imperial pretensions and settling instead for a domestic familial understanding of Britishness. William Whitelaw believed it time "to dispose of the lingering notion that Britain is somehow a haven for all those whose countries we used to rule."[53] His colleagues apparently agreed, arguing in one case that Britain had no "duty—moral or legal—to the inhabitants of those countries that were formerly in the British Empire."[54] Thus, after more than thirty years of placing limits on the practical rights of British subjects, London formally divided all British subjects into categories perceived to be appropriate to their level of "real" Britishness. As a result, the 1981 act appears to represent the explicit and final reconstruction of British nationality to suit preconceived notions of family and culture. It accepted a narrowly conceived domestic community of Britishness based firmly within the United Kingdom and rejected the broader political community based within the wider empire/commonwealth.

According to Home Secretary Whitelaw, the 1981 act provided "the comprehensive and logical overhaul of our citizenship legislation that has so long been required and which it has long been the absolute duty of the Government of the United Kingdom to introduce."[55] Despite the claim of "logical overhaul," British nationality policy remains confused in places. All three categories of citizen created by the 1981 act may travel on a British passport; all three may seek British consular protection; yet only the first enjoys the right to live in the United Kingdom. Perhaps the greatest irony lies in the common passports carried by all three categories of citizen. The first page of every British passport "requests and requires in the name of Her Majesty all those whom it may concern to allow the bearer to pass freely without let or hindrance and to afford the bearer such assistance and protection as may be necessary." For two categories of British citizen, however, as one journalist has observed "the freedom from let or hindrance comes to an abrupt end if they choose to approach our own island shores."[56]

When the link between center and periphery had been reconfirmed in 1948, the Attlee government had not anticipated that the far distant colonial and imperial lands would one day soon run into Britain's "own island shores." Instead, policy makers expected the colonial periphery and the imperial center to remain in separate geographical spheres for a long time to come. They believed this because they also believed that the empire would retain much of its existing shape for some time to come. Policy makers in the immediate postwar era had been sufficiently flexible to recognize that this basic shape might undergo some adjustment: granting independence within the Commonwealth where appropriate and providing funds for economic development within the empire where necessary. In both cases, however, the policies were based on the assumption that Britain would retain its influence in the areas far into the future. A part of this assumption was the belief that residents of the empire would remain malleable and subject to London's direction. Thus, while it was acceptable for the UK to bring Indian and West Indian servicemen to Britain in order to prosecute the war, it was unacceptable for colonials to undertake this migration themselves. Beginning in 1948, this was precisely what they had done, and by that movement they had brought the periphery onto the very shores of the center. By establishing tiers of citizenship and limiting the right of abode, the 1981 act attempted to restore the space between center and periphery to prevent further unlooked-for merging. By this means, the Conservative administration reconstructed British nationality to suit its conceptions of which Britons in law were true Britons at heart.

IV

These conceptions assumed great importance a year after the act was passed, when the Argentinean government authorized the invasion of the Falkland Islands, a small British colony in the South Atlantic, on 2 April 1982. During the parliamentary debates on the 1981 Nationality Act, representatives from both Houses, and both sides of the House, had fought to bring the Falkland Islands within the area providing for British citizenship. The government refused, however, and although many Falkland Islanders received citizenship through familial connections, many others did not, and the colony itself was classified as a Dependent Territory. This might have been taken as a sign that the islands were of little importance to Britain and the islanders not really regarded as kith and kin with the residents of the United Kingdom.

Nonetheless, confronted by an alien invasion of a British colonial possession, Prime Minister Thatcher marshaled the United Kingdom's defense forces and after several weeks of military engagement defeated Argentina and reclaimed the Falklands for Britain. This much might have been expected of a nation which had so recently identified itself as an imperial power. Less expected was the language employed during the conflict. Thatcher asserted the Falkland Islanders to be "British in stock and tradition." Michael Foot, leader of the Opposition, identified the islanders as "our friends and fellow citizens." And even Enoch Powell urged the government to do all that it could to defend "the British people in this . . . remote portion of British territory."[57] Taking their cue from politicians, popular newspapers called on Britain to protect the "British people" living on the islands, spoke of British kith and kin, and in general used language that suggested the Falkland Islanders were British. Notwithstanding the nationality act that had separated them, there appeared to be a common identity between UK residents and Falkland Islanders.

The Falklands War is revealing on a number of levels. It demonstrates that despite the fiasco of Suez, the wave of independence celebrations throughout the empire, and the entry into the European Community, the British national identity still retained an element of imperialism. The jingoism and the patriotism stemmed from a conviction that the invasion constituted a blow to Britain's imperial pride and therefore had to be staunchly resisted. More interesting, however, is the light shed by the war on the changing nationality of one group of people. Over the course of the previous thirty-four years, the Falkland Islanders had been reconstructed five times. The 1948 Nationality Act confirmed their status as British subjects. Defining them as Commonwealth immigrants, the 1962 act placed limits on their right to migrate to the United Kingdom. The 1971 act reclassified the majority as patrials, making them once again free to enter. The 1981 act reconstructed many into citizens of a British Dependent Territory, and they once again lost the right to migrate to the United Kingdom. And after the war, in 1982, under the terms of a special British Nationality (Falkland Islands) Act, they were redefined as British citizens with all the privileges of migration, residence, and franchise.[58] Although the physical nature of the Falkland Islanders obviously remained constant throughout the course of this thirty-year history, their legal identity had changed with each piece of legislation. Effectively their formal national identity was successively reconstructed to suit the demands of the politics of citizenship in Britain.

A similar story, though with an opposite ending, may be told of the residents of Hong Kong, another small island colony, though this time located in the Far East and home to some three million British subjects of color and three million citizens of China. The nationality of the British subjects had also been reconstructed over the course of the postwar decades, and like the Falkland Islanders, under the terms of the 1981 act, the majority of these British subjects were transformed into citizens of a British Dependent Territory. Also like the Falkland Islanders, they risked losing even this version of British nationality in the face of an imminent takeover by an alien power. In this case, however, there was to be no last minute realization of their true position as first-class British citizens. Rather, a tiered understanding of British nationality had developed. In addition to the twenty thousand residents qualifying for British citizenship through descent, an additional fifty thousand heads of household have received this right through the British Nationality (Hong Kong) Act of 1990. Prompted by the events of Tiananmen Square, many Hong Kong residents were leaving the colony to acquire rights of residency elsewhere—most notably Canada, Australia, and the United States. Fearing that too great an exodus would destabilize Hong Kong's economy, the Thatcher government provided full British citizenship to fifty thousand of the colony's key personnel on the grounds that if the right of abode in Britain was ensured, they would choose to remain in Hong Kong. Eligibility for the schemes was limited to those deemed essential to the maintenance of the colony and included health, legal, and educational professionals, technology experts, businesspeople, members of the disciplinary services and other individuals holding "sensitive" jobs. In short, it was a group described by Home Secretary David Waddington as "carefully chosen and highly qualified."[59] This presentation revisits the image of Britain rifling through the refugee camps of continental Europe to select the most suitable for life in Britain. The remaining 2.5 million or so British Dependent Territory citizens are eligible for a travel document bearing the legend British National (Overseas) and have the right to visit Britain without a visa but have neither residency rights nor access to employment, education, or welfare. This "new form of nationality" was later extended to cover much of the remainder of Hong Kong's population.[60] Meanwhile seven thousand Indians and Pakistanis who are likely to become stateless after 1997 have neither free access nor residency but have the promise of settlement rights should they be forced to leave.

The tiered nationality of the residents of Hong Kong well reflects the communities of Britishness which have governed concepts of British nationality since 1948. White-skinned children of the empire, together with migrants of high utility, have gained entry, while most subjects of color have been excluded. The ostensible reason for casting off the residents of Hong Kong was the number involved—perceived as too many for the United Kingdom to sustain. This particular reconstruction of identity is at odds with a 1949 Cabinet decision that in Hong Kong "every endeavor" was to be made to demonstrate that "life under British rule was preferable to life . . . dominated by communism." Fifty years on, the politics of British citizenship demanded an alternative perspective. Notwithstanding the supposed evils of communism, negotiations for the transfer of power following the end of Britain's lease on the New Territories proceed on the assumption that the majority of Hong Kong residents are to become reconciled to their impending transformation into Chinese nationals.

Residents of other member countries in the European Union have always been aliens under British nationality law. Their nationality has not been reconstructed, but their right to enter the United Kingdom has been altered as the aspirations of the 1957 Treaty of Rome are realized and the free movement of labor develops. Although several MPs contrasted the Thatcher government's treatment of the three million Hong Kong British Dependent Territory citizens with the right of abode enjoyed by 250 million Europeans, for the most part anger at the Treaty of Maastricht concentrated on the potential loss of sovereignty rather than fears of "an alien invasion."[61]

In the 1990s official public statements have made few references to race and culture, but the practical effect of the 1981 act and the contrasting responses toward the residents of the Falkland Islands, Hong Kong, and the European Union reflect the persistence of policy makers' racialized perception of the imperial population. As it had done at the outset, this racialized understanding created a demographic hierarchy with a primary split between center and periphery. White-skinned subjects remained at the core of the British national identity and received the most valuable privilege (to UK policy makers) of the right of abode in the United Kingdom. The "rescue" of the Falkland Islanders from their temporary exclusion from the domestic community of Britishness manifests policy makers' continuing attraction to a community of Britishness based around whiteness. Apart from those gaining right of abode through existing residency, the majority of subjects of color received little of actual value in terms of citizenship and were placed on the periphery. The refusal to accept the British Dependent Territory citizens of Hong Kong as potential residents demonstrates that although an entirely white UK community was now out of the question, successive Conservative administrations still seek to ensure that future additions to the domestic community consist largely of white-skinned people.

V

In addition to the contrasting treatment of the Falkland and Hong Kong islands, recent years have revealed another facet of the politics of citizenship. The great efforts put into winning Olympic medals and international trophies suggest that sporting achievements are perceived to add much to a nation's prestige. One area of effort in which the United Kingdom has excelled over the past several years has been in identifying the "true" Britishness of the children of its former colonists. Hence, for Zola Budd, born in South Africa but with a grandfather born in England, the qualifying period for registration as a British citizen was reduced to only twenty-three days in order that she could compete in the 1984 Los Angeles Olympics. In a similar manner, UK fans at Wimbledon in 1995 seemed gratified at the third-round success of British tennis player Greg Rusedski. Yet Rusedski's Britishness consisted of a life spent in Canada as a child of a German-born father and a UK-born mother. In recognizing the true Britishness of all those who hold or could hold British passports, the Home Office might be deemed to be acting expansively and honorably. The circumstances surrounding the sports players' realization of Britishness, however, suggests that it had more to do with convenience than allegiance. Admitting that her "sole motive was to run internationally," Budd later claimed to have "had no affinity for" Britain at the time of the Los Angeles Olympics. Similarly, a former captain of the English Test cricket side pronounced himself to be "a loyal South African" but admitted to a "burning ambition to play Test cricket."[62] In both cases, whereas apartheid and a South African passport denied international competition to these individuals, playing under a Union Jack transformed them into acceptable competitors.

At the same time as the politics of citizenship has been expansive, however, it has also been exclusive, suggesting, as ever, that some potential Britons and indeed some Britons are more British than others. In the 1980s, Cabinet Minister Norman Tebbit introduced the so-called "cricket test," which suggested that a Pakistan-born migrant watching a cricket match between Pakistan and England could not be regarded as assimilated if he [*sic*] cheered for the land of his birth. Taking this test one step further, a freelance contributor to the bible of cricketing, *Wisden Cricket Monthly*, asked whether "an Asian or negro raised in England will . . . feel exactly the same pride and identification with the place as a white man." Answering his own question, the author suggested that in fact a "coloured England-qualified player" will likely share the same "resentful and separatist mentality" as "the general West Indian–derived population" and thus is unlikely to play with the same commitment as those who are "unequivocally English." The general conclusion of the article suggested not only that "interlopers" play with less than full "instinctive" enthusiasm themselves but that their presence undermines the "team spirit" and "camaraderie" of the "unequivocally English players."[63]

The article generated a considerable amount of discussion, with all the major newspapers running stories in response. Most pertinent was the journalist who observed that what was apparently "an esoteric debate about who does and does not belong in the England Test side" was in fact about "who does and does not have a right to live and work in Britain."[64] The incident demonstrates that black Britons, whether sporting heroes or not, still must endure a question mark over their status as "true Britons." As Linford Christie, the sprinter, observed, "As a winner I'm from Great Britain. When I lose sometimes I'm called a native of Jamaica."[65] This potential for flexibility and shifting boundaries exists because there is a perception, based on decades of reconstructive language and a succession of immigration and nationality laws, that black-skinned people are generally immigrants and that immigrants are less than fully British. The same assumptions apply when after claiming England as home, black Britons are pestered as to their "true" origins. Commenting on the *Wisden* article, Gary Younge discussed the frequency with which black Britons must "qualify their nationality." "Asked 'Where are you from?' He answers, 'Hertfordshire.' They ask, 'But before then?' He replies, 'I was born there.' They persist 'Well, where are your parents from?' 'Barbados.' 'Oh so you're from Barbados.' He responds, 'No I'm from Hertfordshire.' "[66]

Again, the qualifying of national identity derives from almost fifty years of manipulation of the politics of citizenship in Britain. A bright side to the debate may be that the journalistic response to *Wisden*'s article was so overwhelmingly negative that the editor subsequently had to apologize for its publication. This response suggests that whatever the internal politics of citizenship, and however close to the internal political discourse of the 1950s, in 1995 it was no longer acceptable to question the patriotism of black Britons publicly, particularly those whose sporting prowess reflects well upon England. This must surely be recognized as an advance of sorts.[67]

VI

The politics of citizenship in postwar Britain is the politics of contradiction and competition. Over the course of the past five decades, succeeding Labour and Conservative administrations have renegotiated the composition of subjecthood and citizenship throughout the empire and within the United Kingdom. In this process, formal definitions of citizenship increasingly have had less influence than racialized images of national identity. Thus skin color and the races which were presumed to follow came to be perceived as natural dividers of peoples, and the common nationality of Britishness came to be seen as a mistake that could be corrected through legislation. As a result of this racialized understanding of nationality, each of the four demographic groups examined in this book underwent a different migration experience. Consequently Britain since 1945 has been home to several communities of Britishness, reflecting distinctly separate spheres of nationality. Within a formal nationality policy that accepted all as equal were layers that distinguished between members and potential members of a domestic community of Britishness, members of a familial imperial community, members of an Irish community, and members of a purely political community of Britishness. Although each of the communities contributed to the changing face of British society during the postwar period, it is the members of this last political community who have suffered the most for their part in the process. More succinctly, British subjects and citizens of color, constituting just under 5.5 percent of the total population in 1991, appear to have borne the brunt of elite and popular anger that the Britain of 1995 is not the Britain of 1945.[68] This suffering was experienced both by those whose British passport proved insufficient as an entry voucher and by those who gained admission only to discover that they did so against the wishes of the policy-making elite. For despite official sanction for integration, the passing of ever narrower nationality and migration laws suggests that theirs is an unwanted and contested presence. As a result, just as alien guestworkers demand the rights of citizenship in continental Europe, so in Britain black Britons must fight for the right to identify themselves as British.

On the contested terrain of British nationality I have outlined, certain measures seem appropriate. First, politicians and officials must recognize that the vision of a singular fixed national identity for all British citizens, of whatever gender, class, or race is as unreal on the verge of the twenty-first century as it was at the end of the Second World War. Second, the various communities within Britain must overcome the divisions that separate them and recognize that the claim to Britishness belongs to all for whom the island is home. And third, a new flexible and inclusive definition of Britishness would more accurately reflect the current demographic makeup of Britain and would not need to be qualified for those born in Britain of parents or grandparents born in the former colonies. While all citizens (and subjects) must participate in this construction of an inclusive identity, a leading role must be played by those with the power to set an example, both in the code of law and through official practice. For only when the concept of Britishness is redefined to include all the competing communities of Britishness and to reconcile separate spheres of nationality, can Britain truly be said to be providing equal citizenship and membership for all.

Notes

Preface

1. In popular understanding, skin color is commonly seen as a signifier of race, as though race were an absolute and natural feature of human society. I do not accept this view. I contend, rather, that race is a social construct, not biological. For the sake of clarity, however, and given the frequency with which the term appears in the text, I have refrained from placing the word *race* within the quotation marks that would indicate my skepticism about it.

2. This literature is useful for its concern with broad questions about how we should define membership and participation in society. See especially William R. Brubaker, ed., *Immigration and the Politics of Citizenship in Europe and North America* (Lanham, Md.: University Press of America, 1989); J. M. Barbelet, *Citizenship* (Minneapolis: University of Minnesota Press, 1988); Michael Walzer, *Spheres of Justice* (New York: Basic Books, 1983); Zig Layton-Henry, *The Political Rights of Migrant Workers in Western Europe* (London: Sage, 1990); Joseph Carens, "Aliens and Citizens: The Case for Open Borders," *Review of Politics* (Spring 1987); Gary Freeman, "Migration and the Political Economy of the Welfare State," *Annals of the American Academy of Political and Social Science* 485 (May 1986).

3. Joseph Carens, "Membership and Morality: Admission to Citizenship in Liberal Democratic States," in *Immigration*, ed. Brubaker, pp. 31–49.

4. Thomas Hammar, "Dual Citizenship and Political Integration," *International Migration Review* 19 (Fall 1985): 3.

5. Brubaker, Introduction to *Immigration*, p. 11.

Introduction. The Road from 1945

1. Labour's commitment to the empire/commonwealth as a means of supporting an international role is most clearly described in William Roger

Louis, *The British Empire in the Middle East, 1945-1951* (Oxford: Clarendon Press, 1984); P. S. Gupta, *Imperialism and the British Labour Movement, 1914-1965* (New York: Holmes and Meier, 1975); Ritchie Ovendale, ed., *The Foreign Policy of the British Labour Governments* (Leicester: Leicester University Press, 1988); Kenneth O. Morgan, *Labour in Power, 1945-1951* (Oxford: Oxford University Press, 1984); Peter Weiler, "British Labour and the Cold War: The Foreign Policy of the Labour Governments, 1945-1951," *Journal of British Studies* 26 (January 1987): 54-82; Peter Weiler, *British Labour and the Cold War* (Stanford, Calif.: Stanford University Press, 1988).

2. FO371/50912 Memorandum by Sir Orme Sargent, 11 July 1945, cited in John Kent, *British Imperial Strategy and the Origins of the Cold War, 1944-1949* (Leicester: Leicester University Press, 1993). Except where otherwise stated, all archival records are located at the Public Records Office, Kew. The current policy in Britain is to make the records available for public viewing only after a minimum of thirty years has passed since the operational date.

3. On British policy makers' use of the sterling area, see P. S. Gupta, "Imperialism and the Labour Government of 1945-51," in *The Working Class in Modern British History: Essays in Honor of Henry Pelling*, ed. Jay Winter (Cambridge: Cambridge University Press, 1983), pp. 99-124. See also D. K. Fieldhouse, "The Labour Governments and the Empire-Commonwealth," in *Foreign Policy of the British Labour Governments*, ed. Ovendale, pp. 83-120. Britain's "economic Dunkirk" was starkly cited in CAB129/1 CP(45)112 Our Overseas Financial Prospects, 14 August 1945, quoted in Kenneth O. Morgan, *The People's Peace* (Oxford: Oxford University Press, 1990), p. 65. See also David Marquand, "Sir Stafford Cripps," in *Age of Austerity*, ed. Michael Sissons and Philip French (London: Penguin, 1963), pp. 173-96.

4. Nicholas Mansergh, *The Commonwealth Experience* (New York: Praeger, 1969); W. David McIntyre, *The Commonwealth of Nations: Origins and Impact, 1869-1971* (Minneapolis: University of Minnesota Press, 1977).

5. Although this new friendship was not formalized until the ANZUS pact of 1951, clearly the foundations rested on the ruins of Singapore. The chairman of the Australian Republican Movement, Thomas Keneally, cited the fall of Singapore as the occasion when Australia realized that its future could no longer be secured solely under a "British umbrella." *Guardian Weekly*, 10 October 1993.

6. John Darwin, *Britain and Decolonization: The Retreat from Empire in the Postwar World* (New York: St. Martin's Press, 1988), pp. 46-47.

7. CAB129/20 CP(47)242, 23 August 1947, cited in Gupta, "Imperialism and the Labour Government," p. 107. Malaya, for example, exported rubber to the United States but was unable to benefit directly from the dollars earned.

8. For an analysis of the full ramifications of this idea, see John Kent, "Bevin's Imperialism and the Idea of Euro-Africa, 1945-49," in *British Foreign Policy, 1945-56*, ed. Michael Dickerill and John W. Young (New York: St. Martin's, 1989), pp. 47-76.

9. CAB129/30 Cabinet Committee on Commonwealth Relations, 4th Report, 21 July 1948, and Draft Statement of Principles; FO800/444 Attlee to Cabinet members, 14 May 1947.

10. Richard A. Soloway, *Demography and Degeneration: Eugenics and the Declining Birthrate in Twentieth-Century Britain* (Chapel Hill: University of North Carolina, 1990), pp. 229, 241–42; *Times*, 9 June 1943.

11. Sir William Beveridge, *Social Insurance and Allied Services*, Cmd. 6404 (London: HMSO, 1942), para. 413.

12. *Parliamentary Debates* (Commons), 5th ser. [1943], v. 391, c. 554, 16 July 1943.

13. *Times*, 15 February 1943.

14. *Times*, 14 June 1945.

15. *Times*, 17 February, 9 June 1943.

16. University of Warwick, Modern Records Centre, TUC Papers, MSS 292/107.5/1 TUC to M. Oliver, 18 October 1945.

17. TUC Papers, MSS 292/107.5/1 National Conference of Trade Union Executives on Production and Manpower, 19 February 1946.

18. CAB129/6 CP(46)32, 30 January 1946, CP(46)35, 1 February 1946; CAB134/301 Foreign Labour Committee, 1st meeting, 14 March 1946. The economic survey forecast a labor shortage of 1.3 million, and the Manpower Committee, less pessimistically, 600,000.

19. *Economic Survey for 1947*, Cmd. 7046 (London: HMSO, 1947), paras. 60–61.

20. CAB129/6 CP(47)20, 7 January 1947.

21. LAB13/257 Isaacs to Arthur Greenwood, Lord Privy Seal, 17 April 1947.

22. CAB134/301 memorandum by Foreign Labour Committee, 14 May 1946.

23. *Report of the Royal Commission on Population*, CMD 7695 (London: HMSO, 1949), paras. 158, 289, 321.

24. *Daily Graphic and Sketch*, 24 January, 11, 13 February 1947.

25. Morgan, *Labour in Power*, pp. 144–50, 341–46.

26. *The Political Diary of Hugh Dalton 1918–40, 1945–60*, ed. Ben Pimlott (London: Jonathan Cape, 1986). See, for example, the entry for 8 August 1947. Dalton felt sufficiently strongly that he threatened to resign unless cuts were made. See also Teddy Brett, Steve Gilliatt, and Andrew Pople, "Planned Trade, Labour Party Policy, and US Intervention: The Successes and Failures of Post-war Reconstruction," *History Workshop* 13 (Spring 1982): 131–42. Brett et al. suggest that "it was the policy of defending the Atlantic Alliance and the Empire which, in fact, incurred the very heavy unproductive costs which reduced the rate of reinvestment and constantly rendered the country vulnerable to balance of payments deficits and the outflow of capital." Peter Weiler suggests that Labour's initial commitment to empire and the American alliance instead of Europe represents "the lost opportunity of the period." Peter Weiler, *Ernest Bevin* (Manchester: Manchester University Press, 1993), p. 166.

27. Jim Tomlinson, "Labour and the Trade Unions, 1945–51," in *The Attlee Years*, ed. Nick Tiratsoo (London: Pinter, 1991), pp. 90–105. A detailed analysis of the role of economic planning within the Attlee governments is to be found in James E. Cronin, *The Politics of State Expansion: War, State, and Society in Twentieth-Century Britain* (London: Routledge, 1991), pp. 153–87. Cronin concludes that Labour presided over "real and sustained" economic recovery in the immediate postwar years but suggests the recovery may have come at the cost of future radical innovations to the economy.

28. CAB128/9 CM8(47), 16 January 1947, CM14(47), 30 January 1947.

29. TUC Papers, MSS292/107.5/1 "Publicity in Relation to Manpower Programmes," no date; *Daily Graphic and Sketch*, 4 January 1947. "Lend a Hand on the Land" volunteers were urged to spend their vacation working on farms helping to bring in the potato harvest. In return for such work they received pay, room and board, reduced railway fares, and recreational facilities. TUC Papers, MSS292/107.5/1, National Conference of Trade Union Executives on Production and Manpower, 19 February 1946; CAB134/469 Secretary of State for Scotland, 5 December 1947.

30. TUC Papers, MSS292/107.5/1 "Publicity in Relation to Manpower Programmes," no date.

31. LAB12/513 Cripps' Press Conference, 29 January 1948. "The mill girl of today," announced Cripps, "is rightly not content with the clog and shawl, she wants to look and can look as attractive as any other girl in the country."

32. Janice Winship, "Nation before Family: *Woman*, the National Home Weekly, 1945–1953," in *Formations of Nation and People* (London: Routledge and Kegan Paul, 1984). Winship contends that the dual role expected of women during wartime extended into the postwar period as women were expected to be both workers and feminine. They were encouraged to look beyond their immediate home circle only so long as it benefited their larger family—the nation. Within the workplace, women continued to receive lower wages than men. In 1949, for example, even as desperate as the Cabinet was to find more nurses, it was reluctant to raise wages as a means of attracting labor for fear that raising female wages would necessitate a similar rise in male wages in order to "preserve some differential between men and women." CAB 128/15 CM 26(49).

33. *Dalton Diary*, 2 October 1947.

34. TUC Papers, MSS292/107.17/4 Joint Consultative Committee, Ministry of Labour, Control of Labour, November 1949, Control of Engagement Order Quiz, October 1947.

35. CAB128/12 CM1(48), 6 January 1948; TUC Papers, MSS292/107.17/4 Ministry of Labour, National Joint Advisory Committee, Review of the Operation of the Control of Engagement Order, October 1948.

36. CAB134/469 LC(47)3, 1 December 1947.

Chapter 1. Subjects and Citizens

1. Ann Dummett and Andrew Nicol, *Subjects, Citizens, Aliens, and Others: Nationality and Immigration Law* (London: Weidenfeld and Nicolson, 1990), pp. 62–67. Labour Home Secretary Herbert Morrison confirmed this precedent during a 1950 parliamentary debate when he declared that "no one has a legal right to a passport" and that all passports remained the property of the issuer and could be impounded at will. *Parliamentary Debates* (Commons), 5th ser., [1950], v. 474, c. 1895. Part of the following discussion draws on material in Kathleen Paul, "British Subjects and 'British Stock': Labour's Post-war Imperialism," *Journal of British Studies* 34 (April 1995): 233–76.

2. HO213/360 Cabinet Memorandum E(B)(30)4, 2d Report of the Inter-departmental Committee on Inter-imperial Relations, 26 June 1930. For clarity, I confine my discussion to British subjects and do not consider the position of individuals residing outside the formal empire who occupy the intermediary status of British Protected Persons.

3. Dummett and Nicol, *Subjects, Citizens*, p. 125.

4. *Parliamentary Debates* (Commons), 5th ser., [1914], v. 62, c. 1201, British Nationality and Status of Aliens Act, 7 August 1914.

5. HO213/360 Cabinet Memorandum E(B)(30), 22 August 1930, Cabinet Memorandum E(B)(30)4, 2d Report of the Inter-departmental Committee on Inter-imperial Relations, 26 June 1930.

6. HO213/360 Note on the Discussions in 1929 and 1930 on the Subject of Nationality, 2 March 1934. The conference declared that "the Members of the British Commonwealth are united by a common allegiance to the Crown, this allegiance being the basis of the common status now possessed by all subjects of His Majesty" in accordance with the 1914 British Nationality and Status of Aliens Act. It is difficult to know precisely what prompted the previously "extreme" dominions to concede the primacy of British subjecthood over dominion citizenship but perhaps one clue might be found in the decision by UK officials to emphasize at the conference the international hardships that would accrue to dominion states should their nationals no longer be regarded as British subjects. These hardships ranged from the forfeiture of extraterritorial jurisdiction in certain foreign countries in favor of treatment under the ordinary criminal code; exclusion from the benefits of commercial treaties currently concluded by the United Kingdom on behalf of all British subjects; denial of protection abroad from British consulates; and the loss of privileges within the Commonwealth currently enjoyed by British subjects. HO213/360 Cabinet Memorandum E(B)(30)4, 2d Report of the Inter-departmental Committee on Inter-imperial Relations, 26 June 1930.

7. A Home Office official observed that "if the United Kingdom wishes to be regarded as a parent nation in the sense which none of the Dominions are it must expect, like parents, to show a consideration in which is not alto-

gether returned." HO213/360 C. G. Markbreiter to Sir Oscar Dowson, 19 May 1937.

8. *Parliamentary Debates* (Commons), 5th ser., [1914], v. 65, c. 1464. During the debate on the 1948 Nationality Bill, one MP resisted the reform of this ruling on the grounds that it represented "a real misunderstanding of the essential nature either of marriage or of nationality to suppose that a woman married to a foreigner, could in every sense and completely, preserve her devotion to the British Crown." *Parliamentary Debates* (Commons), 5th ser., [1948], v. 453, c. 458. Illegitimate children, who took their British mother's nationality, were the exception to paternal transmission. Francesca Klug, " 'Oh to Be in England': The British Case Study," in *Woman-Nation-State*, ed. Nira Yuval-Davis and Floya Anthias (New York: St. Martin's Press, 1989), pp. 16–36.

9. The presumptions that women would be married, not participating in the paid labor force, and economically linked to the state through their employed husbands were incorporated in to the postwar welfare state. See Sir William Beveridge, *Social Insurance and Allied Services*, Cmd. 4606 (London: HMSO, 1942); Carole Pateman, "The Patriarchal Welfare State," in *Democracy and the Welfare State*, ed. Amy Gutman (Princeton: Princeton University Press, 1988); Jane Lewis, ed., *Women's Welfare: Women's Rights* (London: Croom Helm, 1983). Following the same assumptions, the Royal Commission on Population reluctantly acquiesced in the limited, controlled immigration of alien men as a partial, short-term solution to the labor shortage while viewing British women almost exclusively as actual or potential mothers. *Report of the Royal Commission on Population*. Cmd. 7695 (London: HMSO, 1949), paras. 329–37, 401–6.

10. Anna Davin, "Imperialism and Motherhood," *History Workshop* 5 (Spring 1978).

11. Richard A. Soloway, *Demography and Degeneration: Eugenics and the Declining Birthrate in Twentieth-Century Britain* (Chapel Hill: University of North Carolina, 1990), pp. 38–59.

12. T. H. Marshall, "Citizenship and Social Class," in *Class, Citizenship, and Social Development* (New York: Doubleday, 1964).

13. Robert Miles, *Racism* (London: Routledge, 1989), p. 75. See also Bob Carter and Marci Green, " 'Races' and 'Race-Makers': The Politics of Racialisation," *Sage Race Relations Abstracts* 13, no. 2 (London, 1988); and Miles's earlier *Racism and Migrant Labour* (London: Routledge and Kegan Paul, 1982).

14. One example of administrative controls was the Coloured Alien Seamen Order, which purported to distinguish between alien and British seamen but, in fact, was intended to prohibit the landing of black British seamen in Britain. For a more detailed examination of the government's treatment of seamen, see Laura Tabili, "The Construction of Racial Differences in Twentieth Century Britain: The Special Restriction (Coloured Alien Seamen) Order, 1925," *Journal of British Studies* 33 (January 1994): 54–98.

15. Raphael Samuel's three-volume collection of essays, *Patriotism: The Making and Unmaking of British National Identity* (London: Routledge, 1989), provides examples of groups and individuals whose formal equality was compromised by practical inequality. See particularly Dave Douglass, "C Stream on Tyneside," pp. 43–56, Anne Summers, "Pride and Prejudice in the Crimean War," pp. 57–78, David Feldman, "Jews in London, 1880–1914," pp. 207–29. Discrimination faced by subjects of color within an imperial context is detailed in James Walvin, *Black and White: The Negro in English Society, 1555–1945* (London: Penguin, 1973); Peter Fryer, *Staying Power: The History of Black People in Britain* (Atlantic Highlands, N.J.: Humanities Press, 1984); Paul B. Rich, *Race and Empire in British Politics*, 2d ed. (Cambridge: Cambridge University Press, 1990).

16. On the construction and contestation of the notion of "Britishness," see Eric Hobsbawm and Terence Ranger, eds., *The Invention of Tradition* (Cambridge: Cambridge University Press, 1992); Linda Colley, *Britons: Forging the Nation, 1707–1837* (New Haven: Yale University Press, 1992); Robert Colls and Philip Dodd, eds., *Englishness: Politics and Culture, 1880–1920* (London: Croom Helm, 1986); Patrick Wright, *On Living in an Old Country: The National Past in Contemporary Britain* (London: Verso, 1985).

17. PREM8/851 CP(45)287, 16 November 1945.

18. PREM8/851 Norman Brook to Attlee, 21 November 1945.

19. PREM8/851 CP(45)287, 16 November 1945, Canadian Citizenship Bill.

20. Dummett and Nicol suggest that the act "bore all the marks of a plan devised piecemeal to deal with each technical problem as it came up, rather than one based on any clear, guiding theory." *Subjects, Citizens*, p. 134. Similarly, J. M. Evans concentrates exclusively on the technical changes brought about by the act, entirely missing the political implications and debates. *Immigration Law*, 2d ed. (London: Sweet and Maxwell, 1983). Clive Parry suggests that the "common code" was already so fragmented that the 1948 act merely constituted one more change. *Nationality and Citizenship: Laws of the Commonwealth and Ireland* (London: Stevens and Sons, 1957).

21. PREM8/851 CP(45)287, 16 November 1945, Canadian Citizenship Bill.

22. At the time, the rather clumsy term "belonging to" had to be used to differentiate between those British subjects in whose name the treaty was being concluded (generally those resident in the United Kingdom) and the larger class of British subjects resident elsewhere in the empire. PREM8/851 CP(45)287, 16 November 1945, Canadian Citizenship Bill; PREM8/851 CM(45)55, 22 November 1945.

23. PREM8/851 CP(46)305 Changes in British Nationality Law, Joint Memorandum by the Home Secretary and the Secretary of State for Dominion Affairs, 29 July 1946.

24. PREM8/851 CP(45)287, 16 November 1945, Canadian Citizenship Bill.

25. PREM8/851 CP(46)305 Changes in British Nationality Law, Joint Memorandum by the Home Secretary and the Secretary of State for Dominion Affairs, 29 July 1946.

26. Ibid.

27. HO213/202 Cabinet Memorandum, Changes in British Nationality Law, 13 July 1946.

28. PREM8/851 CP(46)331 British Nationality Law, Memorandum by the Secretary of State for the Home Department, 30 August 1946.

29. PREM8/851 CM(46)80, 9 September 1946.

30. PREM8/851 CP(45)287, 16 November 1945, Canadian Citizenship Bill.

31. *Parliamentary Debates* (Commons), 5th ser., [1948], v. 454, c. 48–49, v. 453 (1948), c. 495.

32. Ibid., v. 453, c. 393–98.

33. *Parliamentary Debates* (Lords), 5th ser., (1948), v. 155, c. 762.

34. PREM8/851 CP(48)120 British Nationality Bill, memorandum by the Home Secretary and the Secretary of State for Commonwealth Relations, 4 May 1948; PREM8/851 CM(48)31, 6 May 1948.

35. HO213/202 Foreign Office memorandum, Changes in British Nationality Law: The Question of United Kingdom and Colonial Citizenship, 5 July 1946.

36. HO213/202 Colonial Office Memorandum, British Nationality Proposals for Change in the Law, 5 July 1946. The Colonial Office repeated this argument in CAB130/13 Committee on British Nationality, 1st meeting, 7 August 1946.

37. HO213/200 3d meeting of the Interdepartmental Working Party on British Nationality, 17 May 1946. In resisting the combined UKC option, Sir Oscar Dowson, Home Office chair of the working party, was reiterating the contents of a letter he had received almost a decade previously in which a Home Office colleague had described the idea of packaging the United Kingdom and Colonies as a "distinct class" as "palpably absurd, since among this group of persons is a greater diversity than in the rest of the Empire taken together." HO213/360 Markbreiter to Dowson, 19 May 1937.

38. HO213/202 Colonial Office Memorandum, British Nationality Proposals for Change in the Law, 5 July 1946.

39. HO213/202 Cabinet, Changes in British Nationality Law, Part III, The Question of United Kingdom and Colonial Citizenship, Dowson to Sir Alexander Maxwell, 13 July 1946. The working party suggested that dominion residents might also be granted this option in order to avoid the "unfortunate" appearance that a Jamaican was being privileged over an Australian. This advice was given even though the practical difference between a UK citizen and a British subject was nil.

40. HO213/200 6th meeting of the Interdepartmental Working Party on British Nationality, 15 July 1946.

41. CO323/1869/11 Colonial Office minute, no date. Titles that in-

cluded a reference to Britain or Great Britain were thought particularly unsuitable for the offense they would give to the residents of Northern Ireland, part of the United Kingdom but not part of Great Britain.

42. Dummett and Nicol cite the technical nature of the so-called Experts' Conference as evidence of the perceived unimportance of the 1948 act. *Subjects, Citizens*, p. 134.

43. *Parliamentary Debates* (Commons), 5th ser., [1948], v. 453, c. 483.

44. Ibid., v. 453, c. 417, v. 454, c. 83.

45. Ibid., v. 453, c. 401, 410, 1027–28, 1033.

46. Ibid. (Lords), v. 155, c. 784, 788.

47. Ibid. (Commons), v. 453, c. 417.

48. Ibid., v. 453, c. 393–98.

49. Ibid., v. 453, c. 394–98, (Lords), v. 155, c. 757.

50. Miles, *Racism*.

51. *Parliamentary Debates* (Commons), 5th ser., [1948], v. 453, c. 1042–47.

52. Darwin, *Britain and Decolonization*, p. 139.

53. PREM8/851 CM(45)55, 22 November 1945.

54. *Parliamentary Debates* (Lords), 5th ser., [1948], v. 155, c. 758–62.

Chapter 2. Emigrating British Stock

1. Annual figures fluctuated according to specific stimuli. In the immediate postwar years, for example, emigration totals were heavily inflated by the departure of war brides to the United States. In 1957 the departure of Hungarian and Egyptian immigrants, together with an aggressive immigration campaign by the Canadian government, raised the year's figure to 230,000.

2. Howard Malchow, *Population Pressures: Emigration and Government in Late 19th-Century Britain* (Palo Alto, Calif.: Society for the Promotion of Science and Scholarship, 1979); D. V. Glass and P. A. M. Taylor, eds., *Population and Emigration in Nineteenth-Century Britain* (Dublin: Irish University Press, 1976); H. J. M. Johnston, *British Emigration Policy, 1815–1830* (Oxford: Clarendon Press, 1972); Eric Richards, "How Did Poor People Emigrate from the British Isles to Australia in the Nineteenth Century?" *Journal of British Studies* 32 (July 1993): 250–79.

3. Three-quarters of the emigration passages between 1850 and 1914 were paid for by relatives overseas, leaving the last quarter to be financed by charitable organizations, landlord assistance, independent effort, and government funding—the last constituting a very small portion of the whole.

4. The Poor Law Amendment Act in 1834, for example, had allowed local authorities to use up to half the rates revenue to assist in the emigration of such residents.

5. Charlotte Erickson, *Emigration from Europe, 1815–1914: Select Documents* (London: Adam and Charles Black, 1976), pp. 169–70.

6. The *Freeman's Journal*, a newspaper catering to middle-class farmers

in Ireland, asked plaintively how land, fisheries, and industry could be made productive when "labour becomes scarcer and dearer by the further depletion of the population." *Freeman's Journal*, 1 March, 16, 28 April 1883.

7. Erickson, *Emigration*, p. 131.

8. "Outposts of Empire" was the term used by the Assistant High Commissioner to Australia, W. J. Garnett. DO35/835 Assisted Migration, 25 July 1950.

9. LAB13/199 Migration to Australia—Possible Size of Movement, Spring 1946; DO35/6379 Final Report of the Oversea Migration Board, July 1954.

10. Quoted by Garnett, DO35/835 Assisted Migration, 25 July 1950. Successive imperial conferences in 1923 and 1930 affirmed United Kingdom and dominion commitment to emigration as significant to the well-being of the empire. Stephen Constantine, ed., *Emigrants and Empire: British Settlement in the Dominions between the Wars* (Manchester: Manchester University Press, 1990).

11. DO35/4877 Report of the Inter-departmental Committee on Migration Expenditure. Total emigration for the period 1922–31 was 1.5 million, approximately 150,000 per annum.

12. *Report of the Oversea Settlement Board*, Cmd. 5766 (London: HMSO, May, 1938).

13. PREM4/421 Prime Minister's Memo, 20 October 1942, Dominions Office Memo, 28 October 1942.

14. PREM4/421 Prime Minsters' Meeting, 12 May 1944. Four years later Bevin again proposed demobilization in the dominions as a means of increasing "good British stock" there. The Ministry of Defence rejected the plan on practical grounds. FO800/444 A. V. Alexander to Clement Attlee, 22 April, 24 June 1948; Ernest Bevin to Attlee, 22 April 1948.

15. PREM4/421 Prime Ministers' Meeting, 12 May 1944.

16. PREM4/421 Paymaster General to Prime Minister, 26 April 1944.

17. PREM4/421 WH(45)46, 16 April 1945.

18. *Migration within the British Commonwealth*, Cmd. 6658 (London: HMSO, 1945).

19. PREM8/1479 CM(45)40, 11 October 1945.

20. LAB13/199 Overseas Settlement in Southern Rhodesia; LAB13/204 E. C. F. Whitehead, Southern Rhodesian Minister of Finance, 5 April 1947. Southern Rhodesia's scheme aimed initially for an intake of 100 per month, although this number was expected to increase as more shipping became available.

21. In 1948 prospective migrants and their employers both had to provide financial guarantees, and it was no longer possible for emigrants to enter Southern Rhodesia in search of work. Thus immigration was effectively confined to those with guaranteed employment or with proven individual resources—£1,500 capital or an annual income of £500. Salisbury was particularly keen to ensure that incoming white migrants were of sufficient financial

health to enable them to live above the standard of living of black indigenous labor. LAB13/281 Ministry of Labour Review of Migration Policy, 1949; DO35/4877 Report of the Interdepartmental Committee on Migration Expenditure.

22. LAB13/204 Record of a Meeting at the Commonwealth Relations Office, September 27, 1950. Southern Rhodesian officials stated that the UK proportion of total immigration to Southern Rhodesia had fallen from 50 percent in 1948 to 22 percent in the first six months of 1950, LAB13/204, Memorandum: Immigration, 8 September 1950.

23. LAB13/204 L. B. Walsh Atkins to A. D. Chataway, 10 October 1950; LAB13/204 Assisted Passages for Settlers after Screening, 13 July 1951; LAB13/204 Meeting at Rhodesia House, 24 August 1951. Reflective perhaps of who were deemed to be "British stock," the scheme was open to UK and Eire residents alike.

24. CAB129/107 C(61)201, 1 December 1961, British Emigration Policy: Memorandum by the Secretary of State for Commonwealth Relations.

25. LAB13/281 Joint Memorandum by the Commonwealth Relations Office and the Ministry of Labour and National Service, Problems of Emigration from the United Kingdom with Particular Reference to Movement to the Commonwealth, June, 1950. LAB13/281 Ministry of Labour Review of Migration Policy, 1949; LAB13/835 Report of the Interdepartmental Committee on Migration Policy, 12 December 1950. See also LAB13/835 Note, 1 September 1950.

26. DO35/4877 Report of the Interdepartmental Committee on Migration Expenditure. Separate figures were not recorded for Southern Rhodesia and South Africa until 1948. Thus the total of 105,002 for the period 1946–53 includes, for 1946 and 1947, those UK residents emigrating to Southern Rhodesia as well as those to South Africa. LAB13/30 Reference Paper on Migration, 2/1961.

27. PREM4/421 Prime Ministers' Meeting, 12 May 1944; LAB13/199 Oversea Settlement in the Dominions. Australia and Britain initially shared financial responsibility for the Assisted Passage Scheme, but as the costs increased and Britain's financial position worsened, Australia took on a larger share. Britain paid all the costs associated with the Free Passage Scheme since it was regarded as a resettlement bonus.

28. LAB13/434 Oversea Settlement in Australia, 1950–1953: Commonwealth Hostel Arrangements in Conjunction with the Free and Assisted Passage Schemes. Approved industries included iron, steel, and brick production; construction; engineering; mining; general manufacture. UK policy makers were never too keen on the scheme, disliking the idea of British emigrants living in hostels and being tied to particular employment. The ministry disliked this prospect as much for its own sake as for the fate of the migrants, fearing that the ministry would be blamed if "British migrants find themselves stranded in hostels, and uncongenial work, with no prospects of escape." The ministry believed that such criticism would be partly justified since "we are

too closely associated with the financing and organization of the schemes not to be considered in some degree to have underwritten their success." LAB13/ 434 R. F. Keith to G. C. Veysey, 28 March 1950. The rioting and evictions followed an increase in hostel tariffs which some UK migrants refused to pay on the grounds of poor conditions. The evictions were suspended during June 1953 to avoid embarrassment during the coronation period. A subsequent inquiry blamed the whole episode on communists. LAB13/434 Committee's Report on Migrant Hostel Accommodation, 5 December 1952.

29. CAB129/107 C(61)201, 1 December 1961, British Emigration Policy: Memorandum by the Secretary of State for Commonwealth Relations. This figure constituted 35 percent of total immigration to Australia. The Australian government had contributed £36 million toward the Free and Assisted Passage Schemes.

30. LAB13/836 UK High Commissioner Geoffrey Scoones to Secretary of State for Commonwealth Relations, 25 June 1954.

31. LAB13/277 Oversea Settlement in New Zealand; CAB129/107 C(61)201, 1 December 1961, British Emigration Policy: Memorandum by the Secretary of State for Commonwealth Relations.

32. Canadian Minister for Immigration Walter E. Harris explained his government's refusal to conclude an assisted passage agreement with the United Kingdom: "You do not necessarily get the best type of immigrant if he is wholly subsidized to come." Instead, the Canadian government preferred to retain "absolute" control over immigration by conducting its own recruiting schemes. DO35/6361 Canadian House of Commons, 24 April 1953. See also LAB13/835 Note, 1 September 1950; DO35/6361 Canadian Government's Immigration Policy.

33. Canadian "requirements" included good health, good character, and sufficient means for maintenance pending settlement. LAB13/281 Ministry of Labour Note on Migration Policy, February 1949. Migration to Canada was also facilitated by the provision of an air charter service which was intended to carry 10,000 passengers a year. The service was withdrawn, however, in deference to French Canadian sentiment. In 1948 the amount that intending emigrants could take with them was reduced from £5,000 to £1,000, payable in four equal annual installments. In response to Canadian government complaints that this restriction limited migration, the Treasury agreed to add £250 per dependent up to a maximum of four. In 1954 the restrictions were relaxed again, and emigrants were allowed to take £2,000 at departure. DO35/4863 Brief for Secretary of State's Canadian Tour; LAB13/ 835 Report of the Interdepartmental Committee on Migration Policy, 12 December 1950.

34. LAB13/281 Problems of Emigration from the United Kingdom with Particular Reference to Movement to the Commonwealth, June 1950; DO35/4877 Report of the Interdepartmental Committee on Migration Expenditure, 1954; DO35/6361 Canadian Government's Migration Policy.

35. DO35/6361 UK High Commissioner to Secretary of State for Commonwealth Relations, 5 February 1955.

36. The government undertook to provide $5 for each child per month to cover some of the costs of upkeep until the family became eligible for the real family allowance. The loans were extended to cover the cost of dependents' passages up to any reasonable amount. DO35/6361 Press Release, 16 December 1955; Liverpool *Daily Post*, 4 April 1956.

37. The exchange was later disowned as a joke. DO35/6361 *Evening Standard*, 10 February 1956.

38. DO35/6361 Liverpool *Daily Post*, 4 April 1956; *Daily Telegraph*, 4 January 1957; *Manchester Guardian*, 10 January 1957.

39. DO35/6361 *Daily Telegraph*, 1 March 1957. Eighteen thousand migrants, including five thousand Hungarians, left Britain by air for Canada in the first six months of 1957. LAB13/30 Reference Paper on Migration 3/1957.

40. CAB129/107 C(61)201, 1 December 1961, British Emigration Policy: Memorandum by the Secretary of State for Commonwealth Relations. Total Canadian immigration for 1957 was 282,164. LAB13/30 Reference Paper on Migration 2/1958.

41. LAB13/30 Reference Paper on Migration 2/1961; CAB129/107 C(61)201, 1 December 1961, British Emigration Policy: Memorandum by the Secretary of State for Commonwealth Relations. Despite an attempt to restimulate the flow in 1960, the persistence of unemployment in Canada helped keep movement slow through 1962.

42. CAB129/107 C(61)201, 1 December 1961, British Emigration Policy: Memorandum by the Secretary of State for Commonwealth Relations.

43. *Times*, 12 December 1944, 3 February 1945.

44. Dr. Barnardo's, the Fairbridge Society, the New Zealand Child Migration Society, Northcote Children's Emigration Fund for Australia, the Federal Catholic Immigration Committee of Australia, the Church of England Council for Commonwealth Settlement, the National Children's Home and Orphanage, the Church of Scotland Committee on Social Service, and the Salvation Army all concluded agreements with the UK government under the terms of the Empire Settlement Act. Of the children sent to the dominions, approximately 50 percent were sent by Roman Catholic institutions. This heavy representation owed itself to the scarcity of Catholic homes able to foster children and the reluctance of Catholic officials to place children in non-Catholic settings. DO35/4881, 1956, Interdepartmental Committee on Migration Policy.

45. LAB13/835 Syers Committee—Report of the Interdepartmental Committee on Migration Policy, 12 December 1950; DO35/6379 Annual Report of the Oversea Migration Board, 1954. Assuming an annual rate of 200 children per year, the Home Office estimated that emigration saved the state between £12,000 and £17,000 per year. DO35/4881 Report of the Interdepartmental Committee on Migration Policy, 1956, Annex: Savings to Public Funds Due to Child Migration.

46. LAB13/835 Extract from *Report of the Care of Children Committee* (the "Curtis Committee"), Cmd. 6922 (London: HMSO, 1946).

47. LAB13/836 Inter-departmental Committee on Migration Expenditure, Emigration of "Deprived" Children, Note by the Home Office, 1954. Two years later, as proof of the declining importance of emigration, the Home Office contrasted the 13,000 adoptions between June 1953 and June 1954 with the 204 emigrations. DO35/4881 Report of the Inter-departmental Committee on Migration Policy, 1956.

48. DO35/6381 Fact Finding Mission on Child Migration, Departmental Note; DO35/6380 R. H. Johnson to G. E. B. Shannon, 28 June 1956; Shannon to Sir Saville Garner, 28 June 1956. Officials published the report because the publicity they themselves had generated in anticipation of a favorable account was too great to allow them to bury it. DO35/4881 Report of the Interdepartmental Committee on Migration Policy, 1956.

49. CAB129/107 C(61)201, 1 December 1961, British Emigration Policy: Memorandum by the Secretary of State for Commonwealth Relations. Margaret Humphreys, *Empty Cradles* (London: Doubleday, 1995), is an in-depth journalistic exploration of the issue of child migration which suggests that many postwar child emigrants left without their parents' consent or knowledge and often in ignorance of their own circumstances.

50. Figures for both the SOSBW and the Big Brother Movement are drawn from CAB129/107 C(61)201, 1 December 1961, British Emigration Policy: Memorandum by the Secretary of State for Commonwealth Relations. See successive interdepartmental committee reports for observations upon the effectiveness of these organizations.

51. The exact figure of 1,508,000 is the sum of the numbers given by the dominion governments of Australia, Canada, New Zealand, Rhodesia, and South Africa of arriving UK residents. UK officials believed dominion immigration figures to be more accurate than UK Board of Trade departure statistics since the latter did not include air travel, increasingly important by the end of the 1950s. Dominion figures taken from CAB129/107 C(61)201, 1 December 1961, British Emigration Policy: Memorandum by the Secretary of State for Commonwealth Relations and LAB13/30 Reference Papers on Migration, 1/1957, 2/1958, LAB13/30 E. J. Toogood to Welch, 11 March, 1957.

52. Total UK emigration including that to foreign parts climbed to a postwar high in 1957 of 230,000 or 0.5 percent of the UK population. LAB13/30 Reference Papers on Migration, 2/1958, 3/1958, 4/1958.

53. In the case of Australia, two-thirds of postwar emigrants received assistance. CAB129/107 C(61)201, 1 December 1961, British Emigration Policy: Memorandum by the Secretary of State for Commonwealth Relations.

54. LAB13/281 Assistance Given by Ministry of Labour in Recruitment and Selection under the Australian Assisted Passages Scheme; LAB13/835 Note on the Position of the Ministry of Labour as Regards the Expiry of the Empire Settlement Act and the Australian Assisted Passages Scheme.

55. LAB13/199 Isaacs minute, 1 March 1946. See this whole file and LAB13/24 for the history of the negotiations.

56. *Report of the Royal Commission on Population*, Cmd. 7695 (London: HMSO, 1949), paras. 331, 332, 337.

57. Quoted in DO35/4877 Report of the Interdepartmental Committee on Migration Expenditure, 1954.

58. LAB13/281 Problems of Emigration from the United Kingdom with Particular Reference to Movement to the Commonwealth, June 1950.

59. LAB13/835 Note, 1 September 1950.

60. LAB13/281 Ministry of Labour speech written for Dame Mary Smieton to be delivered to the Society for the Oversea Settlement of British Women, 1950.

61. LAB13/281 Emigration and Manpower Ministry of Labour Policy, 16 April 1952.

62. DO35/4877 Draft Report of the Interdepartmental Committee on Migration Expenditure, 1954.

63. DO35/4877 Draft Report of the Interdepartmental Committee on Migration Expenditure, 1954; DO35/4879 Report of the Interdepartmental Committee on Migration Expenditure, 1954. Employing much the same language, the Ministry of Labour echoed these sentiments in its support of renewal of the Empire Settlement Act in 1956. LAB13/837 Draft Note Review of Long-term Migration Policy.

64. DO35/4881 Report of the Interdepartmental Committee on Migration Policy, 1956.

65. DO35/6368 Memo by G. E. B. Shannon, Migration, 5 June 1956.

66. CAB129/CP(56)240 Memorandum by the Commonwealth Relations Secretary, Assisted Passage Scheme to Australia and the Empire Settlement Act, October 1956.

67. DO35/10194 Extract from *Parliamentary Debates* (Commons), 5th ser., 7 February 1957.

68. Reported in *Parliamentary Debates* (Commons), 5th ser., [1958], v. 583, c. 155.

69. CAB129/107 C(61)201, 1 December 1961 British Emigration Policy: Memorandum by the Secretary of State for Commonwealth Relations.

70. LAB13/277 Emigration to New Zealand, Note of a Meeting, 15 May 1947.

71. LAB13/836 UK High Commissioner Geoffrey Scoones to Secretary of State for Commonwealth Relations, 25 June 1954.

72. LAB13/204 Southern Rhodesia Legislative Assembly Debates, 25 May 1950.

73. LAB13/204 M. A. Bevan to Veysey, 24 January 1947.

74. CAB128/28 CM15 (55), 17 February 1955.

75. DO35/6361 Canada: Immigration into Canada, UK High Commissioner in Canada to Secretary of State for Commonwealth Relations, 5 February 1955.

76. LAB13/199 A. J. S. James, Note, 24, 29 October 1945.

77. LAB13/835 H. E. Holt's Opening speech at Citizenship Convention, 22 January 1951; DO35/6363 White Australia Policy.

78. The only exception to this perspective was Churchill's 1947 party political broadcast, which berated the emigrants for leaving Britain during a time of need. Churchill's prior and subsequent support of imperial migration suggests that his sentiments on this occasion were perhaps inspired more by party politics than conviction. *Times*, 18 August 1947.

79. LAB13/434 H. M. Phillips to Veysey, 9 March 1950.

80. LAB13/199 Gwyllim Myrddin-Evans to Isaacs, 2 January 1947.

81. LAB13/199 Sir Godfrey Ince to Eric Machtig, 3 January 1947.

82. The discrepancy was due both to Britons' superior shipping and living conditions and to the use of international funds for refugees' passage costs. LAB13/434 Extract from the *Sydney Morning Herald*, July 4, 1952; DO35/6368 Allan Noble to Secretary of State, 7 June 1956.

83. LAB13/835 Note on the Position of the Ministry of Labour as Regards the Expiry of the Empire Settlement Acts and the Australian Assisted Passage Agreements, 12 July 1950. LAB13/835 Note, 1 September 1950.

84. LAB13/835 Memorandum, W. J. Garnett, Assistant High Commissioner to Australia, 25 July 1950. Garnett believed it imperative that the inflow of alien stock, which would "take generations to assimilate," should be counterbalanced by British migration.

85. DO35/4881 Report of the Interdepartmental Committee on Migration Policy, 1956.

86. *Parliamentary Debates* (Commons), 5th Ser., [1952], v. 499, c. 501.

87. LAB13/434 H. M. Phillips to Veysey, 9 March 1950; H. M. Phillips to J. R. Davies, 16 March 1950; J. R. Davies to Buxton, 21 March 1950. Other ministry officials suggested helping the Australian building industry by sending out UK technicians to train recruits already in Australia.

88. *Report of the Royal Commission on Population*, paras. 355, 356.

89. LAB13/835 Assisted Migration, Note by Assistant High Commissioner to Australia, 25 July 1950.

90. *Parliamentary Debates* (Lords), [1950], v. 476, c. 88; [1952], v. 176, c. 1217; (Commons) [1952], v. 499, c. 75.

91. DO35/4879 Stephen Holmes to Commonwealth Relations Office, 20 August 1954.

92. DO35/4881 Report of the Interdepartmental Committee on Migration Policy, 1956.

93. The scheme was partially opened in September 1946 for the recruitment of two hundred building workers but did not open fully until 31 March 1947.

94. LAB13/204 G. Grant Minute, 31 January 1947.

95. LAB13/204 L. B. Walsh Atkins to A. D. Chataway, 10 October 1950.

96. LAB13/199 A. Reeder to C. E. Maher, 17 July 1947; PREM8/1479 W. L. Gorrell-Barnes to Attlee, 25, 27 February 1947.

97. *Times*, 18 August 1947.

98. Attlee wrote "I agree" on W. L. Gorrell-Barnes's memo but initiated

no change of policy. Significantly, the Ministry of Labour refused to help finance Italian emigration to the British Commonwealth on the grounds that "our experience in the matter of emigration overseas suggested that it was often the best and most vigorous workers (and moreover those without dependents) who formed the majority of emigrants, and their departure represented an economic loss to the country." LAB13/45 Report of Working Party on Manpower, 21 July 1948.

99. LAB13/281 Problems of Emigration from the United Kingdom with Particular Reference to Movement to the Commonwealth, Annex, June 1950; *Times*, 1 April 1947; LAB13/257 Isaacs to Lord Privy Seal, 17 April 1947; LAB13/278 Migration to Australia: Outline of Requirements of the States for 1947; James to Bevan, 11 March 1947; Occupational Categories of Migrants Required by the States within the First 900 Berths Available to Each State for 1947; Salmon to L. H. Hornsby, 12 November 1948; LAB13/434 H. M. J. Parker to G. L. Veysey, 4 April 1950. LAB13/434 H. D. W. Wesche to R. L. Dixon, 9 April 1951.

100. LAB13/281 Problems of Emigration from the United Kingdom with Particular Reference to Movement to the Commonwealth, Annex, June 1950.

101. LAB13/838 National Institute of Economic and Social Research Memorandum on Postwar Migration to Australia.

102. LAB13/281 Ministry of Labour Note on Migration Policy, February 1949; LAB13/281 Problems of Emigration from the United Kingdom with Particular Reference to Movement to the Commonwealth, June 1950.

103. R. T. Appleyard, *British Emigration to Australia* (Toronto: University of Toronto Press, 1964), pp. 86, 126.

104. *Report of the Royal Commission on Population*, paras. 34, 37, 259.

105. *Manchester Guardian*, 8 February 1960.

106. LAB13/204 L. B. Walsh Atkins to A. D. Chataway, 10 October 1950; LAB13/199 Overseas Settlement in Southern Rhodesia; LAB13/836 Keith to E. C. M. Cullingford, 15 June 1954; LAB13/838 National Institute of Economic and Social Research, Memorandum on Post-war Migration from the United Kingdom, 1951; LAB13/30 Reference Paper on Migration, 1/1957, 4/1957, 4/1958; LAB10/1604 Working Party on Manpower Situation, June 1961.

107. LAB13/278 Bevan to Dixon, 28 February 1947; LAB13/199 Phillips to Dixon, 2 March 1946; *Parliamentary Debates* (Commons), 5th Ser. (1947), v. 443, c. 1082.

108. *Times*, 2 December 1946.

109. *Times*, 18 April 1947.

110. Dame Mary suggested that the percentage gain to Australia was about eight times the percentage loss to Great Britain. LAB13/281, Ministry of Labour speech written for Dame Mary Smieton to be delivered to the Society for the Oversea Settlement of British Women, 1950.

111. LAB13/281 Emigration and Manpower, Ministry of Labour Policy Note, 16 April 1952.

112. Attlee "could hardly contemplate giving active encouragement to a movement of working manpower to Australia from this country on the scale which you have in mind." This reply was erased by senior official Eric Machtig, who hoped instead that the opening would come about shortly and in a manner that would accommodate both countries' labor needs. LAB13/199 Draft Reply to Australian Government, December 1946.

113. LAB13/278 W. T. Piggott minute, 27 March 1947; [illegible] to J. M. Glen, 20 March 1947; H. P. Levy minute, 25 March 1947; LAB13/434 Parker to Veysey, 4 April 1950.

114. The accounting methods were imperfect. Throughout the period under review civil servants complained about the paucity of statistics on the number and occupations of those departing. LAB13/281 Ministry of Labour Review of Migration Policy, 1949; DO35/6379 Report of Oversea Migration Board; DO35/4881 Report of the Interdepartmental Committee on Migration Policy, 1956; LAB13/30 Reference Paper on Migration, 4/1957; LAB13/30 Reference Paper on Migration, 1/1961.

115. LAB13/199 Draft Cabinet Memorandum: Shipping for Migrants to Australia, 18 January 1947.

116. LAB13/835 Patrick Gordon-Walker to Isaacs, 5 July 1950.

117. The Ministries of Labour and Transport favored continued support, and the Treasury, Home Office, and Commonwealth Relations Office opposed. LAB13/835 Interdepartmental Committee on Future Migration Policy, 29 September 1950; LAB13/835 Report of the Interdepartmental Committee on Migration Policy, 12 December 1950; DO35/6368 Brief for I. M. R. Maclennan on setting up of committee to consider renewal of Empire Settlement Act.

118. CAB129/43 CP(50)306 Memorandum by the Secretary of State for Commonwealth Relations, 12 December 1950.

119. CAB129/43 CP(50)320 Memorandum by the Minister of Labour and National Service, 15 December 1950; LAB13/835 Assisted Passages Agreement with Australia: Draft Memorandum by the Minister of Labour and National Service, December 1950.

120. CAB128/18 CM(50)87, 18 December 1950.

121. PREM8/1479 CP(51)178 Migration Policy: Assisted Passage Agreement with Australia Memorandum by the Secretary of State for Commonwealth Relations, 26 June 1951.

122. PREM8/1479 CP(51)218 Migration Policy: Assisted Passages Agreement with Australia Memorandum by the Secretary of State for Commonwealth Relations, 23 July 1951; CM(51)47 28 June 1951. Gordon-Walker hoped that the Australian government would increase its contribution to the cost of the ships by £100,000. Thus Britain's contribution of £250,000 would really be only £150,000.

123. PREM8/1479 CP(51)225 Migration Policy: Assisted Passages Agreement with Australia, Memorandum by the Minister of Labour and National Service, 24 July 1951.

124. CAB128/20 CM(51)55, 26 July 1951.

125. LAB13/835 Lord Ismay to Rab Butler, 5 December 1951.

126. LAB13/835 Draft Cabinet Paper: AAPS with Australia, December 24, 1961; LAB13/835 Butler to Walter Monckton, 17 December 1951; CAB128/23 CM(51) 20, 28 December 1951. Australia and New Zealand both estimated the total cost of resettling an emigrant to be around £2,000. Thus, as the Oversea Migration Board noted in its first report, Britain's £150,000 contribution represented the cost of transporting and settling about 75 migrants. DO35/6379 Report of Oversea Migration Board, 1954. In 1961, £150,000 was reported as representing 4 percent of the scheme's costs.

127. LAB13/752 R. F. Keith to J. R. Lloyd-Davies, 24 October 1952.

128. DO35/6368 Brief for I. M. R. Maclenna on setting up of committee to consider renewal of Empire Settlement Act; LAB12/752 Keith to Lloyd-Davies, 24 October 1952, Lloyd-Davies to Veysey, 28 October 1952; DO35/6379 Viscount Swinton note, 31 July 1954; DO35/6379 Report of Oversea Migration Board, 1954.

129. DO35/6368 Brief for I. M. R. Maclenna on setting up of committee to consider renewal of Empire Settlement Act; DO35/4879 Report of the Interdepartmental Committee on Migration Expenditure, 1954.

130. DO35/4881 Inter-departmental Committee on Migration Policy, 1956.

131. DO35/6368 Migration, G. E. B. Shannon and accompanying minutes, 5, 6 June 1956.

132. *Parliamentary Debates* (Commons), 5th ser., [1963], v. 673, c. 203–5. At least 20 parliamentary questions were raised between January 1957 and March 1963. DO35/6361 *Daily Mail*, 8 January 1957. The Registrar General also noted the public fears around the departure of "scientific craftsmen and technicians." LAB13/30, 10 April 1957.

133. *Parliamentary Debates* (Common), 5th ser., [1960], v. 620, c. 98w. The practice had some success: seven scientists were recruited in 1958 and a further sixteen in 1959.

134. *Parliamentary Debates* (Commons), 5th ser., [1963], v. 673, c. 203–5.

135. CAB129/107 C(61)201, 1 December 1961, British Emigration Policy: Memorandum by the Secretary of State for Commonwealth Relations.

136. CAB128/35 CC(61)67, 5 December 1961.

137. DO35/10285 Text of the Conference of Commonwealth Societies, 29 April 1960; *Guardian* 6, 8 February 1960; DO35/10194 Note of a Meeting between UK High Commissioner in Australia (Stephen Holmes) and Australian Minister for Immigration (H. E. Holt), 16 March 1955.

138. LAB13/281 Memorandum by Keith, February 1949.

139. LAB13/434 Address by the Minister for Immigration to the Australian Citizenship Convention, 24 January 1950. Aboriginal leaders would presumably have questioned Holt's definition of Australia as a British community.

140. LAB13/199 Migration to Australia: Further Statement by Minister, 3 October 1945.

141. LAB13/434 Address by the Minister for Immigration to Australian Citizenship Convention, 24 January 1950; R. F. Keith to R. L. Dixon, 13 February 1950; LAB13/388 Approximate Figures of Potential Migrants to the Dominions during 1949.

142. Canberra noted, for example, that while Australia had spent £A3 million to get 23,000 British migrants, they had had to spend only £A2 million to get 42,000 Europeans. They added that the loss of 40,000 or 50,000 assisted migrants could not "seriously be regarded as weakening [the] mother country or depleting her land force." DO35/10194 T. H. E. Heyes to Holmes, 30 March 1955; LAB13/835 United Kingdom–Australia Assisted Passage Agreement Considerations put forward by the Commonwealth Government of Australia for the Continuation of the United Kingdom Government Financial Contribution, March 1952.

143. LAB13/281 Emigrants from the United Kingdom Traveling Direct by Sea to Places out of Europe and Not within the Mediterranean Area, January 1946–September 1948.

144. LAB13/836 New Zealand Immigration Policy, UK High Commissioner to Secretary of State for Commonwealth Relations, 30 July 1954.

145. DO35/6363 Canada: Immigration into Canada, UK High Commissioner (Archibald Nye) to Secretary of State for Commonwealth Relations, 5 February 1955; LAB13/835 Note by the Minister of Labour, Australian Emigration Policy, 24 December 1951; CAB129/107 C(61)201, 1 December 1961, British Emigration Policy: Memorandum by the Secretary of State for Commonwealth Relations.

146. DO35/6363 Canada: Immigration into Canada, UK High Commissioner (Archibald Nye) to Secretary of State for Commonwealth Relations, 5 February 1955.

147. To appease the Canadians the UK Treasury increased the amount of currency that could be taken out of the country. DO35/4863 Brief for Secretary of State's Canadian Tour.

148. LAB13/204 Meeting at Rhodesia House, 24 August 1951.

149. DO35/10197 Federation Newsletter, 10 August 1957, 25 June, 1 August 1958; *Rhodesia Sunday Mail*, 19 November 1957; East Africa and Rhodesia, 29 May 1958; UK High Commission to Denis Cleary (CRO), 8 June 1960.

150. Given Australia's demands for 200,000 immigrants annually, of which Britain was expected to provide only 70,000, or 35 percent, it was clear that the British element in Australia's total population would inevitably decline. LAB13/838 National Institute of Economic and Social Research: Memo Post-war Emigration from the United Kingdom, 1951. In 1956 British stock constituted 47 percent of the total Canadian population, but current rates of immigration and natural increase were likely to reduce this proportion to 32 percent by the year 2000. DO35/6361 UK High Commissioner Archi-

bald Nye to Secretary of State for Commonwealth Relations, 5 February 1955; *Daily Telegraph*, 19 March 1956. This was the case despite the migration of over 300,000 British people to Canada in the eight years since the end of the war. Overall, Britain's share of Canadian immigration shrank from 71 percent in 1946 to 19 percent by 1960. DO35/4877 Inter-departmental Committee on Migration Expenditure, 1956; CAB129/10 C(61)18, 2 November 1961. While New Zealand and Southern Rhodesia maintained high proportions of British stock in their total populations, Britain's share of postwar immigration had been only 53 percent and 38 percent respectively. CAB129/107 C(61)201, 1 December 1961, British Emigration Policy: Memorandum by the Secretary of State for Commonwealth Relations.

151. LAB13/199 Migration within the British Commonwealth, Australian Government telegram to United Kingdom Government, 11 December 1946.

152. *Parliamentary Debates* (Lords), [1950], v. 166, c. 1217, 1251; (Commons), 5th ser., [1950], v. 476, c. 63, 88, 97–99. The "madness" to which Gordon-Walker referred might well have included those individuals both in and outside the House and bodies such as the Migration Council advocating the mass transfer of population from the United Kingdom to the dominions.

153. *Daily Graphic and Sketch*, 18 April 1947, 19 June 1948; *Times*, 20 January 1947. A few years later, as we have seen, the same newspapers questioned the benefit of losing "young and energetic people."

154. LAB13/248 Marwood and Robertson to Ministry of Labour, 22 January 1948; Frames Tours to Ministry of Labour, 26 January 1948; James Spence and Co. to Ministry of Labour, 23 January 1948.

155. Appleyard, *British Emigration*, p. 97.

156. This number was limited to persons completing application forms, undergoing medical exams, or making some other commitment and thus did not include general or vague enquiries. LAB13/388 Wesche to Keith, 27 January 1950; DO35/6379 Annual Report of the Oversea Migration Board, 1954. The Liverpool *Daily Post* estimated that 1 in every 150 Britons was going to try and go to Canada in 1957. Liverpool *Daily Post*, 9 January 1957; *Times*, 16 December 1957.

157. Appleyard, *British Emigration*, p. 102.

158. *Daily Mail*, 8 January 1957; Liverpool *Daily Post*, 9 January 1957; *Daily Telegraph*, 8 January 1957; *Guardian*, 10 December 1956; *Times*, 16 December 1956; Appleyard, *British Emigration* pp. 98–99, 146–78.

Chapter 3. Recruiting Potential Britons

1. V. G. Kiernan suggested that "wherever Homo Sapiens made his first, and on the whole regrettable appearance it was not in Britain." V. G. Kiernan, "Britons Old and New," in *Immigrants and Minorities in British Society*, ed. Colin Holmes (London: Allen and Unwin, 1978), cited by Holmes in "The Promised Land? Immigration into Britain, 1870–1980," in *Demography of*

Immigrants and Minority Groups in the United Kingdom, ed. D. A. Coleman (London: Academic Press, 1982). Official claim to this nonimmigrant status can be found, amongst other places, in a 1953 Ministry of Labour report to the International Labour Office which stated categorically that "the United Kingdom is not a country of immigration." LAB13/367 Measures Taken to Give Effect to the Convention Concerning Migration for Employment.

2. Following William, successive waves of "foreigners" have worn the "English" crown. For much of the Plantagenet period, the monarchs of England laid as much claim to lands in France as to their English territories. The Tudor and Stuart dynasties of the early modern era owed their origins to Wales and Scotland respectively. And the Glorious Revolution of 1688 replaced Scottish with Dutch monarchs. The drying up of this line prompted English parliamentarians to seek a new line of kings (though distantly related) in Hanover, Germany. The marriage of a descendant of this line to Albert of Saxe-Coburg further Germanized the English ruling family. This German strain persisted despite the renaming of the family as Windsor in 1917. And in addition to his German-descended mother, the current heir to the throne, Charles, can claim a father of recent Greek descent. As a result of this varied heritage, the English Royal Family may truly be said to be a family of European proportions. Yet there is nothing so apparently inherently English as the Royal Family. It is the center of the English tourist trade, and it is at the center of the pageantry that, according to television commentators on the occasion of royal marriages and coronations, dates back over a thousand years. The reconstruction of alien invaders and "foreign" potentates into much-loved British kings and queens has been an "invention of tradition" on a grand scale involving the cooperation of Parliament, press and public over several centuries. For an exploration of this and other "invented traditions," see Eric Hobsbawm and Terence Ranger, eds., *The Invention of Tradition* (Cambridge: Cambridge University Press, 1992). The "myth" surrounding the British Royal Family is detailed in David Cannadine's article in the same book, "The Context, Performance, and Meaning of Ritual: The British Monarchy and the 'Invention of Tradition,' c. 1820–1977." For a more elaborate exploration of the place of monarchy in British society, see, Tom Nairn, *The Enchanted Glass: Britain and Its Monarchy* (London: Picador, 1990).

3. For more detailed histories of Jewish migration and the 1905 Act, see J. A. Garrard, *The English and Immigration: A Comparative Study of the Jewish Influx, 1880–1990* (Oxford: Oxford University Press, 1971); Lloyd Gartner, *The Jewish Immigrant in England* (London: Allen and Unwin, 1960); Colin Holmes, *Anti-Semitism in British Society, 1876–1939* (London: Edward Arnold, 1979); Bernard Gainer, *The Alien Invasion: The Origins of the Aliens Act of 1905* (London: Heinneman, 1972).

4. Ann Dummett and Andrew Nicol, *Subjects, Citizens, Aliens, and Others: Nationality and Immigration Law* (London: Weidenfeld and Nicolson, 1990), p. 112.

5. Louise London, "Jewish Refugees, Anglo-Jewry, and British Govern-

ment Policy, 1930–1940," in *The Making of Modern Anglo-Jewry*, ed. David Cesarani (Oxford: Blackwell, 1990), p. 165. That twenty thousand female refugees took up employment as domestic servants represents both the power of the middle-class constituency, who saw in refugees an answer to the "servant problem," and the weakness of a female trade union, the National Union of Domestic Workers. See also Tony Kushner, "An Alien Occupation—Jewish Refugees and Domestic Service in Britain, 1933–1948," in *Second Chance: Two Centuries of German Speaking Jews in the UK*, ed. Werner E. Mosse (Tubingen: J. C. B. Mohr, 1991), pp. 553–78. See also Ari Sherman, *Island Refuge: Britain and Refugees from the Third Reich, 1933–1939* (Essex, UK: Frank Cass, 1994), which suggests that given unemployment, fears of an immigrant deluge, and a paucity of knowledge about the Jews' fate, Britain's interwar acceptance of refugees was reasonable.

6. University of Warwick, Modern Records Centre, TUC Papers, MSS292/107.5/1 National Conference of Trade Union Executives on Production and Manpower, 19 February 1946; CAB129/5 CP(45)305 Employment of German and Italian Prisoners of War, Memorandum by the Minister of Labour, 26 November 1945.

7. CAB128/5 CM(46)15, 14 February, 1946. The Cabinet also considered recruiting a further 165,000 POWs from Germany. TUC Papers, MSS292/107.5/1 Publicity in Relation to Manpower Programmes, no date; *Daily Graphic and Sketch*, 4 January 1947; LAB12/513 Cripps' Press Conference, 29 January 1948.

8. CAB129/7 CP(46)71, 20 February 1946.

9. CAB128/5 CM(46)15, 14 February 1946. These "useless mouths" were currently costing Britain around £2.5 million per month in addition to using up "slender resources of foreign currency." CAB 134/301 FLC (46), 2d meeting, 3 April 1946.

10. As Poles began to assume the status of potential Britons, responsibility for them passed from a ministerial steering committee to the FLC. CAB134/301 FLC(46), 1st meeting, 14 March 1946. By April 1946, Emanuel Shinwell believed that Poles could be placed in mines only on a permanent basis. CAB134/301 FLC(46), 2d meeting, 3 April 1946.

11. LAB13/249 Settlement of Members of the Polish Armed Forces in Civilian Life, Ministry of Labour note, no date.

12. TUC Papers, MSS292/103.28 Foreign Labour—Note for the TUC. These figures included 1,000 "wastage from death and other causes." The Ministry of Labour cites the figure 120,000 in LAB13/1098 Report on Foreigners Accepted into Great Britain, no date; 125,500 is the figure cited in Jerzy Zubrzycki, *Polish Immigrants in Britain: A Study of Adjustment* (The Hague: Martin Nijhoff, 1956). The difference likely lies in Zubrzycki's inclusion of 2,300 veterans who, though remaining in Britain, did not join the corps, and an additional 1,800 dependents. See also LAB13/1098 Regional Controllers' Conference, Foreign Labour, 13 April 1949.

13. FO371/78192 National Assistance Board, 11 January 1950.

14. LAB13/1098 Regional Controllers' Conference, Foreign Labour, 13 April 1949; CAB134/301 FLC(46), 5th meeting, 26 September 1946. In an effort to overcome Poles' reluctance to work in agriculture, "suitable men" were posted to agricultural hostels while still in the Polish Resettlement Corps, where they were "subjected to intensive recruitment efforts." CAB134/301 FLC(47)21, 23 June 1947, 15th Progress Report. Of the 92,750 Poles available for work, only 4,100 were female. TUC MSS292/103.2/2 L. A. Plowman to Carthy, 19 February 1951.

15. CAB134/301 FLC, 1st meeting, 14 March 1946; FLC(46)2 Memorandum by the Lord Privy Seal, 1 March 1946.

16. CAB134/301 FLC(46), 3d meeting, 23 May 1946; LAB13/1098 Regional Controllers' Conference, Foreign Labour, 13 April 1949.

17. CAB128/6 CM(46)79, 4 September 1946.

18. CAB134/301 FLC(46), 7th meeting, 14 May 1946.

19. *Economic Survey for 1947*, Cmd. 7046 (London: HMSO, 1947), paras. 124–25, 128, 139.

20. CAB128/9 CM(47)7, 16 January 1947; CM9(47), 17 January 1947; CM14(47), 30 January 1947; CAB134/301 FLC(46)4 Recruitment of Displaced Persons, Memorandum by the Ministry of Labour, 12 February 1947.

21. Mark Wyman, *DP: Europe's Displaced Persons, 1945–1951* (Philadelphia: Balch Institute Press, 1989). For additional work on displaced persons, see Diana Kay and Robert Miles, *Refugees or Migrant Workers: European Volunteer Workers in Britain, 1946–1951* (London: Routledge, 1992); J. A. Tannahill, *European Volunteer Workers in Britain* (Manchester: Manchester University Press, 1958); Malcolm J. Proudfoot, *European Refugees* (Evanston, Ill.: Northwestern University Press, 1956); Elizabeth Stadulis, "The Resettlement of Displaced Persons in the United Kingdom," *Population Studies* 3 (1949). See also Michael Marrus, *The Unwanted: European Refugees in the Twentieth Century* (Oxford: Oxford University Press, 1985), pp. 296–345.

22. CAB128/9 CM(47)28, 13 March 1947.

23. CAB134/301 Memo by Lord Privy Seal, 25 February 1947; LAB13/257 Isaacs to Greenwood, 17 April 1947; *Parliamentary Debates* (Commons), 5th ser., [1947], v. 433, c. 329; PREM8/1019 FLC(47), 2d Meeting, 26 February 1947.

24. LAB13/44 Beryl Hughes to Philip Nicholls, 5 January, 1 February 1949, F. Tarrant to G. E. D. Ball, 25 February 1949; HO213/998, P. Hayman to Ian Roy, 25 July 1947, Roy to V. A. Spinks, 23 October 1947.

25. LAB13/43 Foreign Labour; LAB13/257 Isaacs to Greenwood, 17 April 1947.

26. LAB13/257 Isaacs to Attlee, 26 February 1947, Isaacs to Greenwood, 17 April 1947; CAB134/301 Interdepartmental Committee for the Employment of Supplementary Labour, July 1947. The hoped-for figure of four thousand was not reached but during peak recruitment, over two thousand per week entered Britain. Actual recruitment of DPs was placed under the control of the Displaced Persons Operation Committee.

27. LAB13/257 FLC, Second and Third Progress Reports, 1 April, 8 May 1947. The Home Office security exam checked identity, age, and nationality. Only 1 percent failed to pass. Tannahill, *European Volunteer Workers*, chap. 4.

28. CAB134/301 FLC(47)17, 8 May 1947, Third Progress Report by the Minister of Labour and National Service; CAB128/12 CM(48)1, 6 January 1948; LAB13/45 UK Programme for the Year 1948–49, Supplementary Note on Manpower.

29. *Parliamentary Debates*, Commons, 5th ser., [1947], v. 433, c. 791; LAB13/367 Ministry of Labour, Domestic Worker Permits, Position of Employment Agencies, no date; LAB13/43 Foreign Labour, 8 February 1949.

30. LAB13/43 Foreign Labour, 8 February 1949. Prospective employers applied for a work permit, which was then sent to the worker to enable her or him to enter Britain.

31. The North Sea scheme, for example, was attracting only four hundred recruits a month while eight hundred individual work permits were issued for the same employment category for the same period.

32. LAB13/43 Foreign Labour, 29 August 1949. The scheme worked by having potential employers and employees send in applications to the ministry which then dispatched details of the alien to the employer who in turn applied for a work permit for the named alien. This time-consuming procedure perhaps explains why many employers and employees continued to prefer the facilities offered by a private employment agency. Official thought on the scheme was mixed. Some policy makers disliked employment agencies' exploitation of a tight labor market and a ready pool of labor. Others believed that by involving itself in these most intimate contracts, the government was setting itself up for great criticism when employees and employers failed to build a happy relationship. LAB13/367 M. A. Bevan to W. Taylor, 27 May 1949; LAB13/43 Bevan note, 2 June 1949; LAB13/806 F. E. B. Gabbutt to H. A. Pass, 3 April 1950.

33. LAB13/1098 Employment of Foreign Women in Domestic Employment in the United Kingdom, Preliminary Conference on Migration, 8 April 1950. Not all these permit holders would become permanent residents.

34. LAB13/1098 Utilisation of Available Manpower of Participating Countries, Employment of Foreign Women in Domestic Employment in the UK; LAB13/819 Recruitment of Workers from Abroad, General Survey of the Various Schemes Particularly in Relation to Costs; LAB13/44 minute by G. E. D. Ball, 14 July 1949. See also Julius Isaacs, *British Post-war Migration*, Occasional Papers 17 (Cambridge: National Institute for Economic and Social Research, Cambridge University Press, 1954); TUC Papers, MSS292/103. 2/3 Foreign Workers Entering the UK 1947–54.

35. LAB13/1098 National Joint Advisory Council meeting, 4 February 1948.

36. LAB13/44 Ball to Gordon, 27 July 1948. In order to maximize their recruitment potential, London instructed UK officers in the field to work

within a fairly broad age range of potential migrants. LAB13/44 Pass to Ball, 8 December 1948.

37. LAB13/44 Gabbutt to Pass, 26 May 1949.

38. LAB13/813 Cost of Recruiting Workers from Abroad under Official Ministry of Labour Recruiting Schemes, H. F. Rossetti to K. A. L. Parker, 15 March 1951; TUC Papers, MSS292/103.2/2 Foreign Labour 1948–1951, Foreign Workers in Great Britain, 12 May 1950.

39. LAB13/329 Estimated Total Requirements by Sex and Category. These requirements contrast with the ministry's declaration four months later that it was not possible to employ British subjects of color because there were no longer any vacancies.

40. LAB13/329 International Labour Office Report on Requirements of Foreign Manpower and on Resources Available for Emigration in European Countries, 3d report; LAB13/45 UK Programme for 1948–49 Supplementary Note on Manpower. The Minister for Fuel and Power declared coal to be particularly short of labor. CP(50)257, 1 December 1950, Memorandum by the Minister for Fuel and Power.

41. LAB13/813 Parker to Lloyd-Davies 15 May 1951, and reply 29 May 1951; LAB13/817 R. F. Keith to Ball, 4 July 1951. With contracts arranged by agents acting on behalf of respective governments, migrants recruited through the Official Italian Schemes were not quite so vulnerable as displaced persons, having at least the presumption of state protection.

42. LAB13/1098 Organization for European Economic Co-operation Manpower Committee, 13 July 1951; LAB13/817 R. F. Keith to Ball, 4 July 1951; LAB13/817 Recruitment of Foreign Workers for Employment in the United Kingdom under the Permit Scheme, 27 April 1951; LAB13/821 Notes on the Operation of the Scheme for the Recruitment of Italians for Employment with the National Coal Board, 1951–52. The Italian government paid for transport within Italy and some part of the medicals; the UK government paid for transport to England, including subsistence and accommodation as well as an additional two pounds per worker to the Italian government to cover loss of the worker's social security contributions. The NCB paid for English-language instruction as well as coal-mining training. All recruits were provided with food for the journey, but Ministry officials suggested that in addition recruits would most likely need "tea and buns" at Folkestone.

43. LAB13/817 *Times*, 26 March 1951; *News Chronicle*, 27 March 1951.

44. Italians who found jobs in other industries within Britain received £25 compensation; Italians who found work in the Belgian coal mines got £46; and each man who returned to Italy received £60.

45. LAB13/802 Correspondence—British Railways Labour Recruitment.

46. LAB13/821 Notes on the Operation of the Scheme for the Recruitment of Italians for Employment with the National Coal Board, 1951–52; LAB13/805 Organized Recruitment of Italian Labour—Terms and Conditions.

47. TUC Papers, MSS292/103.2/4, 17 October 1956; DO35/4865 Italian Migration to Commonwealth Countries. The last official scheme came to an end in May 1952. LAB13/367 Measures Taken to Give Effect to the Convention Concerning Migration for Employment.

48. TUC Papers, MSS292/103.2/4 Foreign Workers, 23 July 1957.

49. Dummett and Nicol, for example, write of the EVW scheme, that it "was used for a few years to admit small numbers at a time for specific needs, some of them only temporary. Other European countries, and particularly Germany, were eventually to benefit from the labour force scattered in refugee camps throughout Europe and longing to find homes and jobs. The British Government deliberately held back." *Subjects, Citizens*, p. 176. Similarly, both Wyman (*DP*, p. 189) and Michael Marrus (*The Unwanted*, p. 345) cite 86,000 as the total number of displaced persons brought to Britain by the Attlee Government. Wyman gives Britain credit for being the major European recipient of DPs but his figures underestimate nonetheless. Contemporary UK civil servants believed Britain's role in refugee resettlement to be significant, claiming in 1949 that "both absolutely and relative to our population we have resettled more refugees than any other country in the world and far more than are provided for in the current United States Displaced Persons Act." FO371/78202 Foreign Office to British Embassy in Washington, 26 March 1949.

50. LAB13/819 Reviews of Costs as of 31 January 1950. This figure includes £14.6 million for the Poles and £3.5 million for continental recruits, the latter at a cost per head of £42. In addition, the Ministry of Labour paid about £300,000 per year in hostel-operating costs.

51. LAB13/1098 Foreign Labour—Official Schemes; Isaacs, *British Postwar Migration*, pp. 151, 182. The number of aliens recruited by the Attlee government varies according to the source of the figures. Sources that claim 86,000 Westward Ho! recruits are choosing to include the 8,000 Ukrainian POWs who were brought to Britain from the Continent. Given their previous status, I have categorized these individuals within the POW figure. Some estimates of total postwar immigration include only the Polish veterans and the Westward Ho! volunteers, thereby excluding aliens recruited through the later schemes. I include them in the total number of aliens brought to Britain since they were recruited with the same criteria of labor mobility and demographic acceptability in mind. They were viewed as an economic asset, and included in the total of aliens recruited, by the Ministry of Labour in its internal newspaper the *Gazette*. LAB13/1098 Ministry of Labour and National Service and National Joint Advisory Council, Employment of Foreign Workers.

52. CAB129/6 CP(47)19, 7 January 1947.

53. LAB13/257 FLC Third Progress Report, 8 May 1947.

54. CAB134/301 FLC(46), 2d meeting, 3 April 1946.

55. Tannahill, *European Volunteer Workers*, p. 52; LAB13/44 Medical Rules for Recruiting Officers, March 1949.

56. LAB13/44 Ministry of Labour Circular, June 1949; LAB13/257

Fourth Progress Report, 31 July 1947. In addition, London strongly insisted that pregnant women not be sent forward.

57. LAB13/44 Gabbutt to Pass, 23 January 1950.

58. LAB13/817 Recruitment of Italian Workers.

59. FO371/78192 Ball to F. B. A. Rundall, 28 January 1949.

60. LAB13/367 T. J. Weiler to Ministry of Labour, 15 September 1949; CAB134/301 FLC(46)6, 9 May 1946.

61. Both cited in Wyman, *DP*, pp. 189, 193. The International Refugee Organization anticipated that 80,000 "residuals" would be left in the camps. FO371/78192 DP Branch Berlin to Foreign Office, 24 March 1949.

62. LAB13/1098 Ministry of Labour and National Service/National Joint Advisory Council, Employment of Foreign Workers. Figures from Tannahill cited in Diana Kay and Robert Miles, "Migration, Racism, and the Labour Market in Britain, 1945–51," in *Racism and the Labor Market: Historical Studies*, ed. Marcel van der Linden and Jan Lucassen (Bern: Peter Lang, AG European Academic Publishers, 1995), p. 570.

63. LAB13/45 Report for 2d Season of Manpower Programme. The 51,000 consisted of 10,000 Germans, 33,000 displaced persons, and 8,000 Poles.

64. CAB134/301 FLC(46), 2d meeting, 3 April 1946.

65. See, for example, Heather Booth, "Immigration in Perspective: Population Development in the United Kingdom," in *Towards a Just Immigration Policy*, ed. Ann Dummett (London: Cobden Trust, 1986); Stephen Castles, *Here for Good: Western Europe's New Ethnic Minorities* (London: Pluto Press, 1987); Colin Holmes, *A Tolerant Country?* (London: Faber and Faber, 1991); Dummett and Nicol, *Subjects, Citizens*.

66. TUC Papers, MSS103.28 Foreign Labour in Great Britain 1946–47, Isaacs to Sir Vincent Tewson, 6 June 1946.

67. CAB134/301 FLC(47)4 Recruitment of Displaced Persons, Memorandum by the Minister of Labour, 12 February 1947.

68. CAB128/12 CM(48)1, 6 January 1948; CAB134/301 Foreign Labour Committee meetings.

69. CAB134/301 Leaflet for Distribution to Displaced Persons.

70. TUC Papers, MSS103.28 Foreign Labour—Note for the TUC.

71. TUC Papers, MSS103.28/2 Foreign Labour in Great Britain, 1947–51, Reply to Erith Trade Council, July 1949.

72. TUC Papers, MSS103.28 Foreign Workers 1946–47, TUC to Taunton and District Trades Council, 18 July 1946.

73. TUC Papers, MSS103.28 Foreign Workers 1946–47, TUC to Plymouth DTC 13 September 1946; TUC MSS292/103.2/2 Foreign Labour 1948–51, TUC to Poole Trades Council, 7 October 1948, TUC to Chad Trades Council, 13 November 1950; TUC MSS, 103.28/2 Foreign Labour in Great Britain, 1947–51, Reply to Musicians' Union, 29 November 1948. In the case of Poole District Trades Council, TUC officials suggested that in objecting to foreign labor, the council was contradicting the motto on its

letterhead which called on the workers of the world to unite. TUC MSS292/103.2/1 Importation of Foreign Labour, 1929–48, TUC to Sutton District Trades Council, 29 July 1947.

74. TUC Papers, MSS292/103.2/2 Foreign Labour 1948–51, National Joint Advisory Council Meeting, 25 April, 25 July 1950.

75. LAB13/1098 Regional Controllers' Conference, Foreign Labour, 13 April 1949.

76. LAB13/44 Foreign Labour; HO213/1005 Ian Roy to H. Rosetti, 29 October 1948.

77. LAB13/813 Cost of Official Schemes.

78. LAB13/806 J. Shields-Smith to H. A. Pass, 22 September 1949.

79. CAB134/301 FLC(46), 2d meeting, 3 April 1946.

80. CAB134/301 FLC(46), 1st meeting, 14 March 1946. As the historian Keith Sword comments, "At this early stage foreign labour was seen as an interim measure, a short-term expedient to aid the economy through its immediate difficulties. Where avoidable, no long-term commitments were to be entered into." Keith Sword et al., *The Creation of the Polish Community in Britain, 1939–1950* (London: School of Slavonic and East European Studies, 1989), pp. 235–36.

81. CAB134/301 FLC(46)2 Memorandum by the Lord Privy Seal, Preliminary Questions for Consideration, 1 March 1946.

82. LAB13/45 UK Programme for 1948–49, Supplementary Note on Manpower; Kay and Miles, *Refugees or Migrant Workers?* p. 57.

83. *Parliamentary Debates* (Commons), 5th ser., [1947], v. 433, c. 387.

84. TUC Papers, MSS292/103.2/2 *Workers from Abroad*, pamphlet, April 1948; *Parliamentary Debates* (Commons), 5th ser., [1947], v. 433. c. 406, 749–66, 1531.

85. *Parliamentary Debates* (Commons), 5th ser., [1947], v. 433, c. 386–87.

86. Ibid., c. 757.

87. Ibid., [1948], v. 457, c. 1721.

88. Ibid., [1947], v. 433, c. 386–87.

89. LAB13/1005 Notes on an Interdepartmental Conference on the Welfare of EVWs, 18 November 1948.

90. TUC Papers, MSS103.28 Foreign Labour in Great Britain, 1947–51, Joint Consultative Committee Meeting, 25 November 1948.

91. HO213/1005 Roy to Rossetti, 29 October 1948.

92. TUC Papers, MSS292/103.2/1–4, Foreign Workers.

93. LAB13/257 Third Progress Report, 8 May 1947.

94. LAB12/513 Publicity for the Education of Popular Opinion on Foreign Workers, 14 October 1947.

95. LAB13/44 Foreign Labour. Certified to be of uncertain nationality on their passports, once in Britain, Sudetens were to be known as Czechs in order to avoid the recently rewon title of German.

96. CAB134/301 Interdepartmental Committee for the Employment Supplementary Labour, 27 January 1947.

97. TUC Papers, MSS292/103.2/2 *Workers from Abroad*, April 1948.

98. Officials rejected a proposal that five hundred DPs be brought over en masse to set up a self-supporting national community on the grounds that such a move would hinder assimilation. HO213/996 Proposal to Move a DP Camp en Bloc to the UK for Resettlement as a Self-Supporting Community; LAB13/1005 Notes on an Interdepartmental Conference on the Welfare of EVWs, 18 November 1948; LAB13/44 Hughes to Philip Nicholls, 5 January 1949; LAB13/42 Sir Harold Wiles to M. A. Bevan, 8 March 1948; *Parliamentary Debates* (Commons), 5th ser., [1947], v. 433, c. 758; CAB134/301 FLC Recruitment of DPs from Germany for Work in British Hospitals, 14 May 1946.

99. LAB13/329 H. W. Evans to Clifton Robbins, 10 November 1948; PREM11/386 E. B. H. Baker to Montague Browne, 2 April 1953.

100. HO213/1005 Rosetti to Roy, 19 October 1948, Conference of Ukrainian Representatives and Camp Leaders in Scotland, 17 October 1948. In some ways the treatment accorded these recruited aliens and the expectations for their ultimate assimilation prefigured the special handling of an unlooked-for addition to Britain's alien population in the late 1950s. Following the Hungarian Uprising in 1956 approximately fifteen thousand Hungarians entered Britain. From the beginning, those refugees choosing to remain in Britain rather than emigrate elsewhere in the Commonwealth were accorded special care: met upon arrival, accommodated in a hostel, given clothing, and most significant from the Ministry of Labour's point of view, helped into a job. Along with this practical assistance, however, came the assumption that the Hungarians would ultimately become British by learning English and adapting to British ways. To help in this transformation, officials from several departments agreed on the merits of using the news media as a showcase for refugee "success stories." LAB8/2344 Hungarian Refugees: Employment Arrangements; LAB8/2345 Hungarian Refugees: Information, Leaflets and Publicity.

101. HO213/998 Proposed Admission to the UK of Dependents of EVWs, December 1947. The Ministry of Labour urged its officials to beware of acknowledging labor deficits to the International Refugee Organization since "economic needs do not always coincide with political and other aims." LAB13/772 S. G. Holloway to G. E. D. Ball, 27 August 1951.

Chapter 4. Neither Subjects nor Aliens

1. John Megaw, "British Subjects and Eire Citizens," *Northern Ireland Legal Quarterly* 3.8 (November 1949): 139. The uniqueness of the provisions lay more in their content than in their application to Ireland. Citizenship had been an ambiguous area of Anglo-Irish relations ever since the birth of the Irish Free State. For an analysis of the early years, see Joseph P. O'Grady, "The Irish Free State Passport and the Question of Citizenship, 1921–4," *Irish Historical Studies* 26 (1989): 104; see also Gretchen Macmillan, "British

Subjects and Irish Citizens: The Passport Controversy, 1923–24," *Eire-Ireland* 26 (1991): 3; HO213/428 Home Office Circular 48/1949. Much of the following chapter is drawn from Kathleen Paul, "A Case of Mistaken Identity: The Irish in Post-war Britain," *International Labor and Working Class History* (April 1996).

2. Traditionally regarded as the first stage of English colonization, the Norman invasion of 1169 was, in fact, predated by English ecclesiastical interest in Ireland. Among the more recent histories of England's Irish Question and Ireland's English Problem are D. George Boyce, *Nationalism in Ireland*, 2d ed. (London: Routledge, 1991); Roy Foster, *Modern Ireland, 1600–1972* (London: Penguin, 1989); Charles Townshend, *Political Violence in Ireland: Government and Resistance since 1848* (Oxford: Clarendon Press, 1983); Nicholas Canny, "The Marginal Kingdom: Ireland as a Problem in the First British Empire," in *Strangers within the Realm: Cultural Margins of the First British Empire*, ed. Bernard Bailyn and Philip D. Morgan (Chapel Hill: University of North Carolina Press, 1991).

3. Though never formally a colony, Ireland's position within the United Kingdom was in some ways closer to that of India than that of Scotland or Wales. Of the four nations in the United Kingdom, for example, only Ireland had a Governor General and its own civil service and armed militia, and only Ireland waged a sustained physical and constitutional war of independence.

4. Approximately 170,000 Irishmen served in the British Army during World War I, and 40,000 Eire citizens joined in World War II. This latter enlistment matched in numbers though not in proportion Northern Ireland's military contribution. DO35/1230 Comparing Ulster and Eire's Contributions, no date; Julius Isaacs, *British Post-war Migration*, Occasional Papers 17 (Cambridge: National Institute for Economic and Social Research, Cambridge University Press, 1954). During the Depression, emigration from the Free State initially fell but soon recovered, reaching twenty-six thousand in 1937 alone. Joseph Lee, *Ireland, 1912–1985: Politics and Society* (Cambridge: Cambridge University Press, 1989), p. 187. Recent histories of Irish migration include Roger Swift and Sheridan Gilley, eds., *The Irish in Britain, 1815–1939* (London: Pinter, 1989); Lynn H. Lees, *Exiles of Erin: Irish Migrants in Victorian London* (Ithaca: Cornell University Press, 1979); J. G. Williamson, "The Impact of the Irish on British Labour Markets during the Industrial Revolution," *Journal of Economic History* 46 (September 1986): 693–721; M. A. G. O'Tuathaigh, "The Irish in Nineteenth Century Britain and Problems of Interpretation," *Transactions of the Royal Historical Society* (1981).

5. Interview with His Grace, the Archbishop of Liverpool, Derek Warlock, 12 June 1993. In the postwar years His Grace was responsible for initiating and coordinating the Catholic church's reception of Irish migrants.

6. DO35/3917 Ministry of Labour Arrangements for the Transfer of Workers from the Irish Republic to the United Kingdom, 3 August 1951; HO213/1322 Ministry of Labour Circular, 141/30 Movement of Work People between Eire and Great Britain.

7. LAB13/1005 Statistics Relating to Persons Arriving from Overseas Applying for National Insurance Cards during 1960 Compared with 1959, February 1961. See also Commission on Emigration and Other Population Problems, *1948–1954, Reports* (Dublin: Government of Ireland, 1954); *Irish Times*, 16 March 1961. Census figures taken from Liam Ryan, "Irish Emigration to Britain since World War II," in *Migrations: The Irish at Home and Abroad*, ed. Richard Kearney (Dublin: Wolfhound Press, 1990). Over the next thirty years Irish migration held steady. The 1991 UK census recorded an Irish-born population of just under 837,000. *Ethnicity in the 1991 Census*, vol. 2: *The Ethnic Minority Populations of Great Britain*, ed. Cecil Peach (London: HMSO, 1996), p. 224.

8. PREM8/851 CP(45)287, 16 November 1945 Canadian Citizenship Bill.

9. HO213/153 Memorandum by Davies, on the Relationship between British Nationality and Eire Citizenship, 17 March 1944. According to Davies, whatever its intended effect, the Irish Act did not have "any effect one way or the other, in contemplation of British law, on the status of those who come within its operation." HO213/201 Draft Memorandum on Position of Eire, no date.

10. HO213/201 W. E. Beckett to Dowson, 9 May 1946, Draft Memorandum on Position of Eire, no date; PREM8/851 CP(46)305 Changes in British Nationality Law, Joint Memorandum by the Home and Dominion Secretaries, 29 July 1946.

11. CAB133/6 British Commonwealth Conference on Nationality and Citizenship, 2d meeting, 4 February 1947. In addition to the constitutional position, Irish officials were bound by a reluctance to contradict former Taoiseach Eamon de Valera's frequent public assertions that no Eire citizen was a British subject. FO372/5011 Norman Archer to Dixon, 24 January 1947.

12. This was the conclusion of the 1938 Government Committee on Seasonal Migration, cited in Paul Bew, Ellen Hazelkorn, Henry Patterson, *The Dynamics of Irish Politics* (London: Lawrence and Wishart, 1989), p. 75.

13. Of 502,000 persons aged ten to nineteen in 1951, only 303,000 remained in the country by 1961. K. Theodore Hoppen, *Ireland since 1800: Conflict and Conformity* (London: Longman, 1989), p. 218, citing W. E. Vaughn and A. J. Fitzpatrick, eds., *Irish Historical Statistics: Population, 1821–1971* (Dublin, 1978), and P. J. Drudy, "Migration between Ireland and Britain since Independence" in *Ireland and Britain since 1922*, ed. Drudy, Irish Studies 5 (Cambridge; Cambridge University Press, 1986), pp. 107–23. See also Commission on Emigration and Other Problems, *Reports*. This economic dependence extended beyond labor; in 1937, 91 percent of Irish exports went to Britain. Lee, *Ireland*, p. 187.

14. Lee, *Ireland*, p. 227, citing an internal Irish government memorandum, 18 May 1942. Although this last observation was made during the war, the ideology remained true in a postwar era vividly portrayed by contempo-

rary literature as culturally backward and pervaded by a sense of national despair. See particularly the work of Patrick Kavanagh, Austin Clarke, and Brenden Behan. Details of the postwar economy and the importance of emigration within it appear in Terence Brown, *Ireland: A Social and Cultural History, 1922 to the Present* (Ithaca: Cornell University Press, 1985), pp. 162-82; Lee, *Ireland*, pp. 258–328; Bew, Hazelkorn, and Patterson, *Dynamics of Irish Politics*, pp. 41-89; Foster, *Modern Ireland*, pp. 563–82; Ronan Fanning, *Independent Ireland* (Dublin: Helicon, 1983), pp. 143–86.

15. Liam de Paor, "Ireland's Identities," *Crane Bag* 3.1 (1979): 25, cited in Brown, *Ireland*, p. 165.

16. Bew, Hazelkorn, and Patterson, *Dynamics of Irish Politics*, p. 219. So high were postwar emigration figures that the government instituted a Commission on Emigration in 1948, the findings of which suggested that contemporary migrants were leaving not in order to sustain rural lifestyles, as earlier emigrants had done, but in rejection of them. In response to these conclusions and other analyses of the economy, Irish politicians in the late 1950s and 1960s attempted to steer a new economic course for Ireland, determined to halt the hemorrhage of the young by providing opportunity and prosperity at home. In 1946, however, as the British Nationality Act was being written, that new course lay in the future; for the present there was only the fact and the need of continuing emigration. Brown, *Ireland*, pp. 132–82; Foster, *Modern Ireland*, p. 539.

17. These efforts to define and protect the Irish national identity continued after 1922 with, among other examples, the compulsory use of Gaelic in schools, the creation of a censorship board prohibiting the import of much modern foreign literature, and the general idealization of the rural heartland as the "true" Ireland. Brown, *Ireland*.

18. In 1936 the UK and all dominion parliaments had to pass legislation facilitating and acknowledging the abdication of Edward VIII. De Valera used the opportunity to reduce the role of the English Crown in Irish affairs, specifically reserving the relationship between Eire and the Crown to external policy. F. S. L. Lyons, *Ireland since the Famine*, rev. ed. (London: Collins, 1973), pp. 518–519; Fanning, *Independent Ireland*, pp. 117–20.

19. Many contemporary observers condemned Ireland for "opting out of history," but as at least one historian has observed, most Irish men and women understood neutrality as yet another assertion of Ireland's right to do as it pleased and to disregard UK assumptions that it would "naturally" follow its erstwhile foe into war. Neutrality reinforced the image of political independence. Brown, *Ireland*, p. 139. For a more detailed analysis of Irish neutrality, see Robert Fisk, *In Time of War: Ireland, Ulster, and the Price of Neutrality, 1939–1945* (London: Paladin, 1985).

20. Nineteenth-century Irish nationalists experienced similar difficulties. In the 1880s the UK government instituted a number of state-sponsored emigration schemes. The problem for Irish politicians in Westminster was how to denounce the need for the schemes—i.e., the need for emigration—and yet at

the same time extract the best possible terms for Irish people wishing to avail themselves of the opportunity to emigrate to other parts of the dominions.

21. FO372/5011 L. S. Brass to Beckett 11 January 1947. UK officials surmised that the Irish government was "very keen" that Irish citizens should not become aliens in Britain.

22. *Parliamentary Debates* (Commons), 5th ser., [1948], v. 453, c. 1112.

23. HO213/1330 W. H. Hardman to Roy, 20 March 1947; Lee, *Ireland*, p. 227, citing J. P. Walshe to de Valera, 18 May 1942.

24. CAB134/1210 C I (56)5, 18 September 1956.

25. Such at least was the opinion of Lord Rugby, who suspected that Costello, in a possible effort to outbid the more radical de Valera, "had been led by considerations of domestic politics" and had "bungled matters." CAB128/13 CM71(48), 12 November 1948; CAB129/30 CP48(253), November 1948, memorandum by Lord Rugby, the UK Representative in Dublin. Eamon de Valera was the contemporary politician most associated with radical Irish nationalism. It was he who had opposed the Anglo-Irish Treaty of 1921 and he who had introduced both the 1935 Citizenship Act and the 1937 Constitution. A detailed history and analysis of the repeal and the subsequent negotiations may be found in Ian McCabe, *A Diplomatic History of Ireland, 1948–49* (Dublin: Irish Academic Press, 1991). See also Ronan Fanning, "London and Belfast's Response to the Declaration of the Republic of Ireland, 1948–49," *International Affairs* 58.1 (1981–82): 95–114.

26. This choice of date is open to interpretation. Some might suggest that the Irish had been dying for the cause of nationalism since 1169. The date does, however, represent the year in which, during the Easter Rising, a republic was first declared, and it was to this republic that twentieth-century republicans swore allegiance.

27. The Irish Civil War pitted those who favored rejection of the 1921 Anglo-Irish Treaty against those who believed that while short of a republic, the treaty's terms represented the best available at the time. Led by Michael Collins, the pro-Treaty forces constituted the Free State government and were ultimately the victors.

28. Sean MacBride, "Anglo-Irish Relations," *International Affairs* 25.3 (1949): 257–73.

29. The ERA had been the topic of discussion within Irish politics for quite some time, but still it seems likely that Costello's announcement, though later publicly supported by his Cabinet, was unplanned. The ERA had played an earlier role in the politics of emigration. One explanation of de Valera's failure to proclaim a republic in 1937 was that "the merest prospect that the multitude of Irish-born citizens living in Britain might, perhaps, be deprived of their rights there with the consequential prospects of enforced repatriation, to say nothing of the choking off of the safety valve of Irish emigration to the United Kingdom, would give any Irish government nightmares." Fanning, *Independent Ireland*, p. 118. Costello's determination to pursue the logic of his Foreign Secretary's words thus represented a brave step in terms of migration and economics.

30. CAB129/30 CR(48)2, 21 May 1948, CR(48)4, 21 July 1948, CR(48)5, 14 September 1948, Cabinet Committee on Commonwealth Relations, 1948.

31. CAB128/13 CM73(48), 15 November 1948; CAB129/31 CP (48)272, 17 November 1948.

32. DO35/3962 Brief for Prime Minister, 13 October 1948.

33. CAB129/30 CP(48)262 UK Reply to Eire Government, 10 November 1948. The phrase "friendly warning" was used by UK civil servants to describe the kind of message that might be sent to persuade the Eire government to change its mind.

34. CAB128/13 CM71(48), 12 November 1948.

35. CAB129/30 CP(48)263 Possible Measures to Mitigate Possible Disadvantages of the Repeal of the External Relations Act, 10 November 1948, plus Annex—Interdepartmental Note on Possible Mitigatory Measures; CAB129/30 CP(48)254 Ireland and the Commonwealth.

36. CAB129/30 CP(48)258 Account of a Meeting with Eire Ministers on 17 October, 8 November 1948; CAB129/31 Report of Paris Meetings, 14 and 16 November 1948, read at Cabinet meetings, CAB128/13 CM (48)73, 15 November 1948, and CM(48)74, 18 November 1948; DO35/3962 Herbert Evatt to Attlee, 12 October 1948. Attlee invited these dominion leaders because of their Irish populations. McCabe, *Diplomatic History*, p. 60.

37. CAB128/13 CM(48)73, 15 November 1948.

38. CAB129/30 CP(48)258 Account of a Meeting with Eire Ministers, 17 October, 8 November 1948; CAB128/13 71(48), 12 November 1948.

39. UK representatives rejected this argument on the grounds that in 1937, all other members of the Commonwealth had specifically stated that the adoption of the Irish Constitution and the ERA did not alter Eire's relationship with the Commonwealth. CAB129/30 CP(48)262 UK Reply to Eire Government's Aide-Memoire, 10 November 1948; CAB129/31 CP(48)272, 17 November 1948.

40. DO35/3979 Departure of Eire from the Commonwealth; CAB129/30 CP(48)262 Aide-Memoire from Eire Government, 20 October 1948; McCabe, *Diplomatic History*, p. 79.

41. CAB129/31 CP(48)272 Eire's Future Relations with the Commonwealth, Joint Memorandum by the Lord Chancellor and Secretary of State for Commonwealth Relations, 17 November 1948.

42. Ibid. This was not the first time that Irish nationalism was protected by dominion sensibility. In 1931 during the debate on the Statute of Westminster, future Prime Minister Winston Churchill tried to include a clause forbidding Irish revocation of the 1922 Treaty. The Eire government sent a letter warning that such "legislative enactment" would be ill taken. Prime Minister Stanley Baldwin supported the Irish view on the grounds that Churchill's restrictive clause "would offend not only the Irish Free State, not only Irishmen all over the world, but other dominions as well." Lyons, *Ireland since the Famine*, pp. 509–10.

43. CAB128/13 CM74(48), 18 November 1948. The reciprocity as eventually enacted was not complete. Citizens of the United Kingdom, Australia, New Zealand, and Canada were exempt from aliens provisions in Eire but could not vote, whereas Eire citizens possessed the franchise in Britain (but not in other dominion countries). This exceptionalism on the part of Britain may be related to its looked-for metropolitan role.

44. FO371/76369 Minute by G. W. Furlonge, 21 January 1949.

45. CAB128/13 CM74(48), 18 November 1948; *Parliamentary Debates*, (Commons), 5th ser., [1948], v. 458, c. 1414.

46. FO371/76369 G. W. Furlonge note, 21 January 1949.

47. CAB128/13 CM74(48), 18 November 1948.

48. DO35/3917 Irish Chargé d'Affaires to Commonwealth Relations Office, 28 August 1951.

49. DO35/3917 Ministry of Labour Response to Irish Chargé d'Affaires telegram, 5 November 1951; DO35/3917 G. W. Tory (British Embassy, Dublin) to N. E. Costar, (Commonwealth Relations Office), 31 August 1951. Tory claimed that an Irish official had once admitted Ireland's dependence on the annual emigration of thirty thousand citizens and the seasonal migration of many more. At the same time, however, and despite the great need, the Irish government loudly condemned an English announcement that additional recruits for mine work would be sought among the Irish. Private practice was thus different from public policy.

50. PREM11/824 Report of the Committee on the Social and Economic Problems arising from the Growing Influx into the United Kingdom of Coloured Workers from Other Commonwealth Countries, 3 August 1955.

51. Officials suggested that many Irish citizens currently enjoying the franchise would be unsure of their nationality if pressed and would thus be unable to help electoral officers distinguish between Irish aliens and British subjects. In addition, officials believed that the Conservative Party's support for the Republic of Ireland Act of 1949 tied them to the continuation of its provisions. CAB134/1210 CI(56)5, 18 September 1956, Committee on Colonial Immigrants: Immigration from the Irish Republic; CAB134/1210 CP(56) [no additional number given], October 1956, Colonial Immigrants: Supplementary Report of the Committee of Ministers.

52. PREM11/824 Report of the Committee on the Social and Economic Problems Arising from the Growing Influx into the United Kingdom of Coloured Workers from Other Commonwealth Countries, 3 August 1955; CAB134/1210 CP(56) [no additional number given], October 1956, Colonial Immigrants: Supplementary Report of the Committee of Ministers; CAB134/1210 CI(56)5, 18 September 1956, Committee on Colonial Immigrants: Immigration from the Irish Republic; CO1032/121 Commonwealth Relations Office Re-draft of Social and Economic Report, August 1955.

53. A Colonial Office official noted somewhat acerbically: "The objections of principle to letting in the Irish, while keeping out British subjects, are patent. The arguments of commonsense in favour of allowing the Irish to get

away with it yet again are perhaps more convincing." CO1032/195 Ian Watt memo, 1 May 1958. These "arguments of commonsense" were sufficiently strong to enable the government to resist two parliamentary calls for the imposition of control on Irish migration as early as 1957. *Parliamentary Debates* (Commons), 5th ser., [1957], v. 566, c. 514. Although willing to let the Irish pass uncontrolled, officials were less willing to publicize their leniency; the Home Office reminded the Ministry of Labour to adopt "a very cautious line as regards drawing attention to the special position of the Irish here." LAB13/774 Kent to Keith, 9 February 1955.

54. CAB129/103 C(60)165, 15 November 1960, Coloured Immigration from the Commonwealth, Memorandum by the Secretary of State for the Home Department.

55. CAB134/1469 CGM(61)3, 8 February 1961, Commonwealth Migrants Committee, Coloured Immigration, Memorandum by the Secretary of State for the Home Department; CAB134/1469 Working Party to Report on the Social and Economic Problems Arising from the Growing Influx into the United Kingdom of Coloured Workers from Other Commonwealth Countries, 25 July 1961.

56. CAB129/105 C(61)69, 26 May 1961 Commonwealth Migrants, Memorandum by the Secretary of State for Commonwealth Relations.

57. CAB134/1469 CGM(61) Commonwealth Migrants Committee, 3d meeting, Monday, 31 July 1961; CAB/1469 CGM(61) Commonwealth Migrants Committee, 4th meeting, 29 September 1961; CAB129/107 C(61)153, 6 October 1961, Commonwealth Migrants Memorandum by the Secretary of State for the Home Department.

58. CAB128/35 CC61(61), 9 November 1961; CAB129/10 C(61)180, 8 November 1961, Commonwealth Immigrants Bill: Application to the Irish Republic, Memorandum by the Secretary of State for the Home Department.

59. CAB128/35 CC(61)63, 16 November 1961; PREM11/3238 Henry Brooke to Prime Minister, 8 November 1961.

60. As we will see in Chapter 6, however, the children of the "old dominions" were in practice to be allowed free entry to Britain. This free entry was purely administrative, however, whereas the Irish position was safeguarded by law.

61. CAB134/1469 Citizenship in Relation to the Commonwealth Immigrants Bill; Working Party to Report on the Social and Economic Problems Arising from the Growing Influx into the United Kingdom of Coloured Workers from other Commonwealth Countries: Report to Ministerial Committee. This proposal would hardly have been well received in Dublin and showed little appreciation of the depth of Irish nationalism.

62. *Parliamentary Debates* (Commons), 5th ser., [1961], v. 650, c. 1186.

Chapter 5. Keeping Britain White

1. A good review of the state of the historiographical debate on the *Empire Windrush* and its significance for future policy making and the making of

race in Britain can be found in Kenneth Lunn, "The British State and Immigration, 1945–51: New Light on the *Empire Windrush*," in *The Politics of Marginality: Race, the Radical Right, and Minorities in Twentieth Century Britain*, ed. Tony Kushner and Lunn (London: Frank Cass, 1990), pp. 161–74. The number of passengers varies in some accounts. Lydia Lyndsey attributes this poor accounting to the independent nature of the sailing and the presence of stowaways. Lydia Lyndsey, "Halting the Tide: Responses to West Indian Immigration to Britain, 1946–52," *Journal of Caribbean History* 26.1 (1992): p. 68. The Colonial Office reported 492 fare-paying passengers and 20 stowaways. HO213/244 *Empire Windrush* Interim Progress Report, 30 June 1948.

2. The image of the Attlee government as precursor of future, more famous debates on race and immigration appears also in Shirley Joshi and Bob Carter, "The Role of Labour in the Creation of a Racist Britain," *Race and Class* 25.3 (1984). These authors say that the Attlee government's construction of race as a problem effectively defined the discourse of race and immigration for the next decade and a half. See also Kathleen Paul, "The Politics of Citizenship in Post-war Britain," *Contemporary Record* 6 (Winter 1992): 452–73.

3. Dilip Hiro, *Black British, White British: A History of Race Relations in Britain* (London: Paladin, 1992), pp. 13–16. Only Trinidad escaped the poverty of its neighbors, being sufficiently wealthy to require incoming migrant labor of its own. Hiro reports that for every migrant who traveled to the United Kingdom, nine migrated to the United States. This equation was to reverse following the implementation of the McCarran-Walter Act. Ceri Peach, *West Indian Migration to Britain: A Social Geography* (London: Oxford University Press, 1969), pp. 1–7.

4. Peter Fryer, *Staying Power: The History of Black People in Britain* (Atlantic Highlands, N.J.: Humanities Press, 1984); James Walvin, *Black and White: The Negro and English Society, 1555–1945* (London: Penguin, 1973); Edward Scobie, *Black Britannia: A History of Blacks in Britain* (Chicago: Johnson, 1972).

5. Twelve thousand West Indians enlisted during World War II, serving as foresters, RAF ground crew, and munitions workers. CAB129/40 CP(50)113, 18 May 1950. The formal color bar preventing black commissions was removed in 1939 for the duration of the war, but unofficially blacks were still prohibited from service as officers. Marika Sherwood, *Many Struggles: West Indian Workers and Service Personnel in Britain (1939–45)* (London: Karia Press, 1985), pp. 3–6.

6. Ann Dummett and Andrew Nicol, *Subjects, Citizens, Aliens, and Others: Nationality and Immigration Law* (London: Weidenfeld and Nicolson, 1990), pp. 167–69.

7. Laura Tabili, *"We Ask for British Justice": Black Workers and the Construction of Racial Difference in Late Imperial Britain* (Ithaca: Cornell University Press, 1994), pp. 113–35. The order remained in force until 1942 when

the need for "bodies on ships" temporarily took precedence over fears for the purity of the so-called British race.

8. Sherwood refers to 15,000 (*Many Struggles*, p. 3). Hiro refers to a 1919 "racial minority" of 30,000 (*Black British, White British*, p. 37). E. Ellis Cashmore refers to a 1948 black community of 10,000. Cashmore, *United Kingdom? Class, Race, and Gender since the War* (London: Unwin Hyman, 1989), p. 79. The Colonial Office estimated a population of color of around 15,000 in 1939. CO1006/2 Colonial Office Experience of Colonial Workers in the United Kingdom. This estimate was later revised to between 20,000 and 30,000 by 1950. CAB129/40 CP(50)113 Coloured People from British Colonial Territories, 18 May 1950. The 1951 census recorded a West Indian–born population of 15,000. CO1032/195 Some Aspects of West Indian Migration. Government sources in 1956 referred to a prewar population of color of 7,000, which was presumed to have grown to "rather more than 40,000" by 1953. CAB134/1210 CI(56)1 Cabinet Committee on Colonial Immigrants, Memorandum by the Lord Chancellor, 10 February 1956.

9. Peach, *West Indian Migration*, pp. 2, 23–25; Hiro, *Black British, White British*, p. 16. Peach argues convincingly that West Indian migration was determined more by the pull factor of jobs in Britain than the push factor of unemployment in the West Indies.

10. Lydia Lyndsey points out that Ministry of Labour officials had earlier reacted negatively to the arrival of the *Ormonde*. Thus, the Cabinet reaction to the *Empire Windrush* had some precedent. Lyndsey, "Halting the Tide," p. 63.

11. PREM8/827 Economic Policy Committee (48), 23d meeting, 15 June 1948. Clearly, ministers believed somebody or something must be responsible for the migration. Lyndsey suggests that much of the Colonial Office response was shaped by the need to prove to other departments that it was not involved. In fact, Lyndsey suggests that the Treasury was partly responsible by insisting that a troopship chartered by the UK government recoup some of its expenses by picking up passengers on an otherwise empty return journey to England. Lyndsey, "Halting the Tide," p. 70. The groundnut scheme was part of a plan to develop and harvest the natural resources of East Africa. Established in 1949, it cost a great deal of money during its short lifetime and was abandoned in 1951 as a fiasco. Kenneth O. Morgan, *Labour in Power, 1945–1951* (Oxford: Oxford University Press, 1984), pp. 201–2.

12. Gordon Lewis, "Race Relations in Britain: A View from the Caribbean," *Race Today* 1 (July, 1969): 79, cited in Hiro, *Black British, White British*, p. 199.

13. CAB129/28 CP(48)154 Memo by Secretary of State for the Colonies, Arrival in the United Kingdom of Jamaican Unemployed, June 1948.

14. PREM8/827 Arrival of 419 [*sic*] Jamaicans. The migrants were sorted into three groups; those intending to enlist; those with jobs or friends to go to; those with no fixed arrangements. The first group consisted of 54, the second 204, and the third 236. HO213/244 Empire Windrush Interim Progress Report, 30 June 1948.

15. These steps involved using the Jamaican press and sending a senior civil servant to the West Indies to publicize the likelihood that colonials would face unemployment in England. CAB129/28 CP(48)154 Arrival in the UK of Jamaican Unemployed, June 1948.

16. Paul Rich argues that the Colonial Office was continuing its wartime role as caretaker and provider, dispersing the migrants so as to avoid the development of racism. Paul B. Rich, *Race and Empire in British Politics* (Cambridge: Cambridge University Press, 1986), p. 163.

17. *Parliamentary Debates* (Commons), [1948], 5th ser., v. 451, c. 1851, v. 452, c. 225–26, 422.

18. Lunn, "The British State and Immigration," p. 169.

19. P. Wright, *The Coloured Worker in British Industry* (London: Oxford University Press, 1968), p. 42, cited in Cashmore, *United Kingdom?* p. 81.

20. In addition to Isaacs's and Edwards's statements, Creech Jones recognized "the need for some vetting" of migrants, although he also stated their right as British subjects to travel freely. *Parliamentary Debates* (Commons), 5th ser., [1948], v. 452, c. 422.

21. Zig Layton-Henry, *The Politics of Immigration* (Oxford: Blackwell, 1992), pp. 44–53; Cashmore, *United Kingdom?* pp. 106–17; John Rex and Sally Tomlinson, *Colonial Immigrants in a British City* (London: Routledge and Kegan Paul, 1979); William. W. Daniel, *Racial Discrimination in England* (Harmondsworth: Penguin, 1968).

22. West Indian women who had served in the Auxiliary Territorial Service during the war spoke of having been "brought up to think of England as the Mother country." *Birthrights*, BBC2 Television, broadcast, 5 July 1992. Ben Bousquet and Colin Douglas, *West Indian Women at War: British Racism in World War II* (London: Lawrence and Wishart, 1991). West Indian children rehearsed English nursery rhymes, sang "God Save the Queen," and studied British history syllabi in schools. Hiro, *Black British, White British*, pp. 15–25. See also Trevor Carter, *Shattering Illusions: West Indians in British Politics* (London: Lawrence and Wishart, 1986); John Rex and Robert Moore, *Race, Community, and Conflict* (London: Oxford University Press, 1967); "Personal Experiences of Multi-ethnic Britain," in *"Race" in Britain: Continuity and Change*, ed. Charles Husband (London: Hutchinson, 1982), pp. 175–93; Winston James, "The Making of Black Identities," and Hanif Kureishi, "London and Karachi," in *Patriotism: The Making and Unmaking of British National Identity*, vol. 2: *Minorities and Outsiders*, ed. Raphael Samuel (London: Routledge, 1989). These personal stories describe the confusion for colonial migrants and their children, growing up black in a society of black stereotypes and white privilege. Lunn presents an alternative viewpoint, suggesting that neither the migrants on board the *Windrush* nor those who followed were so naive as to think that Britain would be a perfect "motherland," and "thus the experiences in Britain were less of a surprise than has been indicated." Lunn, "The British State and Immigration," p. 168. Lyndsey suggests something of an intermediate position, arguing that migrants anticipated dif-

ficult economic conditions within England and expected to have to work hard but did not foresee such hostility to their presence. Lyndsey, "Halting the Tide," p. 73.

23. LAB13/42 Sir Thomas Lloyd to Sir Godfrey Ince, 5 March 1948.

24. LAB13/42 Ince to Lloyd, 6 May 1948.

25. LAB13/42 Bevan minute, 15 April 1948; LAB13/42, Veysey to Wiles, 3 May 1948; LAB13/42 C. W. K. MacMullan minute, 28 September 1948; LAB8/1571 Unidentifiable minute addressed to P. Goldberg, 2 October 1948.

26. LAB13/42 Lloyd to Departmental Representatives, 9 September 1948.

27. Discussing this issue, one civil servant outlined the ministry's plan: "It is our hope that, so far as male labour is concerned, the representatives of our labour supply department may be able to convince the Working Party that there is not in fact now any general shortage of male labour in this country. It will not, however, be possible to show the same where women are concerned, in particular there is a well-known shortage of operatives to man-up the textile industry." LAB8/1571 Rossetti to A. Handyside, 19 October 1948.

28. CO1006/2 Working Party on the Employment in the UK of Surplus Colonial Labour.

29. LAB13/329 Estimated Total Requirements by Sex and Category; LAB13/329 International Labour Organization Report on Requirements of Foreign Manpower and on Resources Available for Emigration in European Countries, 3d Report.

30. LAB13/42 Goldberg to MacMullan, 8 October 1948.

31. CO1006/2 Working Party on the Employment in the UK of Surplus Colonial Labour.

32. LAB8/1571 Goldberg to Tarrant, 27 August 1949; Tarrant to Goldberg, 29 August 1949. Goldberg wrote "I clearly could not say . . . that no approach of any kind had been made. . . . I accordingly made it appear in the Report as though (1) the views of the two sides had been informally taken . . . (2) both parties concerned had in the result advised against resorting to the use of coloured labour in present circumstances."

33. LAB8/1571 Goldberg to MacMullan, 15 October 1948; LAB8/1571 Proposed Employment of Colonial Workers in Great Britain, February 1949.

34. LAB13/42 Lloyd to Ince, 5 March 1948, and again 10 August 1949.

35. LAB13/42 Goldberg to Hardman, 10 May 1950.

36. Robert Miles, *Racism* (London: Routledge, 1989), p. 74, cited in Floya Anthias and Nira Yuval-Davis, *Racialized Boundaries: Race, Nation, Gender, Colour, and Class and the Anti-racist Struggle* (London: Routledge, 1992), p. 11.

37. CO1006/2 CLWP(48)5 Working Party on Surplus Colonial Labour, Colonial Office Memorandum, Experience of Colonial Workers in the United Kingdom; LAB13/42 Report of the Working Party on Surplus Colonial Labour, 4th meeting; LAB8/1571 Surplus Colonial Labour Committee, Rosetti

to Handyside, 19 October 1948; LAB8/1571 Proposed Employment of Colonial Workers in Great Britain, February 1949.

38. LAB13/42 Report of the 4th Meeting of the Working Party on Surplus Colonial Labour. The role of the creation of "absolutes" such as "race" and nationality in dividing black and white Britons is fully explored in Paul Gilroy, *There Ain't No Black in the Union Jack: The Cultural Politics of Race and Nation* (London: Unwin Hyman, 1987).

39. LAB13/42 Note by Bevan, 11 October 1948.

40. LAB13/42 Wiles to Bevan, 8 March 1948; LAB13/42 Report of the Committee to "enquire into the possibility of employing in the United Kingdom surplus manpower of certain Colonial territories in order to assist the manpower situation in this country and to relieve unemployment in those Colonial territories"; LAB8/1571 Proposed Employment of Colonial Workers in Great Britain, February 1949, Rosetti to Goldberg, 19 October 1948.

41. LAB13/42 Wiles to Bevan, 8 March 1948.

42. LAB 13/42 Ince to Lloyd, 6 May 1948. The comparison with EVWs was in any case unfair since in reality the controls upon the aliens could not be enforced as rigidly as the existence of contracts would suggest.

43. LAB13/42 Bevan to Veysey, 10 August 1948.

44. CO1006/2 CLWP(48)4 Working Party on Surplus Colonial Labour, the Possibilities of Employing Colonial Labour in the United Kingdom, with Notes on the Number of Vacancies Outstanding in the Principal Undermanned Industries, October 1948.

45. LAB13/42 Report of the Committee on Surplus Colonial Manpower.

46. HO213/244 J. D. Murray et al. to Prime Minister, 22 June 1948, cited by Bob Carter, Shirley Joshi, and Clive Harris in *No Blacks Please, We're British* (London: Routledge, forthcoming).

47. Commissioners evaluated all the negative consequences of a population increase—greater competition for scarce resources on an already densely populated isle and an inflexible labor market—and yet declared in favor of the same. Whether an inflexible labor market would be seen as a disadvantage would depend on whether one was a potential employer or a potential employee.

48. *Report of the Royal Commission on Population*. Cmd. 7695 (London: HMSO, 1949), paras. 321, 518, 587, 647.

49. Ibid., paras. 328, 329, 331, 337.

50. CAB128/16 CM49(49), 27 July 1949; CAB128/17 CM13(50), 20 March 1950. London dockers had struck in sympathy with the Communist-led Canadian Seamen's Union but were probably inspired as much by their own grievances against the Dock Labour Scheme as by communism. For a detailed analysis of the strike which downplays the role of communism see Peter Weiler, "British Labour and the Cold War: The London Dock Strike of 1949," in *Social Conflict and the Political Order in Modern Britain*, ed. James Cronin and Jon Schneer (London: Croom Helm, 1982), pp. 146–78.

51. CAB128/16 CM49(49), 27 July 1949.
52. CAB129/28 CP(48)154 Arrival in the UK of Jamaican Unemployed, June 1948.

Chapter 6. Tinkering at the Edges of Nationality

1. *Economist*, 29 November 1958. Cited in Ira Katznelson, *Black Men, White Cities* (London: Institute for Race Relations and Oxford University Press, 1973).
2. *Daily Mirror*, 3 September 1958.
3. CO1032/196 Press Comment on Race Riots, September 1958.
4. The earliest "traditional" history is perhaps Nicholas Deakin, *Colour, Citizenship, and British Society* (London: Panther, 1970). This abridged version of the Institute of Race Relations' 5-year study *Colour and Citizenship*, asserts that would-be migrants to Britain were hampered by controls imposed by their own governments, not Britain, and that when Britain finally acted, it was on the basis of expediency not principle. A year earlier the Liberal MP David Steel described the 1962 act as the "capitulation of the leaders to the baying of the constituency rank and file and the knights of the shires." David Steel, *No Entry: The Background and Implications of the Commonwealth Immigrants Act, 1968* (London: C. Hurst, 1969). Thus, the "traditional" history while accusing policy makers of pragmatism absolves them of racism. Both Deakin's and Steel's studies were written without the benefit of public records but their message is still current. Peter Fryer, *Staying Power: The History of Black People in Britain* (Atlantic Highlands, N.J.: Humanities Press, 1984), p. 381, claims that successive British governments failed to formulate any policy initiatives to deal with the new migrants and that "between 1958 and 1968 black settlers in Britain watched the racist tail wag the Parliamentary dog." Kenneth O. Morgan, *The People's Peace* (Oxford: Oxford University Press, 1990), pp. 202–4, suggests that the Cabinet attitude toward "coloured immigration" was one of "extraordinary complacency" and that it was only in 1962 that Macmillan "felt compelled" to take action. Robert Miles and Annie Phizacklea, *White Man's Country* (London: Pluto Press, 1987) pp. 31–37, recognize the Conservative government's long-term discomfort with black "immigration" but still contend that in 1958 the current administration had not realized that the "solution" was to impose control and suggest that "more effort was required to push [the government] firmly on to the slippery slope of state racism." Dilip Hiro, *Black British, White British: A History of Race Relations in Britain* (London: Paladin, 1992), p. 207, writes that the Conservative government followed "a laissez-faire policy . . . regarding coloured immigration until popular anxiety forced its hand in 1961." Paul B. Rich, *Race and Empire in British Politics*, 2d ed. (Cambridge: Cambridge University Press, 1990), pp. 189–90, suggests that British society and government were "caught out" by the sudden and dramatic increase in immigrant numbers. Andrew Roberts, *Eminent Churchillians* (London: Phoenix, 1995), pp. 211–43, suggests that while Churchill and a few of his Cabinet perceived the issue

to be of immense importance, the liberal tone of the majority of the government prevented decisive action.

5. Ann Dummett and Andrew Nicol, *Subjects, Citizens, Aliens, and Others: Nationality and Immigration Law* (London: Weidenfeld and Nicolson, 1990), pp. 177–83, also contest the "traditional" view, suggesting that the government's presentation of itself as liberal was "disingenuous, to say the least," and that the pace for control was being set by the Home Office and Cabinet Secretary. Bob Carter, Clive Harris and Shirley Joshi's article "The 1951–55 Conservative Government and the Racialization of Black Immigration," *Immigrants and Minorities* 6 (November 1987), takes a similar viewpoint, detailing the administration's reluctance to accept the migrants as British and the efforts made to problematize the presence of black migrants in Britain. These arguments are pursued yet further in a later article of the same title by the same authors in *Inside Babylon: The Caribbean Diaspora in Britain*, ed. Winston James and Clive Harris (London: Verso, 1993), pp. 55–72. Along the same lines, Michael and Ann Dummett "believe that the activities of the politicians have not merely mirrored, but have been the primary cause of, the grave inflammation of racialist attitudes that has taken place in this decade." Michael Dummett and Ann Dummett, "The Role of Government in Britain's Racial Crisis," in *"Race" in Britain: Continuity and Change*, ed. Charles Husband (London: Hutchinson, 1982), p. 100.

6. CO1032/120 J. L. Keith Memo, 23 November 1954; CAB129/78 CP(56)145 Colonial Immigrants: Report of the Committee of Ministers, 22 June 1956; CAB134/1469 CCM(61)2 Progress Report by the Inter-departmental Committee on the Social and Economic Problems Arising from the Growing Influx into the United Kingdom of Coloured Workers from Other Commonwealth Countries, 1 February 1961; CAB134/1465 CCI(63)4 Commonwealth Immigrants Committee, Rate of Issue of Vouchers, 1 November 1963. Hiro, *Black British, White British*, p. 331.

7. The mere existence of these committees does not constitute proof of policy makers' hostility toward colonial migration, but the absence of any such committees to investigate the continuing Irish and Italian immigration does suggest that colonial migrants received special attention.

8. CAB129/40 CP(50)113, 18 May 1950.

9. CAB128/17 CM13(50), 20 March 1950.

10. CAB128/19 CM15(51), 22 February 1951.

11. PREM11/824 Post Office, Employment of Coloured Workers: Memorandum by the Postmaster General, 16 December 1952; CAB128/25 CM106(52), 18 December 1952.

12. CO1032/119 Report of the Working Party on Coloured People Seeking Employment in the United Kingdom, 17 December 1953.

13. Caroline Knowles, *Race, Discourse, and Labourism* (London: Routledge, 1992), p. 92.

14. Ira Katznelson explores this process of "making blacks" in *Black Men, White Cities* (London: Institute for Race Relations and Oxford University Press, 1973).

15. A detailed account of the construction of the postwar "race/immigration" problem appears in Miles and Phizacklea, *White Man's Country*, pp. 20–44. Though looking at several European countries in a later period, Teun A. van Dijk's work provides a useful context for much of the argument in this chapter. Van Dijk illustrates how elite racism, propagated through the controlled use of language and the presentation of implicit problems, shapes popular understanding. Teun A. van Dijk, *Elite Discourse and Racism* (Beverly Hills, Calif.: Sage, 1993).

16. CO1032/119 Report of the Working Party on Coloured People Seeking Employment in the United Kingdom, 17 December 1953. Suggested grounds for deportation included conviction of a serious criminal offense, inability to hold a job for a given length of time, or perpetual reliance on National Assistance.

17. CAB128/27 CC7(54), 3 February 1954.

18. CAB128/27 CC17(54), 10 March 1954.

19. CO1032/119 Lord Salisbury to Viscount Swinton, 20 March 1954.

20. CO1032/119 Oliver Lyttelton to Swinton, 31 March 1954.

21. Nicholas Deakin, "The Immigration Issue in British Politics" (Ph.D. thesis, University of Sussex, 1972), cited in Zig Layton-Henry, *The Politics of Immigration* (Oxford: Blackwell, 1992), p. 31.

22. PREM11/824 Norman Brook's memo to Prime Minister, March 1954.

23. PREM11/824 C(54)354, 22 November 1954; CO1032/120 Frank Newsam to Sir Thomas Lloyd, 8 November 1954.

24. CAB128/27 CM(78)54, 24 November 1954.

25. PREM11/824 C(54)379, 6 December 1954.

26. *Parliamentary Debates* (Commons), 5th ser., [1954], v. 532, c. 831.

27. Ibid., v. 527, c. 2092.

28. CO1032/120 J. L. Keith, Memo, 23 November 1954.

29. *Sunday Graphic*, 26 October 1952.

30. Thus the rioters did not represent a new phenomenon in UK society but could be linked to other outbreaks of violence over the course of the past hundred years or so. Both postwar "race riots," for example, shared a sudden and growing competition for jobs between demobilized white and black soldiers and seamen, an increased tolerance for aggression on the part of veterans, a tradition of imperial racial hierarchy, and a presumption of state racism. Panikos Panayi, "Anti-immigrant Riots in Nineteenth and Twentieth Century Britain," in *Racial Violence in Britain, 1840–1950*, ed. Panayi (Leicester: Leicester University Press, 1993), pp. 1–21. In Liverpool, for example, white attacks on black seamen followed white seamen's establishment of committees designed to verify black seamen's claim to British nationality and thus eligibility for common jobs on board ships. E. Ellis Cashmore, *United Kingdom? Class, Race, and Gender since the War* (London: Unwin Hyman, 1989), p. 79.

31. Michael Banton, "Beware of Strangers," *Listener*, 3 April 1958, p. 565, cited in Edward Pilkington, *Beyond the Mother Country: West Indians and*

the Notting Hill White Riots (London: I. B. Tauris, 1988), p. 83. Contemporary sociologists' accounts, constituting the first elements of a new "race relations" field, include Michael Banton, *White and Coloured: The Behaviour of British People toward Coloured Immigrants* (New Brunswick, N.J.: Rutgers University Press, 1960). Banton's title betrays his participation in the separation of black and white Britons. Since both black and white were British, his title actually makes little sense unless one accepts that "coloured immigrants" are not really British. Kenneth Little, *Negroes in Britain: A Study of Racial Relations in English Society* (London: Kegan Paul, Trench, Trubner, 1947); Anthony Richmond, *The Colour Problem* (Harmondsworth: Penguin, 1955); Sheila Patterson, *Dark Strangers: A Sociological Study of the Absorption of a Recent West Indian Migrants Group in Brixton, South London* (London, 1963); W. W. Daniel, *Racial Discrimination in England* (Harmondsworth: Penguin, 1968). An authoritative study was produced in 1969 in response to the passing of the 1968 Commonwealth Immigrants Act and the growing public attention given "immigration" in Britain, E. J. B. Rose et al., *Colour and Citizenship* (London: Institute for Race Relations and Oxford University Press, 1969). Although open to criticism for accepting "racial" groups, translating "racial" attributes into cultural differences, and in Richmond's case for a little too conveniently dividing up the population, the work produced by the early practitioners of this new field still stands as testament to the perceived possibilities for acceptance and tolerance in the early 1950s and the goodwill of those trying to comprehend the migrants.

32. Dummett and Dummett, "The Role of Government," pp. 97–127.

33. University of Warwick, Modern Records Center, TUC Papers, MSS292/805.7/2 Commonwealth Workers in Great Britain, 1954–57. According to Paul Foot, a journalist, "the degree of hostility and bitterness at work was remarkably small" in the 1950s. Paul Foot, *Immigration and Race in British Politics* (Harmondsworth: Penguin, 1965), p. 127.

34. TUC Papers, MSS292/103.2/3 Bournemouth Trades Council to TUC, 12 August 1955, MSS292/103.2/4 Andover and District Trades Council to TUC, 28 October 1955, Shingfield District Council to TUC, no date, TUC Advisory Committee Midland Region, 13 August 1958, Bedford and District Trades Council, 17 October 1959.

35. *Daily Sketch*, 3 November 1954. The *Sketch* also condemned the suggestion by a judge that Jamaicans should not be allowed to buy property containing white tenants, 8 December 1954.

36. The *Economist* found it difficult to believe that even ten thousand immigrants a year could represent a serious additional complication for the British economy and wondered whether the alarm would be raised if the ten thousand were Irish workers. The real issue was the attitude of UK residents to the migrants' skin color: "If their skins were white there would be no problem." *Economist*, 6 June 1953, 13 November 1954.

37. Ruth Glass and Harold Pollins, *The Newcomers: The West Indians in London* (London: Allen and Unwin, 1960), pp. 58–61. Colonial migrants'

personal accounts document UK indigenous prejudice with tales of available rooms suddenly becoming unavailable, blatant refusals based on skin color, and subtler rejections on the grounds of other tenants or employees' prejudices. Pilkington, *Beyond the Mother Country*, esp. pp. 41–52.

38. CAB128/27 CM82(54), 6 December 1954.

39. PREM11/824 C(54)356 Colonial Immigrants: Memorandum by the Commonwealth Relations Secretary, 23 November 1954.

40. CO1032/119 Swinton to Salisbury, March 1954.

41. PREM11/824, CP(55)113, 2 September 1955.

42. Roberts, *Eminent Churchillians*, p. 225.

43. CO1032/119 Swinton note.

44. CO1032/119 Report of the Working Party on Coloured People Seeking Employment in the United Kingdom, 17 December 1953.

45. CO1032/121 Commonwealth Relations Office Re-draft of Social and Economic Report, August 1955.

46. PREM11/824 CP(55)113 Memorandum by the Commonwealth Relations Secretary, 2 September 1955.

47. CAB128/30 CM39(55), 3 November 1955.

48. CO1032/119 Report of the Working Party on Coloured People Seeking Employment in the United Kingdom, 17 December 1953.

49. PREM11/824 Brook's memo to Prime Minister, 12 January 1955.

50. DO35/5216 Report of the Working Party to Consider Certain Proposals to Restrict the Right of British Subjects from Overseas to Enter and Remain in the United Kingdom, 10 July 1954.

51. PREM11/824 C(54)354, 22 November 1954, Colonial Immigrants: Memorandum by the Home Secretary; PREM11/824 C(54)356, 23 November 1954, Colonial Immigrants: Memorandum by the Commonwealth Relations Secretary; CP(55)113 Memorandum by the Commonwealth Relations Secretary, 2 September 1955.

52. CAB128/28 CM3(55), 13 January 1955.

53. CAB128/30 CM39(55), 3 November 1955.

54. CAB128/28 CM3(55), 13 January 1955; CAB128/30 CM39(55), 3 November 1955.

55. CAB128/28 CM3(55), 13 January 1955; CM15(55), 17 February 1955; PREM11/824 Brook to Churchill, 17 February 1955.

56. CAB128/28 CC6(55), 24 January 1955; CC8(55), 31 January 1955.

57. PREM11/824 Colonial Immigrants: Memorandum by the Home Secretary, 3 May 1955; CAB128/30 CM9(55), 9 May 1955.

58. PREM11/824 Brook's memo to Prime Minister, 14 June 1955.

59. CAB128/30 CM14(55), 14 June 1955; CAB134/1210 CI(56)1, 10 February 1956, first meeting of Cabinet Committee on Colonial Immigrants.

60. CAB128/30 CM31(55), 15 September 1955.

61. PREM11/824 Report of the Committee on the Social and Economic Problems Arising from the Growing Influx into the United Kingdom of Coloured Workers from Other Commonwealth Countries, 3 August 1955, hereafter Working Party on Social and Economic Problems.

62. The committee was established to determine the form of any legislation, the likely effect of it on actual immigration, and how it could be justified to Parliament, the public, and the rest of the Commonwealth. CAB134/1210 CI(55)1 Committee on Colonial Immigrants, 7 December 1955.

63. CAB129/78 CP(56)145, 22 June 1956; CAB128/29 CM48(56), 11 July 1956; CAB134/1210 CI(56)3, 17 May 1956, Cabinet Committee on Colonial Immigrants, Revised Draft Report to the Cabinet.

64. CO1032/119 Report of the Working Party to Consider Certain Proposals to Restrict the Right of British Subjects from Overseas to Enter and Remain in the United Kingdom, 10 July 1954.

65. A proposal for a quota system had first been put forward in 1951 by Anthony Wedgewood-Benn, a Member of Parliament on the left of the Labour Party, who believed that it would put UK immigration policy on to a "rational footing." The Home Office rejected the proposal in favor of maintaining government discretion and freedom of maneuver. *Parliamentary Debates* (Commons), 5th ser., [1951], v. 491, c. 811–12. Five years later, the working party suggested that even if the 1951 census were used as a basis for assigning quotas, thus avoiding the recent "abnormal" West Indian immigration, it would include the 137,000 born in British India. Many of these people were undoubtedly of European ancestry, but it would be impossible to reduce the quota accordingly. CO1032/195 Second Report of the Working Party on Social and Economic Problems, 26 March 1957.

66. CAB129/78 CP(56)145, 22 June 1956; CAB134/1210 CI(56)3, 17 May 1956, Cabinet Committee on Colonial Immigrants, Revised Draft Report to the Cabinet.

67. CO1032/195 Working Party on Social and Economic Problems, 17 April 1957.

68. Hiro, *Black British, White British*, p. 16. Hiro estimates that it cost an average of six months' unskilled wages to pay for a trip to England. Thus in the early years, only skilled workers and professionals were able to afford it. By 1955, however, as the numbers began to increase and the potential of England's labor market began to be proved, not only did more people of different classes travel, but travel agents began to offer loans, sure of their return, and early travelers began to send back passage money. As late as 1956, Sir Hugh Foot, Governor General of Jamaica, observed that the vast majority of emigrating Jamaicans came from the "better-off" sectors of society, frequently leaving jobs behind. CO1032/195 Report on Jamaican Political and Economic Situation by Sir Hugh Foot, 5 November 1956.

69. CO1032/195 Minutes of Working Party on Social and Economic Problems, 16 January 1958.

70. CO1032/195 Watt minute, 21 February 1958.

71. CO1032/195 CC1(58)1 Committee on Colonial Immigrants, Progress Report: Brief for Parliamentary Under Secretary of State, January 1958, Minutes, Ian Watt, 21 February, 1 May 1958, CAB129/93 C(58)129 Commonwealth Immigrants: Memorandum by the Lord President of the Council, 20 June 1958.

72. CO1032/195 Minutes of Working Party on Social and Economic Problems, 24 January 1958.

73. CAB128/31 CM57(57), 25 July 1957.

74. CAB134/1466 Cabinet Committee on Colonial Immigrants, 6 June 1957.

75. CAB134/1466 Coloured Immigration: Review of Developments, 11 March 1958.

76. CAB129/93 C(58)129 Commonwealth Immigrants: Memorandum by the Lord President of the Council, 20 June 1958; CAB128/32 CM51(58), 1 July 1958.

77. CAB128/32 CC17(58), March 1958; CAB128/31 CM50(57), 9 July 1957.

78. DO35/6403 Gwylim Lloyd George to Alec Douglas-Home, 9 April 1956; DO35/6404 British Nationality Bill, Memorandum by A. W. Snelling, 8 November 1957.

79. DO35/6403 Malcolm MacDonald to Sir Gilbert Laithwaite (CRO), 23 April 1956.

80. DO35/6404 Note on Section 12(6) of the British Nationality Act, 1948. The 1957 act also recognized Rhodesia's enactment of independent nationality legislation, authorized high commissioners to register births and deaths abroad and recognized Ghanaian independent citizenship.

81. DO35/6403 K. B. Paice to J. M. R. Maclennan, 27 November 1956, note by D. W. H. Dickson, 29 June 1957.

82. CAB134/1466 Committee on Colonial Immigrants, Control of Indian and Pakistani Migration, Memorandum by Secretary of State for Commonwealth Relations, 9 May 1958. Prime Minister Jawaharlal Nehru stated his belief that the migration of people without resources or educational background would not bring credit to India and therefore should not be allowed.

83. CO1032/119 Report of the Working Party on Coloured People Seeking Employment in the United Kingdom, 17 December 1953; CO1032/195 Indian High Commissioner to Commonwealth Relations Office, 10 May 1958, Pakistan High Commissioner to Commonwealth Relations Office, 16 May 1958. In refusing a passport to applicants thought unlikely to be able establish themselves, the governments of India and Pakistan were continuing a colonial policy, not instituting a new policy. New, however, was the Indian government's practice of "encouraging" intending migrants with passports issued before 1955 to reapply for a passport. Although not required by law, this practice enabled the government to assert greater control over the migration process. In 1958 the Pakistani government increased the repatriation deposit from 1,100 rupees (£82) to 1,800 rupees (£135). DO35/10416 Recent Information about Coloured Immigration.

84. CAB134/1466 West Indian Government Steps against Emigration, no date; CAB134/1466 Committee on Colonial immigrants, 20 May 1958.

85. CAB134/1466 Cabinet Committee on Colonial Immigrants, Progress Report by Working Party on Social and Economic Problems, 17 February 1958.

86. CAB129/40 CP(50)113, 18 May 1950.

87. CO1032/121 Colonial Office to Colonial Governors, 8 August 1956; CO1032/121 Sir Hugh Foot to A. H. Poynton, 15 August 1956. Sir Patrick Renison, governor of Guiana, had suggested that the Colonial Office send out propaganda material deliberately aimed at combating West Indian emigration. Although appreciative of the advice, the Colonial Office feared that it would prove too difficult to maintain a steady flow of negative material since most material available showed West Indians to be settling down well. The case was made worse by the fact that the negative material available tended to reflect badly upon the United Kingdom, not the emigrants, since it consisted of color bar experiences. CO1032/122, Colonial Office to Sir Patrick Renison, 20 November 1956.

88. CAB134/1466 Cabinet Committee on Colonial Immigrants, 6 June 1957.

89. CO1032/196 Colonial Office to West Indies Governors, 29 August 1958.

90. DO35/10416 Recent Information on Coloured Immigration; CAB134/1210 Cabinet Committee on Colonial Immigrants, 1 March 1956.

91. CAB134/1466 Committee on Colonial Immigrants; Control of Indian and Pakistani Migration, Memorandum by Secretary of Sate for Commonwealth Relations, 9 May 1958.

92. CO1032/196 Colonial Office to West Indies Governors, 29 August 1958.

93. CAB134/1466 Cabinet Committee on Colonial Immigrants: Progress Report by Working Party on Social and Economic Problems, 4 September 1958.

94. Ian Watt of the Colonial Office, who had earlier commended the "industriousness" and "Britishness" of the West Indians, commented, "I do think that it would be better to put it strongly to the West Indies Governments that they themselves co-operate with us in helping to solve this problem than that H.M.G. should be forced to decide that the only thing to do was to legislate and control immigration that way." CO1032/196, Watt minute, 22 August 1958. The Commonwealth Relations Office advised the high commissioners to point out to the governments that "the movement in increasing numbers of illiterate, unskilled labourers to the United Kingdom from India and Pakistan is a new phenomenon which it will be impossible for the United Kingdom Government to allow to continue unchecked. However, the UK Government would prefer it possible, that the necessary steps to stop it should be taken by the Governments of India and Pakistan themselves." CO1032/195 Commonwealth Relations Office to High Commissioners of India and Pakistan, 2 April 1958.

95. CO1032/121 Telegram, Secretary of State for the Colonies to West Indian Governments, 8 August 1956; CO1032/196 Colonial Office to West Indies Governors, 29 August 1958.

96. Pilkington, *Beyond the Mother Country*, remains the most comprehensive account of the riots.

97. CAB128/32 CM66(58), 31 July 1958; CM73(58), 29 September 1958.

98. Cashmore, *United Kingdom?* p. 85.

99. CO1032/196 Philip Rogers Memo, 15 September 1958; CO1032/141 Rogers minute, 2 February 1959.

100. Ian Watt, for example, recognized that "the disturbances certainly make it difficult for us to present our proposal publicly as one which we were convinced was desirable before the disturbances began, but I do not think that, simply because of the riots, it should be withdrawn." CO1032/196 Watt Memo, 8 September 1958.

101. CO1032/196 Colonial Governors' replies to Colonial Office, 8 September 1958.

102. CO1032/196 Press Comment on Race Riots, September 1958.

103. CO1032/196 Home Office Meeting, 8 September 1958.

104. *Parliamentary Debates* (Commons), 5th ser. [1958], v. 594, c. 196–202, v. 596, c. 1561–64, 1579–88.

105. CO1032/197 Working Party on Social and Economic Problems, 25 June 1959.

106. CAB134/1467 Progress Reports from the Working Party on Social and Economic Problems, 3 July and 1 December 1959.

107. CAB134/1466 Cabinet Committee on Colonial Immigrants Meeting, 7 November 1958.

108. CAB134/1467 Cabinet Committee on Colonial Immigrants Meetings, 14 January and 22 July 1959.

109. CAB129/102 C(60)102, 19 July 1960.

110. CAB129/103 C(60)165, 15 November 1960; CAB128/34 CC(60)59, 25 November 1960.

111. CAB129/103 C(60)165, 15 November 1960.

112. CAB134/1469 Commonwealth Migrants Committee CCM(61), 1st meeting, 16 February 1961; CAB134/1469 CCMC(61)2 Progress Report from the Working Party on Social and Economic Problems, 1 February 1961.

113. CAB128/35 16 February 1961; CAB134/1469 CCM(61) Commonwealth Migrants Committee, 1st Meeting, 16 February 1961.

114. PREM11/3625 Brief for Macmillan, 3 April 1961.

115. CAB128/35 CC(61)29, 30 May 1961; CAB129/105 C(61)67 Commonwealth Migrants Memorandum by the Lord Chancellor, 26 May 1961; CAB129/105 C(61)69 Commonwealth Migrants Memorandum by the Secretary of State for Commonwealth Relations, 26 May 1961.

116. CAB134/1469 CCM(61) Commonwealth Migrants Committee, 1st meeting, 16 February 1961. Housing permits were rejected because they would be too difficult to enforce and health permits because the real problem was not illness but color. Working Party on Social and Economic Problems, Report to Ministerial Committee, 25 July 1961.

117. CAB134/1469 Working Party on Social and Economic Problems, Curtailment of Immigration by Employment Control, Note by the Ministry of Labour, 28 April 1961.

118. CAB134/1469 CCM(61), 3d Meeting, 31 July 1961, Cabinet: Commonwealth Migrants Committee; CAB134/1469 Working Party on Social and Economic Problems, Report to Ministerial Committee, 25 July 1961.

119. CAB134/1469 CCM(61), 3d meeting, 31 July 1961, Cabinet: Commonwealth Migrants Committee.

120. CAB134/1469 Enoch Powell to Viscount Kilmuir, 11 April 1961.

121. CAB134/1469 CCM(61) Commonwealth Migrants Committee, 2d meeting, 17 May 1961.

122. Ibid. In addition to the problems I have outlined, the government foresaw a potential difficulty should Britain join the European Economic Community and, in consequence, commit to the free movement of labor between member states. Officials concluded, however, that EEC membership would not preclude the UK from administering the same controls to Europeans as to British subjects.

123. CAB134/1469 Working Party on Social and Economic Problems, Report to Ministerial Committee, 25 July 1961.

124. CAB128/35 CC(61)55, 10 October 1961 CAB129/107 C(61)153, 6 October 1961 Commonwealth Migrants: Memorandum by the Secretary of State for the Home Department.

125. *Guardian*, 12 October 1961; J. M. Evans, *Immigration Law*, 2d ed. (London: Sweet and Maxwell, 1983), p. 63.

126. CAB134/1469 CCM(61), 4th meeting, 29 September 1961.

127. Anthony Messina, *Race and Party Competition in Britain* (Oxford: Clarendon Press, 1989), p. 27.

128. CAB129/107 C(61)153, 6 October 1961 Commonwealth Migrants: Memorandum by the Secretary of State for the Home Department. The Cabinet Committee recognized that it could not include a statement denying racial discrimination since the practical effect of the bill would be felt most keenly by people of color. CAB134/1469 CCM(61), 4th meeting, Commonwealth Migrants Committee, 29 September 1961.

129. Dummett and Nicol, *Subjects and Citizens*, p. 188.

130. Messina, *Race and Party Competition*, p. 28.

131. *Parliamentary Debates* (Commons), 5th ser. [1961], v. 649, c. 687–93.

132. Evans, *Immigration Law*, p. 63; Katznelson, *Black Men*, p. 137; Zig Layton-Henry, *Politics of Race* (London: Allen and Unwin, 1984).

Chapter 7. Still the Same Old Story

1. CAB134/1507 CIC(62)1, 3 May 1962, CIC(62)2, 15 May 1962.

2. CAB134/1507 CIC(62)4, 23 July 1962, CIC(62)5, 21 September 1962.

3. CAB134/1508 CIC(63)1, 23 January 1963.

4. CAB134/1508 CIC(63)3, 13 May 1963, CIC(63)4, 8 July 1963.

5. CAB134/1508 CIC(63)5, 2 October 1963.

6. CAB128/38 CM(64)44, 30 July 1964.

7. CAB134/1468 CCI(64)2, 4 February 1964, Memorandum by the Home Secretary, Immigration in the Last Six Months of 1963 and Future Trends; CAB134/1465 CCI(64)11, 31 August 1964, Memorandum by Officials of the Home Department and the Ministry of Labour Control of Commonwealth Immigration.

8. CAB134/1468 CCI(63), 2d meeting, 18 December 1963; CCI(63)5, 9 December 1963, Memorandum by the Minister for Education, Entry of Teachers under the Commonwealth Immigrants Act. To further limit the numbers admitted, the new criteria were applied to B applicants already in the queue and those failing to meet them were reallocated to the nonpriority C waiting list.

9. CAB134/1465 CCI(64)3, 21 February 1964, Memorandum by the Minister of Labour Operation of the Voucher Scheme; CAB134/1508 CIC(63)4, 8 July 1963. Applicants from other countries could expect to wait three years. Nonpriority applicants were those who had not served in the British armed forces.

10. CAB134/1465 CCI(64)6 Operation of Part I of the Commonwealth Immigrants Act, Memorandum by the Home Secretary, 18 June 1964; CAB134/1468 CCI(64)2, 6 July 1964.

11. CAB129/122 C(65)109 Commonwealth Immigrants: Memorandum by the Lord President of the Council, 23 July 1965.

12. CAB134/1465 CCI(64)6 Operation of Part 1 of the Commonwealth Immigrants Act, Memorandum by the Home Secretary, 18 June 1964.

13. CAB128/38 CM(64)47, 10 September 1964.

14. CAB134/1465 CCI(64)11, 31 August 1964, Memorandum by Officials of the Home Department and the Ministry of Labour Control of Commonwealth Immigration.

15. CAB134/1465 CCI(64)8, 21 July 1964, Memorandum by the Secretary of State for the Home Department Control of Commonwealth Immigration.

16. CAB128/38 CM(64)44, 30 July 1964.

17. CAB134/1468 CCI(63)7, 13 December 1963, Memorandum by the Home Secretary, Position of Female Shorthand Typists.

18. CAB134/1465 CCI(64)11 Memorandum by Officials of the Home Office and the Ministry of Labour, Control of Commonwealth Immigration, 31 August 1964.

19. Ibid.

20. CAB129/119 C(64)11, 3 November 1964; CAB128/39 CC(64)6, 5 November 1964. The backlog of applicants had grown to 437, 237 by mid-October 1964. By this date, a total of 84,115 vouchers had been issued and 47,687 voucher holders had been admitted. *Parliamentary Debates* (Commons), 5th ser. [1964], v. 716, c. 237–38.

21. CAB134/1504 CI(64)4 The Working of the Commonwealth Immigrants Act, 1962, Memorandum by the Home Secretary, 10 November 1964.

While official memorandums might well follow a pattern already established, it remained open to Soskice to change the direction of Home Office thinking to suit a new government.

22. CAB134/1504 CI(64)2, 21 December 1964.

23. CAB129/39 CC(65)6, 1 February 1965.

24. Gordon-Walker Papers, Churchill College, 1/16 Smethwick Letters, Harold Wilson to Patrick Gordon-Walker, 13 February 1965.

25. CAB129/122 C(65)109 Commonwealth Immigration, Memorandum by the Lord President of the Council, 23 July 1965.

26. CAB128/39 CC(65)36, 8 July 1965, CC(65)42, 27 July 1965. Ministers made special provision for Malta on the rationale that its need for emigration was a direct result of London's decision to run down the military significance of the island. Ministers recognized that these criteria exposed them to the criticism that Britain was depriving the Commonwealth of the services of its skilled professional workers and drawing up a migration scheme entirely according to its own needs but justified the policy by referring to the valuable experience such elite migrants would gain before returning "home."

27. CAB129/121 C(65)92 Commonwealth Immigration, Memorandum by the Home Secretary, 7 July 1965.

28. CAB128/39 CC(65)36, 8 July 1965, CC(65)42, 27 July 1965. Entry certificates for dependents became obligatory in 1969. Robert Miles and Annie Phizacklea, *White Man's Country* (London: Pluto Press, 1987), p. 67.

29. Miles and Phizacklea, *White Man's Country*, p. 55.

30. CAB128/39 CC(65)11, 22 February 1965, CC(65)31, 20 May 1965.

31. Zig Layton-Henry, *The Politics of Immigration* (Oxford: Blackwell, 1992), p. 217.

32. CAB128/38 CM(64)47, 10 September 1964.

33. Richard Crossman, *The Diaries of a Cabinet Minister* (London: Hamish Hamilton and Jonathan Cape, 1975–76), 1:149, cited in Colin Holmes, *A Tolerant Country?* (London: Faber and Faber, 1991), p. 57. For a contemporary analysis of Smethwick—still one of the best—see Paul Foot, *Immigration and Race in British Politics* (Harmondsworth: Penguin, 1965).

34. Miles and Phizacklea explore this relationship between working-class racism and the state's "failure . . . to house and educate adequately." Miles and Phizacklea, *White Man's Country*, pp. 51–52.

35. National Front references taken from Holmes, *A Tolerant Country?* p. 57.

36. Quoted in Anthony Messina, *Race and Party Competition in Britain* (Oxford: Clarendon Press, 1989), p. 40.

37. Paul Foot, *The Rise of Enoch Powell* (London: Penguin, 1969), p. 119.

38. Quoted in Messina, *Race and Party Competition*, p. 40. Messina suggests that Powell's true crime was to have "violated the rule of silence" surrounding policy makers' manipulation of race and immigration.

39. Crossman went on to write, "There are some 200,000 of them who

are now threatened as a result of the Black-Africa policy. It's quite clear we couldn't allow some 50,000 Asians from Kenya to pour into Britain each year. On the other hand it's doubtful whether we have any legal or constitutional right to deny entry." Crossman, *Diaries* 2:526, cited in Ann Dummett and Andrew Nichol, *Subjects, Citizens, Aliens, and Others: Nationality and Immigration Law* (London: Weidenfeld and Nicolson, 1990), p. 200.

40. The UK government also ensured that Kenyans of European descent received financial compensation upon Kenyan independence. Dummett and Nicol, *Subjects, Citizens*, p. 198.

41. The *Times* referred to the act as "probably the most shameful measure that Labour members have ever been asked . . . to support." Two years later, the newspaper again referred to the betrayal of African Asians by the British for "racialist" reasons and wrote of the hardship many of these individuals were currently suffering as a consequence. *Times*, 27 February 1968, 18 February 1970. *Institute of Race Relations Newsletter*, London (June 1968). All cited in Dummett and Nicol, *Subjects, Citizens*, p. 202. B. Hepple, "Statutes: Commonwealth Immigrants Act 1968," *Modern Law Review* 31 (1968).

42. CAB134/1504 CI(65)13, 29 July 1965, CI(65)14, 21 September 1965.

43. CO537/1910 Colonial Office Draft Memo.

44. CAB134/1468 CCI(63)3, 30 October 1963, Position of Asians in Kenya, Memorandum by the Secretary of State for the Home Department.

45. CAB134/1504 CI(65)13, 29 July 1965, CI(65)14, 21 September 1965.

46. Dummett and Nicol, *Subjects, Citizens*, pp. 216-22.

47. Heather Booth, "Immigration in Perspective: Population Development in the United Kingdom," in *Towards a Just Immigration Policy*, ed. Ann Dummett (London: Cobden Trust, 1986). This figure refers to residents of the United Kingdom born in Eire. J. M. Evans suggested that "in so far as immigration policy reflects a nation's international relationships the Act recognises that Britain is no longer the metropolitan centre of the Commonwealth." Evans was right up to a point. The act confirmed that Britain was no longer the center of the "coloured" Commonwealth, but by confirming the right of patrials to enter, the act confirmed policy makers' vision of the United Kingdom as the center of the white Commonwealth. J. M. Evans, "Statutes: Immigration Act, 1971," *Modern Law Review* 35 (1972).

48. Dummett and Nicol detail the reception arrangements, the pressure on the "Ugandan Asians" to disperse, as well as the patronizing attitude of UK volunteers. Dummett and Nicol, *Subjects, Citizens*, pp. 221, 234–35.

49. Messina, *Race and Party Competition*, p. 122.

50. *Parliamentary Debates* (Commons), 5th ser. [1981], v. 997, c. 935.

51. Home Office Circular, BN 2, British Overseas Citizens, British Nationality Act, 1981; Home Office Circular BN 8, Information about Registration as a British Citizen. Layton-Henry, *Politics of Immigration*, p. 192; Dummett and Nicol, *Subjects, Citizens*, pp. 241–48.

52. J. M. Evans, *Immigration Law*, 2d ed. (London: Sweet and Maxwell, 1983), p. 74.

53. *Parliamentary Debates* (Commons), 5th ser., [1981], v. 997, c. 997.

54. Ibid., c. 983.

55. Ibid., c. 9 45.

56. *Guardian*, April 1991.

57. *Parliamentary Debates* (Commons) 6th ser., [1982], v. 21, c. 633–34, 639, 643.

58. Ibid., v. 26, c. 164.

59. Ibid., [1990], v. 170, c. 1566.

60. Ibid., [1985], v. 72, c. 1067. The travel documents became valid in 1987 and were linked to Hong Kong's acceptance of the 1984 Sino-Anglo agreement. *Guardian*, 5 March 1996. Extending visa-free access was regarded by the government as a sign of support for Hong Kong's future under Chinese rule and a preventive move to secure continued UK access to Hong Kong— critical to continued British participation in the Hong Kong economy.

61. *Parliamentary Debates* (Commons), 6th ser., [1990], v. 170, c. 1589, 1602.

62. *Times*, 4 July 1995. The player is Tony Grieg.

63. Robert Henderson, "Is It in the Blood?" *Wisden Cricket Monthly* (July 1995).

64. *Guardian*, 4 July 1995.

65. *Times*, 4 July 1995.

66. *Guardian*, 4 July 1995.

67. A similar ambiguous advance was evident two years earlier when Conservative MP Winston Churchill, grandson of the wartime leader, declared that the "British way of life" was threatened by an annual inflow of immigrants equal in size to a small British town. The Conservative Central Office distanced itself from the comments, and the media condemned the remark as divisive and inflammatory. The condemnation was contextualized, however, with the almost reassuring information that actual immigration was much lower than Churchill suggested. *Guardian*, 29, 31 May 1993; Sunday *Times*, 30 May 1993; *Gleaner*, 8 June 1993.

68. *Ethnicity in the 1991 Census*, p. 8.

Index

247

Sandys, Duncan, 108, 162, 171
Shawcross, Sir Hartley, 15, 16, 21
Shinwell, Emanuel, 6, 67
skin color (as basis of imperial inequality), xii, 12, 13–14, 22–23, 26, 43, 47, 105–6, 108, 120, 124–30, 134–39, 141, 156, 162, 165, 173, 175–76, 189, 198n.39
Smieton, Dame Edith, 40, 51
social services budget, 135, 156, 157, 174, 244n.34
Soskice, Frank, 174, 175
South Africa, 2, 188; emigration to, 25, 28, 30, 31, 37, 44, 60; and non-whites, 44, 45
Southern Rhodesia: "British stock" in, 182, 211n.150; color bar in, 43–44, 200n.21; emigration to, 25, 30–31, 37, 43–44, 47, 59–60
Soviet Union (Russia), 1–3, 27, 29, 41, 60, 66, 83
sports, 187–89
Statute of Westminster, 2
steel industry, 5, 49, 72
stowaways, 133, 152
Sudeten women, 75, 79, 86, 119
Suez crisis, 34, 60, 62, 150, 185

textiles. *See* industries
Thatcher, Margaret, 170, 182, 185–87
trade unions, 4; and alien workers, 65, 76, 81–82, 85, 118, 123, 140; and immigrants of color, 123, 125, 140, 144
Treasury Office, 76, 122, 164

"Ugandan Asians," 182
UKC. *See* United Kingdom and Colonies citizenship
Ukrainians, 72, 78, 86, 88
United Kingdom (UK): postwar economic problems of, 1, 4–5, 27, 47–60; right of, to legislate its own citizenship laws, 16; self-interest over imperial interests of, 58–60. *See also* British Empire and Commonwealth; citizenship; policy makers
United Kingdom and Colonies citizenship, 16, 17–24, 150–51, 165–67, 170, 179–82
United Nations, 42, 71, 79, 95, 101
United States, 41, 67, 163; anti-imperialist stance of, 7, 10; emigration to, xiv, 93, 186, by West Indians, 112, 141–42, 163; immigration restrictions in, 111, 142, 228n.3; as world power, 1–3, 27, 29, 41, 60

veterans. *See* military forces
voting rights, 10, 107, 226n.43
vouchers (immigration), 166, 167, 171–75

welfare state, 5, 13, 61, 120, 136, 138, 157, 159. *See also* National Assistance; social services budget
West Indian Federation, 163, 165
West Indians: as British war veterans, 44, 123–24, 184, 228n.5, 230n.22; compared to "Asians," 148–49; compared to "British stock," 57–58; economic contributions of, 116, 119, 139, 140–41, 144, 146, 161, 240n.87; migration of, to UK, 38, 111–30; not welcome as migrants, 90–91, 107, 109, 110, 122, 130, 153–54, 184; number of migrants to Britain from, 119, 161, 162; screening of, 152, 153–55, 159, 161, 162, 240n.94; skill level of migrating, 114, 120, 148. *See also* Commonwealth citizens
"Westward Ho!" scheme, 72–73, 78, 79
Whitelaw, William, 182, 183
White Papers (on immigration), 30, 144, 174–75, 177
Wiles, Sir Harold, 87, 125, 126, 136
Wilson, Harold, 170, 173–76, 178, 179–80
women: alien, as laborers, 69, 72, 75, 78, 79, 86, 119, 124; of color, 123, 126, 130; emigration of, 30, 34, 37, 199n.1; as laborers, 6–7, 67, 72, 122–24, 126, 130, 194n.32; as labor force reproducers, 12, 87–88, 196n.9; nationality of married, 12, 14–15, 24; as subsidiary British subjects, 12–15, 49, 196n.9
working parties: on alien labor, 86; on British nationality, 18–19, 23; on colonial immigrants, 106, 122–27, 130, 134–36, 138, 143, 145–48, 150, 161, 162–63, 171–72; failures of, 156; on migration expenditures, 41, 56; on migration policy, 35, 37, 45, 46, 53
work permits, 74–75, 78, 95, 136, 164, 181
World War I, 3, 66, 112
World War II, 29, 67; economic effects of, on Britain, 1, 4; and Ireland, 92, 97, 98; and nationalism, 29, 185; and war brides, 34, 199n.1; and West Indian migration, 112–13

Younge, Gary, 189
Yugoslavians, 72, 84